THE
SEVENTH
DECADE

THE SEVENTH DECADE

The New Shape
of Nuclear Danger

Jonathan Schell

Metropolitan Books
Henry Holt and Company
New York

Metropolitan Books
Henry Holt and Company, LLC
Publishers since 1866
175 Fifth Avenue
New York, New York 10010
www.henryholt.com

Library of Congress Cataloging-in-Publication Data

Schell, Jonathan, 1943–
 The seventh decade : the new shape of nuclear danger / Jonathan Schell. — 1st ed.
  p. cm. — (The American empire project)
 Includes bibliographical references and index.
 ISBN-13: 978-0-8050-8129-9
 ISBN-10: 0-8050-8129-1
 1. Nuclear nonproliferation—United States. 2. Nuclear weapons—United States. 3.
Nuclear disarmament—United States. 4. National security—United States. 5. United
States—Military policy. 6. United States—Defenses. 7. United States—Foreign
relations. I. Title.
U264.3.S43 2007
355.02'170973—dc22   2007014238

First Edition 2007

Designed by Meryl Sussman Levavi

Printed in the United States of America
10 9 8 7 6 5 4 3 2 1

This book was written under the auspices of the Yale Center for the Study of Globalization, where I was a Distinguished Visiting Fellow in the fall of 2005 and spring of 2006. The center is expanding its program dealing with the nuclear question, and it provided the ideal atmosphere for doing this work. I would like to express my gratitude to its director, President Ernesto Zedillo, and its associate director, Ms. Haynie Wheeler, for their support, advice, patience, and encouragement. The views expressed in the book are of course mine alone.

"Ten years from now, [President Reagan] would be a very old man. He and Gorbachev would come to Iceland and each of them would bring the last nuclear missile from each country with them. And they would give a tremendous party for the whole world. . . . He would be very old by then, and Gorbachev would not recognize him. The President would say, 'Hello, Mikhail.' And Gorbachev would say, 'Ron, is it you?' And then they would destroy the last missiles."

—Account by the rapporteur, in the official memorandum of conversation, of comments made by President Ronald Reagan to General Secretary Mikhail Gorbachev at their summit meeting in Reykjavik, Iceland, on October 12, 1986, when, for a moment, they appeared to have agreed to the elimination of all nuclear weapons within ten years.

CONTENTS

THE
SEVENTH
DECADE

THE BOMB
IN THE MIND

CHAPTER 1

THE SEVENTH DECADE

*"He said with great seriousness that the existence of
nuclear arms made a secure and rational world
impossible."*

—DAVID ORMSBY-GORE,

British ambassador to the United States, reporting to
London on a conversation with his friend President
John F. Kennedy at the height of the Cuban missile
crisis of 1962.[1]

The nuclear age has entered its seventh decade. If it were a person,
it would be thinking about retirement—reckoning up its pension
funds, weighing different medical plans. But historical periods,
unlike human lives, have no fixed limit, and the nuclear age is in
fact displaying youthful vigor. The birth of nuclear weapons in
1945 opened a wide, unobstructed pathway to the end of the
world. Along that route was an end to cities, an end to countries,
an end to continents, an end to human life itself. Sometimes one of
these perils has moved to the fore, sometimes another, but all have
continuously cast their shadows over the earth. After the end of
the Cold War, the world's nuclear arsenals seemed to have been
tamed to a certain extent, but now they are growling and baring
their teeth again. Indeed, the bomb is staging a revival, as if to

declare: the twenty-first century, like the one before it, belongs to me.*

During the Cold War, the United States and the Soviet Union made every preparation for annihilation but held back from the final step—launching their globe-wrecking arsenals. With the Cold War's end, those stockpiles were reduced, and the threat of apocalypse receded. But even as the number of warheads was declining the number of nations that possessed such weapons was growing. Nuclear danger, it seemed, did not so much wane as change shape. There were fewer bombs but they were in more hands. The bomb's potential, recognized by all informed observers from the first days of the nuclear age, not only to threaten life on Earth but also, as the deadly know-how spread, to spring up at any point of the compass, was advancing toward realization. In that respect, the bomb is only now truly coming into its own. Having outgrown its parochial Cold War breeding ground, it is moving to take up residence in every part of the globe. India, Pakistan, and North Korea have acquired nuclear arsenals. China, a nuclear power since 1964, is doing likewise. Pakistan now targets India, while India targets Pakistan and, perhaps, China, in a new three-way nuclear arms race. Soon after North Korea's first nuclear test, on October 9, 2006, the prime minister of Japan, Shinzo Abe, called for his country to open a new discussion regarding his country's decision to do without nuclear weapons. Iran has embarked on a program to create nuclear power fuels that would carry it most of the distance to having the bomb, and Iran's neighbors in the Middle East are showing fresh interest in nuclear energy and weapon programs. Israel, which has possessed nuclear weapons since the late 1960s, continues to improve its delivery systems.

Unfortunately, the new sources of nuclear danger have by no

---

*By the handy, popular shorthand "the bomb," which usefully fuses every aspect of the nuclear dilemma into an indivisible whole, I mean to refer to all aspects of the presence of the bomb and its technology and science in our world.

means replaced the old ones. The Cold War antagonists, rather than dispatching their gigantic arsenals into the historical dustbin that swallowed their geopolitical struggle, have held on to them. What is more, they have begun to refurbish their warheads and delivery systems, build new generations of nuclear weapons, and redeploy and retarget them. The seminal event was the attack of September 11, 2001, which set in motion one of the few true revolutions in American nuclear policy since 1945. In a radical reversal of former practice, which had been to seek to stop the spread of nuclear weapons through diplomacy and treaties, the United States now turned to military means, including overthrow of the offending governments—"regime change." This policy was a corollary of a far more ambitious one, rightly called imperial by supporters and detractors alike, of asserting "unchallengeable" American military dominance over the entire globe. One result was the Iraq war, launched in the name of dismantling weapons of mass destruction and programs for building of them, of which the most dangerous was said to be an active nuclear program. Confusingly, Iraq, which of course had no such weapons or programs, turned out not to be an example of the evil in question; yet the idea of stopping proliferation by force, though as yet practiced nowhere else, has continued to enjoy wide acceptance and continues to inform policy.

Far less visible but no less important has been an equally radical change in American nuclear strategic policy—that is, the guidance given the United States' nuclear forces. To the old Cold War targets have been added new ones in the third world. The *Nuclear Posture Review* of late 2002 specifically assigned nuclear weapons a counterproliferation role, soon rendered operational in a new Pentagon command called Global Strike, whose mission is to deliver "conventional or nuclear" strikes on any target anywhere on the planet at a moment's notice. Other Western nations have followed suit, declaring that state supporters of terrorist groups around the world are fitting targets for attack by their nuclear forces. France opposed the Iraq war, but it is building a new, nuclear-capable bomber, the Rafale, and a new submarine-launched ballistic missile, and its former president, Jacques Chirac, has declared that terrorist threats to France may be met with a nuclear response. The British government has similarly announced that Britain will replace its fleet of aging nuclear-armed submarines with a new, improved model, whose Trident missiles are to be purchased, like the last ones, from the United States. Britain, too, cited the dangers of proliferation and terrorism as reasons for remaining nuclear armed deep into the twenty-first century.

The old and new arsenals have thus begun to hone in on one another, as nuclear weapons always do, missile targeting missile, bomb countering bomb. A highly volatile and violent contest—no longer bipolar but global—between some of the existing possessors of the bomb and new entrants or petitioners to the club, who hope to "deter" the great ones with tiny but potent arsenals, has begun to churn international affairs. Already, it has helped to produce the misbegotten American invasion of Iraq, launched in pursuit of weapons of mass destruction that weren't there, and could in time produce other wars—with Iran, North Korea, or countries as yet unknown. As in the Cold War, the nuclear danger has become an axle around which the wheel of geopolitical events is turning.

In an inseparably related and long-predicted development, the world is also awash in nuclear-weapon technology, adding a new dimension to the dangers of proliferation, and raising the terrifying specter of a terrorist group that acquires and uses a nuclear weapon, or perhaps several of them, to lash out against a great city somewhere in the world. Tens of thousands or perhaps hundreds of thousands of people might die. The city would be rendered uninhabitable by radiation for decades. If it were a national capital, the nation's government could be destroyed. Beyond these direct consequences lie indirect ones that are no less real for being veiled in great uncertainty. For example, if the country were the United States, would the government survive? What emergency measures might it adopt, and for how long? Would the Constitution remain in effect, and, if it were suspended, would it ever be restored? Would liberty around the globe be taken away by governments straining every nerve to prevent new attacks? Would terror-stricken populations of other cities flee to the countryside? Might the global economy collapse? Although such an attack, involving only one or a few of the world's twenty-seven thousand or so existing nuclear warheads, would be the merest fraction of the kind of global holocaust that seemed so near at hand during the Cold War, its consequences bring us to a verge beyond which the imagination falters.

Talking Our Extinction to Death

Yet while the bomb has been showing fresh energy, the people have grown tired. Even as the bomb was setting forth on new, worldwide adventures, the issue of the bomb was acquiring a stale, anachronistic air in the public mind, a sort of 1960s feeling, as if a youth entering his prime were forced to go abroad in antique clothing. One reason for the waning attention has been the peculiar structure of the nuclear dilemma, which tends to circumvent ordinary mechanisms of response to danger. Consider the ways in which it differs from global warming—the only other catastrophe on the horizon whose consequences are in the same league with a nuclear holocaust. The two perils have a great deal in common. Both are the fruit of swollen human power—in the one case, the destructive power of war; in the other, the productive power of fossil-fuel energy. Both put stakes on the table of a magnitude never present before in human decision making. Both threaten life on a planetary scale. Both require a fully global response. Anyone concerned by the one should be concerned with the other. It would be a shame to save the Earth from slowly warming only to burn it up in an instant in a nuclear war.

Yet the two menaces obtrude in life in very different ways. Global warming has conformed to a pattern that is familiar from other gathering dangers, such as the AIDS epidemic or the threat to the ozone layer from man-made chemicals. First, the peril appears and is disclosed to the world in specialized journals and to a certain extent in the press but is largely ignored by politicians and the public. Then the evidence grows, and alarm increases. As the predictions begin to come true, frightening reading material is supplemented by disturbing concrete experiences. In the case of global warming, these have included hotter summers, more frequent and powerful hurricanes, rising sea levels, more flooding in low-lying areas and more drought elsewhere, vanishing species, disintegrating coral reefs, melting glaciers and polar ice. Photographic evidence becomes available, and the problem can be shown on television—or made into a film, such as former vice president Al Gore's *An Inconvenient Truth*. Apathy and denial now have a potent competitor in the pressure of events. The question, complex in practice but simple in principle, becomes whether the unpleasant initial consequences can inspire political action fast enough to head off utter calamity later on.

No such sequence has been exhibited in the evolution of the nuclear danger. The most important reason is that the transition from warning to experience has not—most fortunately—occurred. No nuclear weapon has been exploded in anger since the destruction of Nagasaki on August 9, 1945. Instead, a welcome if tenuous "tradition of nonuse" has developed. To be sure, the worldwide buildup of the machinery of nuclear power and nuclear war has exacted a significant medical and environmental price. The fallout from nuclear tests has caused a worldwide increase in deaths from cancer. The Chernobyl disaster of 1986, in which a nuclear power plant exploded in Ukraine, contaminated several hundred square miles of the surrounding territory with radiation. Nuclear wastes from both nuclear weapon production and nuclear plants, some of which will remain radioactive for as long as a million years, are heaping up around the world, and no one is certain what to do with them over the long run. However, grave as these costs may be, they obviously have not had the overwhelming impact on the public mind that would be produced by the sudden, colossal devastation of a nuclear war, which continues to hide its face.

In this singular situation, in which nuclear war has yet to happen, and so sheer foresight is asked to play the role usually played by punishing experience, the awful facts of nuclear life have repeatedly been taught and learned, only to be forgotten again, in a pattern of boom and bust. In 1945, many of the scientists in the United States who created the bomb in the wartime Manhattan Project tried to make use of their authority to wage a campaign to educate the public about nuclear arms and to call for their elimination. From them, the world learned that an aspirin-size quantity of mass, when released as energy in a nuclear explosion, can, in obedience to Einstein's law that the energy released from a split atom equals mass times the speed of light squared ($E = mc^2$), level a city. It learned that any city on Earth could be destroyed, together with its population, by a nuclear weapon of the appropriate size. It learned that although the United States was the first to acquire an atomic bomb, other nations would be able to do the same before long, and that the bomb could be mass produced. However, with the onset of the Cold War in the late 1940s, fear of the Soviet Union eclipsed fear of the bomb in Western opinion, and awareness of the nuclear danger faded.

It revived after the explosion of the first H-bomb by the United States, on November 1, 1952, on Eniwetok atoll, in the South Pacific, followed by the first Soviet H-bomb test, called "Joe 1," after the Soviet dictator Joseph Stalin, less than a year later. The moral issues raised by weapons that could kill tens of millions of people in an instant weighed on the public mind. Using a newly current word, a majority of the General Advisory Committee created by President Harry S. Truman to counsel him on whether or not to build the H-bomb—a weapon that could release hundreds of times the explosive power of the Hiroshima bomb—warned that it "might become a weapon of genocide."[2] A lively antinuclear movement developed on both sides of the Atlantic. Statesmen, too, spoke in a new tone of awed horror. Winston Churchill, who had embraced the A-bomb, now found that "there is an immense gulf between the atomic and the hydrogen bomb." For "the atomic bomb, with all its terrors, did not carry us outside the scope of human control or manageable events in thought or in action, in peace or in war. But [with the H-bomb], the entire foundation of human affairs was revolutionized, and mankind placed in a situation both measureless and laden with doom."[3]

Yet even this somber awareness faded, and, after the resolution of the Cuban missile crisis in the autumn of 1962 and the signing in 1963 of a treaty banning nuclear tests in the atmosphere, once again died away. Widespread public concern about the nuclear danger did not revive until the early 1980s, when President Ronald Reagan's nuclear buildup and the breakdown of arms control negotiations with the Soviet Union inspired a "nuclear freeze" movement. Teams of physicians toured the country with slide shows depicting how just a few hundred such weapons targeted on American cities could wipe out two-thirds of the population of the United States; how a single Ohio-class submarine, with its twenty-four Trident ballistic missiles capable of carrying almost two hundred warheads, was a nation- or continent-smashing boat; how a "nuclear winter," in which dust and smoke would be hurled into the atmosphere by nuclear explosions, would bring on a catastrophic cooling of the earth; and how the other global ecological effects of nuclear war would put the world's ecosphere, including its human component, at risk. But when, in the mid-1980s, arms control negotiations resumed and Cold War tensions began to wane, the awareness yet again died away, in obedience to the familiar pattern.

With the Cold War's end, consciousness of the dilemma sank to its lowest ebb yet, apparently in the mistaken belief that the Cold War and the nuclear predicament had been one and the same, and that the end of the first must mean the end of the second. Liquidation of the global quarrel did indeed increase the world's safety as well as permit a continued reduction of nuclear arsenals. But at the same time it left immense arsenals in place. The issue of nuclear arms had died but the nuclear arms themselves remained, now curiously untethered from political justifications for their existence. Meanwhile, a new, post–Cold War generation, largely innocent of nuclear knowledge, was growing up. Its elders, having dropped the issue themselves, also forgot to impart even the most basic information regarding nuclear matters to their children. The press neglected the issue, as did schools at every level. And so to elderly amnesia was added an ocean of fresh, young, pure ignorance. The moment of greatest opportunity for disarmament since 1945 thus became the moment of least action.

Looking at this record, which contrasts so sharply with the responses to other dangers of global consequence, it seems as if Robert Lowell's line from his poem "Fall, 1961," written at the height of the Berlin crisis, had finally come true: "We have talked our extinction to death." He meant, of course, that the talking, not the threat of extinction, had died. Like a bone stuck in the world's throat, nuclear weapons, neither detonated nor discarded, by the 1990s appeared to have installed themselves in a kind of limbo. Known to all yet somehow forgotten, lying in plain sight yet unseen, feared and yet deeply accepted, the bomb—evidently an even more inconvenient truth than global warming—seemed to have gravitated, as if guided by a genius all its own, to some location in the human order to which neither the mind nor heart nor will could follow. Worse, in addition to its destructive physical effects, from the thermal pulse to the shock wave to radiation sickness to ozone depletion to nuclear winter, it seemed to possess a capacity to disable every effort to come to grips with it—to blur the vision that tried to see it, to fog the minds that tried to grasp it, to numb the feelings that might register its human significance. To the nuclear dilemma, then, must be added what might be called the dilemma of the nuclear dilemma—the unique riddle of the vacillating, intermittent, and currently stalled human encounter, now more than sixty years old, with what is still the only technology that can put an end to all human beings.

A New Wave of Concern?

Today, however, as nuclear danger continues to mount, there are signs that another bout of public concern may be in the offing. For one thing, the recent rise in awareness of global warming may indirectly call attention to its forgotten elder nuclear sibling in the family of planetary threats. For another, the revolution in nuclear policy inaugurated by the Bush administration after September 11 has taken a severe beating at the hands of events. Proliferation and terrorism, including the nuclear variety, were and remain growing dangers, but the measures the administration chose to deal with them turn out to have been based on misconceptions. One was the apparent assumption, by no means restricted to this administration, that nuclear danger arose only from the spread of nuclear weapons, not from existing arsenals. A second was the conviction that proliferation could be stopped on a global basis by the application of overwhelming force. A third was the belief that the deed could be accomplished by an international community whose leading nations were themselves nuclear powers and were determined to remain so. And all three of these misconceptions were entangled in the more comprehensive misconception that the world of the twenty-first century could be managed by the unilateral decisions of a single power, the United States.

The miscarriage of the Iraq war, North Korea's nuclear test, and the persistence of Iran's nuclear program, among many other developments, have pulled the rug out from under each of these propositions, and there is a palpable need for rethinking across the board and for new nuclear policies. Many recent studies have been devoted to ideas for addressing the proliferation threat, but most of them seem to share the assumption that the nuclear danger consists wholly of the acquisition of nuclear arms by new parties. Few address the problem of existing arsenals. Fewer still address the connections between proliferation and possession. This book will do so. It will consider the nuclear dilemma as an indivisible whole as it enters its seventh decade. I shall argue that proliferation and possession cannot be considered in isolation from each other; that a solution to the former requires dealing with the latter; and that this can only mean a commitment to the elimination of all nuclear arms.

That vision—as old as the nuclear age itself—has recently won fresh support in a surprising quarter. In an article in the *Wall Street Journal* in January 2007, former secretary of state George P. Shultz, former secretary of defense William J. Perry, former secretary of state Henry A. Kissinger, and former senator Sam Nunn—about as impressive a chunk of the nuclear establishment in the United States as could be represented by four authors—called for "a world free of nuclear weapons."[4] The article, which was also endorsed by dozens of other former officials, also reminded readers that the most ardent defender of nuclear abolition ever to occupy the White House was a conservative Republican, President Ronald Reagan. Breaking with nuclear orthodoxy, which has held that a large nuclear arsenal is a necessity for the indefinite future, the authors endorsed the goal of eliminating nuclear arms. A recent poll has shown that 66 percent of the American public agree.[5] The article noted that when this idea had been championed by President Ronald Reagan and the Soviet leader Mikhail Gorbachev at the Reykjavik summit in 1986, it had "shocked many officials." Since some of the signers and supporters of the article had been among the shocked (Shultz, who as secretary of state was present at the summit, is a notable exception), the shift in mainstream official opinion seems significant.

However that may be, any fresh effort to seriously tackle the nuclear dilemma will face a formidable array of new obstacles and puzzles along with many of the old ones. The bomb, always a Pandora's box of deceptions and self-deceptions, has added new disguises, mask upon mask. It is obvious that nuclear dangers are real and again growing, but the policies that have generated them have become more convoluted and obscure. It is not easy to determine why Britain is about to spend £20 billion to rebuild its nuclear forces from the ground up by renewing its Trident submarine system, its only nuclear weapon platform. Why does France need to improve its arsenal? In order to attack whom? It is perhaps even more difficult to explain why, almost twenty years after the end of the Cold War, the United States and Russia still insist on holding each other's populations hostage to nuclear annihilation. It is scarcely less tricky to fathom the relationship of nuclear policy to antiterror policy, two things that seem to have fused in the minds of the administration of President George W. Bush. Are nuclear arsenals truly an appropriate instrument for stopping nuclear proliferation or nuclear terrorism? Or, on the contrary, do they encourage these dangers? No less riddlesome is the relationship of America's nuclear arsenal to its global power. Does the bomb, once called "the absolute weapon," enhance American power or is its existence on the contrary now a source of weakness, as Shultz and his coauthors intimate in their article?

It would be convenient if the nuclear dilemma consisted simply of a definite, concrete set of dangers posed by certain states, but it is not so. Nuclear policy has always been a scene of rampant illusion and obfuscation, and just recently the maze's trap doors, dead ends, false bottoms, illusory exits, mirages, and misleading appearances have multiplied. By comparison, the Cold War order, for all its doom-laden contradictions and icy paradoxes, now seems almost a model of clarity and rationality. Certainly, no understanding of the current moment in the nuclear story is possible without first unraveling the new snarl of confusion added by the evasions, misunderstandings, distortions, factual errors, and missteps of the Bush administration as well as other governments in recent years. In sum, the policies of the the United States and the other nuclear powers have become less intelligible, less feasible, more self-contradictory, more liable to self-defeat, more drastically at odds with the basic realities of the nuclear age, and more prone to catastrophe than at any time since 1945. In consequence, the world as a whole drifts toward what some have termed "nuclear anarchy." Not since the world's second nuclear bomb was dropped on Nagasaki has history's third use of a nuclear weapon seemed more likely.

The Limits of Theory

How did we arrive at this point more than six decades into the nuclear age? Even as the protean flexibility and remarkable staying power of the bomb seem to have worn out its opponents, the long historical record thereby created does offer new advantages for understanding. The most important of these may be that in broad areas historical guidance can now take over from the prescriptions of abstract thought. The fortunate absence of actual nuclear conflict during the Cold War created a vacuum of direct experience, which for decades was filled chiefly by a profusion of war gaming and strategic theories composed in academia and in think tanks. At their core was the doctrine of deterrence, whose central teaching was that a nation could defend itself against nuclear arms only by possessing nuclear arms or allying itself with a nation that did. Any power contemplating nuclear attack, the doctrine taught, would be confronted with its own annihilation and hold back.

The answers to many important questions still remain hidden behind the veil created by the tradition of nonuse. For example, no one knows how a nuclear war would actually develop, since none has ever occurred. (The bombing of Hiroshima and Nagasaki were nuclear attacks, but Japan, of course, was unable to respond in kind.) Could such a war, once under way, be restrained, or would it run to its limit? Theory can offer its answers, but they are only speculation. The consequences of a large-scale nuclear attack are even more imponderable than those of a terrorist use of a single weapon. Would it disable electrical equipment all over the world through the creation of an electromagnetic pulse, devastate the ozone layer, bring on nuclear winter, or otherwise impair or ruin the global ecosphere?* Judgments

---

*A new study by Richard Turco of UCLA's Department of Atmospheric and Ocean Sciences and Owen Brien Toon, an atmospheric scientist at the University of Colorado, used newly developed climate models to report that even a regional nuclear war in South Asia could loft enough soot into the atmosphere to severely cool the atmosphere and cripple agriculture in large parts of the globe for up to ten years. See http://www.copernicus.org/EGU/acp/acpd/6/11745/acpd-6-11745.pdf.

can be hazarded on each of these perils, but they will be misleading unless accompanied by a confession of vast uncertainties. What would the extent of the devastation be? Would the injured or devastated nation retaliate if it could? How would the world respond to the event or to the retaliation? Might the conflagration become general?

On the other hand, an abundance of historical experience bears on an array of other essential questions that press on us with new urgency today. Perhaps the most obvious of them—though the hardest to answer—is why states want nuclear weapons. What advantages, if any, do they confer on their possessors? What are the liabilities of possession? Why do many states that are fully capable of producing the bomb nevertheless reject it? What accounts for the remarkable immunity of nuclear arsenals, once established, to political changes and reversals, including even globally revolutionary ones, such as the end of the Cold War? What relationship do existing arsenals have to proliferation? Which characteristics of the nuclear dilemma are unchangeable—written into what we might call its genetic code—and which are subject to historical change and so can bend to human will? Which policies, therefore, butt our heads against immovable realities and which might open the way to deliverance from nuclear danger? Which measures are likely to be successful in stopping proliferation? What role can diplomacy and treaties play in this effort? What can force accomplish? Above all, where should we look for the pathways that will provide what Mohammed ElBaradei, the chairman of the International Atomic Energy Agency, has termed an "exit strategy from the nuclear age?" The six-decade record since Nagasaki is a rich storehouse of events, near events, terrors, opportunities, and missed opportunities that shed light on all of these critical questions.

In the foreground of our attention must be the bold nuclear policies of the Bush administration, but behind them lies a broader governing philosophy, or doctrine, behind which, in turn, lie important decisions made—as well as ones left unmade—during the post–Cold War era. And behind *them* lies the long experience of the

Cold War and the much shorter period, a mere historical instant but full of consequence for the future, that lies between the first atomic bomb test, in Alamogordo, New Mexico, on July 16, 1945, and the end of the Second World War, on September 2 of that same year. Let us start with that beginning and then, making use of the extended historical record now open to view, proceed forward to examine the self-made nuclear labyrinth in which we now wander lost.

CHAPTER 2

A POWER OUT
OF OUR POWER

Even as the bomb was born into the world, it seemed to be propelled by a momentum that no one knew how to stop. Every page of the nuclear story, including the current one, is stamped by a profound fatalism—an anxiety or conviction that the bomb, though a human creation, is somehow immune to human control. Rarely, if ever, have human beings seemed to bow down more abjectly before an artifice of their own creation.

That momentum was in full force as the B-29 *Enola Gay* took off from Tinian island in the Pacific to bomb Hiroshima on August 6, 1945. One of the first to sense it was Deke Parsons, a scientist charged with arming the bomb as the plane approached the doomed city. In a flash of insight occurring at exactly the moment the bomb was released from the plane, he understood that it was slipping out of the grasp of its makers. "The bomb was now independent of the plane," he remembers. "It was a peculiar sensation. I had a feeling the bomb had a life of its own now that had nothing to do with us."[1] It was not just entering history; it was taking charge of it, a sovereign master. Einstein gave voice to a similar understanding a few years later when he wrote, "Radioactive poisoning of the atmosphere and hence annihilation of any life on earth has been brought within the range of technical possibilities. The ghostlike character of this development lies in its apparently compulsory trend. Every step appears as the unavoidable consequence of the preceding one. In the end, there beckons more and more clearly general annihilation."[2] And we hear the diplomat and scholar George Kennan, principal author of the Cold War policy of "containing" the Soviet Union, sounding the same note thirty years later, when, as he witnessed the nuclear buildup of President Reagan's first term, he wrote, "We have gone on piling weapon upon weapon, missile upon missile, helplessly, almost involuntarily, like the victims of some kind of hypnosis, like men in a dream, like lemmings heading for the sea."[3]

The bomb's greatest champions have also been possessed by a feeling that the nuclear arms race was somehow fated. But theirs has been an enabling fatalism, like a wind at their backs, assuring them that what they were doing would happen whether they participated in it or not. This feeling eased the qualms that many of the atomic scientists had about participating in such an obviously barbaric undertaking. For example, the radio-chemist George Cowan spoke of the decision to build the H-bomb in the following terms: "Knowing that it was going to work encouraged those people to go ahead and do it. . . . *There was no longer an option.*" (Emphasis added.) He went on, "Despite all the debates, no responsible government would ever voluntarily forgo developing a very powerful new weapon if it knew how to do it. . . . If you are in the government it is not an option."[4] J. Robert Oppenheimer, the scientific leader of the American atomic bomb project, was of like mind. Although he at first opposed the H-bomb, he ended his opposition once the theoretical obstacles to its production had been overcome. He wrote, "It is my judgment in these things that when you see something that is technically sweet, you go ahead and do it and you argue about what to do about it only after you have had your technical success. That is the way it was with the atomic bomb. I do not think anybody opposed making it; there were some debates what to do with it after it was made."[5] But the most categorical expression of the momentum of the H-bomb came from one of its "fathers," Edward Teller. In 1945, seven years before the first H-bomb test, he commented, "There is among my scientific colleagues some hesitancy as to the advisability of this development on the grounds that it might make the international problems even more difficult than they are now. My opinion is that this is a fallacy. If the development is possible, it is out of our power to prevent it."[6] Here, the future inventor of the hydrogen bomb finds himself so utterly helpless *not* to create the device that, more than a half decade before the deed, he seems to wait for his own action to descend upon him as if from the heavens. In other words, the momentum generated by the H-bomb was operating on its creators even before it came into existence. Later, the mathematician John von Neumann, who contributed to the H-bomb work, generalized Teller's intuition to encompass all scientific inventions when he said, "If it can be made, it will be made"—a principle that, if applied, might one day be a fitting epitaph for the human species.

An Open Secret

Were it not that the bomb's opponents recorded a similar fatalism, we might suspect that Teller and Neumann, both enthusiasts of the bomb, were merely rationalizing their actions. Yet both camps were obviously responding to a reality of the nuclear dilemma whose origins lay deeper than either acceptance or rejection of nuclear weapons. In truth, the sources of the bomb's momentum were rooted in the structure of the modern scientific enterprise. In the beginning, the bomb was a thought. More specifically, it was a thought in the mind of the Hungarian scientist Leo Szilard, who, while crossing a street in London one day in 1933, came to believe that a nuclear chain reaction was possible, and that, if it were so, the very survival of human life would be in jeopardy.[7] The thought was the marriage of a scientific experiment (James Chadwick's discovery of the neutron in 1932) and a work of science fiction (H. G. Wells's futuristic novel of 1914, *The World Set Free*, in which he foresaw atomic war). A few years later, Szilard obtained patents on some of the processes involved in chain reactions and deeded them to the British Admiralty, which, he hoped, would keep them secret from the war-bound world. It was history's first attempt at nuclear nonproliferation, and it of course failed.

On the eve of the Second World War, Szilard and others tried again to halt proliferation by successfully advocating the withholding of certain findings relating to nuclear fission from scientific journals. The effort again failed, this time for a reason that shone a powerful light on the nature of both nuclear proliferation and the momentum behind it. Instead of fooling Soviet scientists, the gaps in the scientific literature tipped them off to the Western scientists' belief that a bomb was feasible. Their very secrecy became disclosure. The reason was simple and lodged deeply in the nature of modern scientific inquiry. Science was and remains a fully international, cooperative undertaking—sometimes referred to as the Republic of Science—in which each scientist is able to lay a new brick on the rising edifice of a given body of knowledge only because he knows which bricks have just been laid by others and which gaps remain to be filled. In 1940, scientists were so well acquainted with the state of play in nuclear physics that a conspicuous gap aroused curiosity. No clearer demonstration could have been given, if any were needed, of the unconfinable character of scientific findings.

The normal method of scientific dissemination was simply publication in a scientific journal. At bottom, nuclear proliferation was then, as it is now, the export not of centrifuges and reactor parts or any other machinery or physical object but of knowledge, the world's most transferable substance, especially in an "information age" like ours. No power can stop it and no limit can be set upon it. Soon after 1945, the Soviets would acquire most of the rest of what they needed to make an atomic bomb by means of highly successful spying—another way that knowledge can spread. In the first place, then, the momentum of the bomb stems from the momentum of all scientific knowledge as it spreads uncontrollably and universally from its points of origin.

As for the scientific community per se—the company of individuals who performed the work—its international character was perhaps most clearly displayed by the Manhattan Project, many of whose most important scientists were from other countries. It was the singular good fortune of the United States at that moment to be able to assemble, in one land, a significant proportion of the era's best minds in physics. Szilard, Teller, and Neumann were Hungarian Jews. Enrico Fermi, leader of the team that built the first reactor, was Italian. Klaus Fuchs and James Franck were German. Victor Weisskopf was Austrian. Niels Bohr, who did not work for the project yet was apprised of it and gave occasional advice, was Danish. James Chadwick and William Penney were British.

An underappreciated contribution to the bomb is the French one. A few days after the news of the bombing of Hiroshima broke, many were startled to read that the French physicist Frédéric Joliot, one of the world's most respected nuclear scientists, had asserted that the discovery had been made in France. There was a measure of truth in the claim. Until its fall to Nazi Germany in 1940, France had indeed had an active and productive nuclear program under the leadership of Joliot. So advanced was it that in November 1939, Joliot had written a letter to the French prime minister, Édouard Daladier, apprising him of the feasibility of an atomic bomb and requesting funds to purchase uranium and heavy water, which Joliot then obtained. After France's fall to Nazi Germany, French scientists delivered the heavy water—the only supply of it in the world—to the British and also shared with them important research results, especially on "slow neutron work"—that is, nuclear power technology. Subsequently, several of the French scientists were dispatched to Canada, where they led a program on nuclear reactor development. Canada thus also played an important role in the development of the bomb. In fact, the uranium used in the Hiroshima bomb came from a mine at Great Bear Lake in the Northwest Territories, and it was thus literally a tiny piece of Canada, extracted by mining and then refined, whose fissioning obliterated the Japanese city.

It's customary to say that the United States invented the bomb, but the Manhattan Project can also be seen as an attempt to nationalize a technology that, like all fruits of basic science, was in essence international. Indeed, the first government to awaken to the technical feasibility of the bomb was not the American but the British, and the scientists who did the work involved, Otto Frisch and Rudolf Peierls, were German Jewish refugees from Hitler. And it was their work, conveyed to the United States in a seminal document called the Maud report, which persuaded President Franklin Delano Roosevelt and his advisers to embark on the United States' top secret program to build the bomb, the Manhattan Project.

Around this time, as it happens, the Soviet spy John Cairncross (the "fifth man" in the famous Cambridge spy ring that also included Kim Philby) was delivering the Maud report to Stalin. (As a result, that report contributed to all three of the world's first atomic bomb programs.)[8] Or consider the spy Klaus Fuchs, also German and Jewish and a refugee from Hitler. He fled to Britain and then, as a British citizen, was sent to work on the Manhattan Project. But when he decided to act as a spy, it was not of course for his native Germany but for the Soviet Union. This fully internationalized scientist was a one-man nemesis of nonproliferation. His motive, in addition to his left-wing sympathies, was one that would inspire many scientists to build nuclear bombs in many countries in years to come: he thought it dangerous for just *one* country to possess such a weapon. It was precisely this justification, for instance, that inspired Andrei Sakharov, the inventor of the Soviet H-bomb, to work under the direction of the odious Lavrenti Beria, the head of Stalin's secret police organization, the NKVD, to deliver the H-bomb into the hands of the totalitarian despot Stalin. As he explained later, "We (and here I must speak not only in my own behalf, for in such cases moral principles are formulated in a collective psychological way) believed that our work was absolutely necessary as a means of achieving a balance in the world."[9]

A righted balance was exactly what Stalin had asked of his

scientists. After Hiroshima, he told them, "A single demand of you, comrades, provide us with atomic weapons in the shortest possible time. You know that Hiroshima has shaken the whole world. The equilibrium has been destroyed. Provide the bomb—it will remove a great danger from us."[10] Sakharov's motivation, like Fuchs's, was in a sense to *reinternationalize* a technology that the United States was trying to nationalize.

The tension between the international and open character of science and the secrecy imposed by a strictly national effort to build the bomb is a thread that also runs through the history of the Manhattan Project. Its military director, General Leslie Groves, sought to impose a strict security regime on the effort, confining and restricting both the scientific knowledge and the scientists, who for their part yearned for the openness and freedom that were intrinsic to true science. Thanks to Fuchs and others, his effort failed as thoroughly as Szilard's earlier attempts to patent chain reactions.

The atomic spies were in any event only the cutting edge of the spread of nuclear know-how. Groves was in the unenviable position of trying to suppress the scientific process even as he sought, in a limited sphere, to foster it. It was a battle, destined to be lost, wherever and whenever people have imagined that there is a secret of the bomb and have tried to keep it to themselves. (Perhaps the most farcical and self-defeating of these efforts was the decision by the Atomic Energy Commission to seek to protect nuclear secrets by stripping Oppenheimer of his security clearance, owing to his left-wing connections of the 1930s, which had been known to the government even before he was hired as the scientific director of the Manhattan Project.)

The Bomb in the Mind

Such were the origins of the bomb. It did not spring from the brains of any one country; it was crossbred, multiethnic, and multinational, and it was predestined to stay that way. The momentum conferred on the bomb by its origin in the scientific realm carried over into the political realm. The story again begins with that enterprising and imaginative scientific and political maverick Leo Szilard.

The world was on the brink of war. The bomb, he understood, would very likely give a decisive advantage to the nation that developed it first. A refugee from Europe, Szilard did not want that country to be Germany. Appalled by the prospect of any atomic destruction, but even more by the prospect that Hitler would wreak it on the Allies (the discovery of fission, after all, had been a German achievement), he took a seminal step. In August 1939, he persuaded Einstein, who also hated the thought of using atomic energy for war and also hated Hitler more, to write a letter to President Roosevelt informing him that such a thing was possible. When the businessman Alexander Sachs brought Einstein's letter to a meeting with Roosevelt, the president responded, "Alex, what you are after is to see that the Nazis don't blow us up." He then authorized the program that would become the Manhattan Project. In 1939, the bomb existed only on paper, yet it was so powerful a reality that it propelled the American president to secretly inaugurate what would turn out to be history's most extensive and expensive single military project to date. The fact that Roosevelt acted in the ominous and unpredictable year of 1939, a month before the outbreak of the Second World War and more than two years before the United States entered the war, shows the exceptional power of nuclear weapon developments even before the bomb existed.

By the time the Manhattan Project got under way in earnest, in January of 1943, the Allied forces, victorious in the Pacific in the Battle of Midway and on their way to victory at Stalingrad in the heart of Russia, seemed likely to win the war. But what if Hitler got the bomb and the Allies had none? The British, still tenuously holding on to their empire, felt a more generalized version of the same pressure. The Maud report, which in 1942 prompted Roosevelt to step up the Manhattan Project, argued that England would need the bomb *even if* Hitler failed to get it first, for no nation "would care to risk being caught without a weapon of such decisive capabilities."[11] If we seek the point of origin of the nuclear dilemma, it lies here. Before there was a physical bomb, there was a virtual bomb, a bomb in the mind. The first bomb was not the one built by Groves and Oppenheimer that turned night into day at Alamogordo on July 16, 1945; it was the one that sprang to life in the brain of Leo Szilard more than a decade earlier as he crossed the street in London. It is this bomb in the mind, more durable than any material object, that stands at the heart of the nuclear dilemma, holding our age in thrall with its terror and allure. And if we ask why people want the bomb, the first answer lies here also. They want it because they fear others having it. And they fear others having it because they know that unlike any physical bomb, which at any given moment may be in the hands of only a few states, the mental one is destined to be available to all.

If the bomb possessed an irresistible momentum even before it existed, the reason was that, in a globe at war, it already seemed to be coming at the world from all directions at once. For the mental template of the bomb, radiating its terror outward to all lands and forward to all future ages, perpetually invites physical bombs into being. Owing to the virtual bomb's existence, not even the builders of the first physical bomb believed they were initiating a nuclear arms race. Like all their successors, they thought they were reacting to someone else, even if this was a future person. None of them thought they were acting aggressively; all believed they were acting defensively. More than any physical arsenal, it is this mental construct, inscribed forever in the human species' common heritage of thought, that has for more than sixty years defeated every attempt to deliver the world from the danger of atomic annihilation.

The Bomb in War

The momentum that pushed Roosevelt to act even more strongly affected his vice president and successor, Harry Truman, the bomb's first possessor and only user, who arrived in office on the eve of the bomb's advent with no knowledge that the Manhattan Project even existed. He was pitched without warning into the swift-running and powerful current of the bomb preparations, now on the verge of completion, as well as the deliberations regarding its use against Japan. The extent to which use of the bomb rested on a widely unchallenged tacit assumption that it *would* be dropped is illustrated by the striking fact that the historical record contains no specific order for its use signed by Truman. The omission was keenly felt by General Carl Spaatz, commander of the U.S. Strategic Forces in the Pacific, who had been asked to arrange that the bomb be used but did not want, as he said, to "blow off the south half of Japan" merely on his own authority. In a strange reversal of the usual military procedure, his request went *up* the military chain of command, whereupon an order was duly penned by General Groves, approved by army chief of staff George C. Marshall and Secretary of War Henry Stimson, and delivered to Spaatz.[12] No signature from Truman was thought necessary. Moreover, the order was not confined to the bomb to be dropped on Hiroshima. Rather, it authorized the use of atomic bombs on four cities (Hiroshima, Kokura, Niigata, and Nagasaki), stating, "Additional bombs will be delivered on the above targets as soon as made ready by the project staff."[13]

For sixty years, historians have debated "the decision" to drop the bomb "Little Boy" on Hiroshima. However, what was actually approved in the order to Spaatz was something subtly different: not the use of *a* bomb on a particular city, but the use of a new *type* of bomb on *many* cities, with the timing to depend on the speed of production, which in turn would be governed by "the staff." Thereafter, the order stated, "instructions" (not orders) "will be issued concerning targets" in addition to the four already named.[14]

Truman's first public statement regarding the bomb's use conveys a similar feeling of an existing process unfolding rather than a decision made. In his announcement of the bombing of Hiroshima, he said that the "battle of the laboratories" had been won, and then devoted most of the rest of his statement to the scientific achievement.

There is no mention of any decision to drop the bomb, or even of any weighing of pros and cons or alternatives. After the city of Nagasaki had been destroyed by a second atomic bomb, he stated that "having found the bomb, we have used it"—a sentence construction that, by making the use of the bomb a mere corollary of finding the bomb, seemed to purge any element of choice from the proceeding.

Several historians have argued that in fact there never was a "decision" to drop the bomb per se. They suggest that there was, at most, a failure to stop its use. For example, Martin Sherwin has written, "Policymakers never seriously questioned the assumption that the bomb should be used."[15] Barton Bernstein has commented, "Its use did not create ethical or political problems for them."[16] David McCullough refers to "the decision that was no decision." Many contemporary figures also saw the matter in this light. Winston Churchill, who was at the Potsdam conference when news of the success of the Alamogordo test was brought to Truman, said, "There was never a moment's discussion as to whether the atomic bomb should be used or not."[17] None other than Leslie Groves, the personification of the bomb's momentum, later insultingly likened Truman to a "little boy on a toboggan" that was already hurtling down a hill when he became president.[18] Groves also said, "Truman did not so much say 'yes' as not say 'no,'" and insisted that "I didn't have to have the president press the button on this."[19] We would not expect to find, nor do we find, any objection from Stalin to the bomb's first use. When, at Potsdam, Truman informed him somewhat circumspectly of the bomb's existence (Stalin already knew about the program from his spies), he merely answered that he hoped Truman would make "good use of it."

On the other hand, some historians have rightly pointed out that even if no moment came when, after full-dress deliberation with his advisers (perhaps with appropriate moral agonizing), Truman chose to go ahead and use the bomb, he nevertheless took several positive steps to clear obstacles out of the way of use. In the summer of 1945, the military defeat of Japan, now cut off from all external support and exposed to relentless conventional bombing by the U.S. Air Force, was a foregone conclusion. (Before Hiroshima, sixty-one Japanese cities had been burned to the ground by incendiary bombing.) Most historians now believe that there were several steps short of an American invasion of the home islands that might have ended the war without use of the bomb. One would have been to tell the Japanese, who were signaling a will to surrender if only the emperor could remain on the throne, that he could do so (as, after the war, he in fact did). Another would have been to persist in the blockade and conventional bombing. (No invasion was possible until the fall in any case.)

Still another would have been to hold off using the bomb until after the Soviet invasion of Manchuria, which was scheduled for early August. Japan's last hope, however delusional, of avoiding final defeat and occupation, rested on the fantasy that Russia, which had until then been neutral in the Pacific war, might retain that stance and perhaps even broker a more favorable peace agreement with the United States. (The historian Tsuyoshi Hasegawa has recently argued that the Soviet entry into the war, occurring only two days after Hiroshima, was actually more important in Japan's decision to surrender than the atomic bomb.)* Stalin indeed was speeding up his timetable for attack precisely in order to be able to seize spoils in East

---

*The implications of this conclusion are interesting to reflect upon. To say that the Russian invasion was in fact more important in ending the war than the bomb is not the same as to say that the bomb, had its use continued beyond Nagasaki, would not have brought surrender. It does suggest that the use of more atomic bombs might have been required. Here, however, an important consideration invites thought. Truman's administration had decided on four Japanese cities as targets, with more to come. In his announcement of Hiroshima, Truman had said, "If they do not now accept our terms they may expect a rain of ruin from the air, the like of which has never been seen on this earth." Yet in actuality Truman desisted from using atomic bombs after Nagasaki, explaining to Vice President Henry Wallace that "the thought of wiping out another 100,000 people was too horrible." For "he didn't like the idea of killing, as he said, 'all those kids.' " In other words, even if Truman had unleashed the rain of ruin without giving an order, he *did* reverse his own nondecision, and order its halt. Thus there *was* a decision regarding nuclear weapons in August 1945, and it was a decision not to drop a third bomb.

Asia before the war ended. Truman took care to steer clear of both of these alternative paths to war's end. In the Potsdam Declaration, which spelled out surrender conditions to Japan, he left out any reference to the emperor. The omission was notable because a draft of the declaration prepared by his advisers had included a paragraph 12 that would have announced American readiness to leave the emperor in place, thus possibly leading to an early surrender. And instead of waiting to see what the consequences of a Soviet invasion were, Truman used the bomb at the very first moment possible.

This record shows that, in a negative sense, there certainly *was* a kind of "decision" to use the bomb. If you have deliberately foreclosed every solution to a problem but one, you have chosen that one. However, Truman's rejection of the alternative paths to the war's end is not incompatible with emphasis on the bomb's momentum. The rejection of alternatives may only show that the underlying pressure to use the bomb was so great that alternatives were brushed aside. Missing from the record is any sustained discussion among the top American decision makers of the other ways to end the war. A decision to *stop* the bomb's use and to pursue other paths to Japan's surrender would have been a decision indeed.

All Power of Operation

The deep-rooted feeling among both scientists and statesmen that inventing the bomb and using it were scarcely distinguishable stages in a single process also had roots in the nature of modern science. In ancient times, science proceeded mainly by thought. Scientific theories, like philosophic theories, won acceptance when they appealed directly to enough of the best minds. The hallmark of modern science, on the other hand, was the turn to empirical proof.

Experimentation became the gateway through which scientific theory had to pass if it was to be accepted as knowledge. But even experiment needed validation—by a second experiment, and then a third, and so forth—demonstrating that anyone repeating the procedure would arrive at the same result. (The results of many experiments have been dismissed when colleagues were unable to repeat them.) The need for repetition to confirm knowledge further blurred the distinction between knowing and doing. What is an assembly line of, say, cathode ray tubes but the repetition ad infinitum of the experiment that demonstrated the possibility of cathode ray tubes in the first place?

The great sixteenth-century philosopher of modern science Francis Bacon used a word that captured these fundamental aspects of scientific method better than the word "experiment" does. He spoke of "operation," meaning both what we call experimentation and the productive power that flows from it. As he wrote, ". . . nor can nature be commanded except by being obeyed. And so those twin objects, human knowledge and human power, do really meet in one; and it is from ignorance of causes that operation fails." When he stated his renowned dictum "knowledge is power," he did not merely mean that new knowledge would endow the knower with new power, true as that was; he meant that the very acts of acquiring knowledge and acquiring power were one and the same. He rightly said that knowledge *is* power, not that knowledge *brings* power. In his words, "For the matter in hand is no mere felicity [of thought], but the real business and fortunes of the human race, and all power of operation."

The gulf between thought and action that characterized previous scientific efforts had been closed forever. Thereafter, to be a scientist was to be a doer, an actor, an "operator," and even the purest science carried scientists deep into the zone of action. If they felt a curious, helpless inability *not* to introduce revolutionary change into the world—*not* to make the A-bomb, *not* to make the H-bomb—one reason was that by virtue of the nature of their quest, they had already left the quiet precincts of contemplation behind.

This blurring of the border between thought and action, which characterizes all modern scientific inventions, was manifested in the

bombing of Hiroshima. To begin with, the bombing itself was literally an experiment. The test at Alamogordo the month before had
been of a plutonium bomb—the kind dropped three days later on
Nagasaki, which thus *was* tested in New Mexico before it was used.
The Hiroshima bomb employed uranium, and was a very different
device. So certain had the scientists been of its success that they felt
no need to test it first. The test and first use of the uranium bomb
were the same event—the bombing of Hiroshima. The experimental
character of the explosion was important to the policy makers, who
were eager to learn the effects of atomic weapons not just on desert
sand but on a human population. The stated criterion for a target—
"a vital war plant employing a large number of workers and closely
surrounded by workers' houses" (in other words, a city)—was
shaped by this consideration.[20]

To create an impression of destructive power of a new order of
magnitude was not easy in Japan in August 1945. The devastation of
so many cities by firebombing led the Target Committee to fear that
no unruined city large enough to show the full effects of an atomic
explosion would be available. Several Japanese cities had to be taken
off the conventional target list in order to reserve them for the
bomb. The problem was especially acute because Secretary of War
Stimson had ruled out bombing Kyoto, Japan's ancient capital and
repository of much of its finest art, which he had visited in the
1920s and found beautiful. Groves was upset because he judged Kyoto to be the perfect laboratory for studying the effects of his
creation. "I particularly wanted Kyoto as a target," he later wrote,
"because . . . it was large enough in area for us to gain complete
knowledge of the effects of an atomic bomb."[21]

"A Profound Psychological Impression"

Thus gaining the knowledge of how to make the atomic bomb im-
perceptibly spilled over into gaining "complete knowledge" of the
bomb's effects in war. Gaining *that* knowledge—an important

objective for the newborn nuclear power—was in turn inseparable from the central political objective of the bombing. It was not to crush the Japanese military machine (though the United States accompanied the bombing with false and unconvincing statements that the targets had been "military"). Rather, the objective was to bypass the military by shocking the Japanese government and public through the sheer hopeless horror of the spectacle into directly surrendering. Later, Secretary of War Henry Stimson explained that "to extract a genuine surrender from the Emperor and his military advisers, they must be administered a tremendous shock which would carry convincing proof of our power to destroy the Empire." For the bomb "was more than a weapon of terrible destruction; it was a psychological weapon."[22] In the decisive words of the minutes of the Interim Committee, which recommended the bomb's use to Truman, "We should seek to make a profound psychological impression on as many of the inhabitants as possible."[23] Or, as the Target Committee wrote, the aim was "obtaining the greatest psychological effect against Japan" and, in addition, "making the initial use sufficiently spectacular for the importance of the weapon to be internationally recognized when publicity on it is released."[24]

In other words, the knowledge acquired by the bombing not only had to be gathered but broadcast. The prime audience would not be the physical city or population of Hiroshima but the population of the whole of Japan, with the intent to crush its will to continue fighting. The secondary audience was the entire onlooking world, but especially America's emerging rival on the international scene, the Soviet Union. For as soon as the bomb was tested, policy makers began to calculate its usefulness in the gathering confrontation with the Soviets, already under way in Eastern Europe. This multilayered "psychological" character of atomic policy, so tightly linked to the science that made it possible, was to prove a central characteristic of the nuclear dilemma during the Cold War and after.

None of this is to say that the decision to drop the bomb was foreordained or might not have been avoided by a statesman of exceptional imagination and resolve. (Some have suggested that Roosevelt, had he lived, might have been such a statesman.) But there can be no question that when the bomb was delivered into the hands of the new president, it was attended by a powerful momentum flowing from the very nature of the innovation. In Groves's words, "It would . . . have taken a lot of nerve to say 'no' at that time."[25]

And so in the very first moments of the nuclear age, several of the basic characteristics of the nuclear dilemma—of its genetic code—were put on display and immediately began operating in the world. Well before any physical bomb had been built, science had created the bomb in the mind, an intangible thing. Thereafter, the bomb would be as much a mental as a physical object. Because scientific findings are uncontainable, the know-how for building the bomb was destined to be universally available. Like the rain in the Sermon on the Mount, knowledge of the bomb would fall on the just and the unjust alike. Because uranium was widely dispersed around the globe, its availability had practical meaning for other nations. (Einstein commented, "There are atoms in all countries.") Because scientific findings, once discovered, cannot be repealed from human consciousness, the world forever after would be, if not nuclear-armed, then at least nuclear-capable: the nuclear dilemma, that is, would be everlasting. Nuclear arsenals might be abolished, but no one could ever abolish the bomb in the mind. Because the destructive power of the bomb was effectively unlimited, any country fearing that another would get it would be tempted to seek it for itself. (Roosevelt opposed preemptive war, but he practiced preemptive acquisition of the bomb.) Because the bomb concentrated that power into a very small object and could be delivered by any form of transportation, from a donkey cart to an intercontinental ballistic missile, defenses against it were unlikely to be successful. And because the danger was universal, everlasting, unlimited, and immune to defenses, it formed an indivisible, global unified field, in which the disturbance of one part immediately reverberated throughout the whole system.*

Atoms for Peace and War

All of these characteristics of the bomb, which set the fundamental, unvarying terms of the nuclear predicament, have remained in force throughout the nuclear age, framing the choices available at every key juncture. American presidents, Soviet general secretaries, and other statesmen struggled with them in different ways, sometimes

---

*It is telling that nuclear momentum appears prominently in the decisions regarding nuclear programs in other countries. For example, the official historian of the British program, Margaret Gowing, writes that the decision to make plutonium was "what can only be called a non-decision." As late as the mid-1940s, "the need for atomic bombs went unquestioned in all these [governmental] discussions, and again no one pointed out that the decision to make them had never been taken." We read that with minor exceptions "the Cabinet as a body was excluded from all the major decisions on atomic policy. It took no part in the decisions to establish a research establishment, to build piles to produce plutonium, or, later, to build gaseous diffusion plants . . . no part in the decisions to make and test an atomic bomb, and about the planned place of atomic bombs in British strategy." Nevertheless, "the general assumption was that Britain was going to make atomic weapons." As for parliament, it also played no role. Churchill finessed the nondecision by merely stating in the House of Commons in 1945, "This I take is already agreed, we should make atomic bombs." There were no questions.

France's program presents a similar picture. In a review of its history, McGeorge Bundy concludes, "If the Fourth Republic had lasted beyond the spring of 1958, we might have a full case history of a country that acquired nuclear weapons mainly because the government never decided not to." But when Charles de Gaulle came to power in that year, the atmosphere changed, with results that are instructive. De Gaulle was bent on developing the bomb, but strong public opposition inside and outside the National Assembly developed. His prime minister, Michel Debré, had recourse to an emergency article of the newly established constitution, giving the government the right to pass a bill without a vote unless, within twenty-four hours, a motion to censure the entire government was passed. De Gaulle thus staked the existence of his government on the bomb. When the question was framed in that fashion, the assembly folded, and he had his way. But the assembly never did vote directly whether France should build the bomb. Indeed, it is a striking fact of the nuclear age that no legislative body has ever voted to develop the bomb. As in the United States, the decision, or lack of same, has always been in the hands of the executive branch and has usually been taken in secret.

accepting them, sometimes fighting against them. Today, nuclear proliferation, a term unknown in 1945, stems from the same unstanchable spread of scientific know-how that broke the U.S. nuclear monopoly when the Soviet Union acquired the bomb in 1949. The central choice, now as before, has been and remains whether, bowing to the bomb's long-term universal availability, to address the bomb as a common danger afflicting all nations or whether, denying the fact of that availability (at least for a while), to try to assert national ownership of the bomb and seek military advantage from it. In 1945, it was the United States that sought to maintain its monopoly.

The decisions made by the first three presidents to deal with the nuclear question—Roosevelt, Truman, and Eisenhower—illustrate the terms of the basic choices involved. When Roosevelt initiated the Manhattan Project, he was "responding" to the bomb in the mind in its prospective Nazi incarnation (which of course never came close to occurring). He obviously understood that the bomb would be available to others (starting with Germany) and suffered from no delusion that an American monopoly could be preserved. He apparently had what later would be called "deterrence" in mind.

Truman's understanding was different. When he bombed Hiroshima, he was taking advantage of the first moment of the United States' brief atomic monopoly to end a world war and intimidate the Soviet Union. When the Soviet Union acquired the bomb, Truman sought to renew and extend the United States' advantage by ordering the H-bomb. In doing so, he fostered an illusion that would endure—that the maintenance of atomic superiority was a feasible objective for the United States over the long term. If Roosevelt laid the foundation in 1939 for the tradition of deterrence, Truman laid the foundations in 1945 and 1949 for the quest for nuclear superiority. Of course, it could not last: less than a year after the United States tested its first H-bomb, the Soviet Union did likewise.

It's true that in 1946 Truman proposed the Baruch Plan, for the abolition of nuclear arms. Yet in practice, this proposal and the Soviet counterproposal, both aiming at disarmament, became, through their failure, a kind of moral license for the ensuing Cold War arms race. Each side said to itself and the world: *we* don't want nuclear arms, but as you can see, the other side refuses to accept our reasonable plan for eliminating them, so we are reluctantly compelled to build up our arsenal. As Glenn Seaborg, head of the Atomic Energy Commission under Presidents Kennedy, Johnson, and Nixon, has written, "One is left with the conviction that, in offering a proposal that was virtually certain to be rejected, U.S. policymakers had made the fateful decision to rely on our prowess in nuclear arms to keep us safe, rather than on international agreements. Meanwhile, we would be satisfied with the propaganda victory made possible by the apparent generosity of the Baruch Plan."[26] The Soviet Union, bent on getting the bomb at all costs, made the same calculation, and a world that had attached real hope to the nuclear disarmament negotiations of 1946 was left with a runaway arms race accompanied by a counterpoint of high-sounding, empty phrases.

Under Truman's successor, President Dwight D. Eisenhower, the tension between seeking unilateral advantage and addressing the common danger again appeared, but in a new form. Choosing superiority over meeting the common danger, Eisenhower bought a decade of American numerical preponderance over the Soviet Union at the cost of fueling future proliferation. The vehicle for this unfortunate bargain was his Atoms for Peace program. In 1953, his first year in office, Eisenhower was planning a major nuclear buildup in support of his "massive retaliation" policy, which, at least theoretically, placed new reliance on nuclear threats to repel local threats by Communist forces around the world. To this end, during his two terms in office, he increased the American nuclear arsenal from 1,436 to 20,464 warheads. (The Soviet Union, still struggling to catch up, meanwhile increased its arsenal from 120 to 1,065 warheads. It would draw even with the United States in the 1960s and 1970s.)[27]

By 1953, however, in the wake of both American and Soviet H-bomb tests, international pressure to head off an arms race was growing. While Eisenhower did not wish for a nuclear arms control agreement, because it might interfere with his buildup, he did wish to *appear* to want one. In the words of Secretary of State John Foster Dulles, a public posture of desiring negotiations was needed as a "holding operation," because "of international opinion and governmental opinion."[28] As the National Security Council Planning Board put it later that year, arms talks were needed "principally because our political position would suffer at this time by any indication that the United States lacks interest in disarmament."[29]

As a substitute for the arms control proposal he didn't want, Eisenhower came up with something very different, his Atoms for Peace proposal. It recommended that the nuclear powers contribute fissionable materials to an atomic energy commission, which would in turn disburse them to nonnuclear powers, but only for peaceful purposes, such as nuclear power and nuclear medicine. Its professed aim was to beat nuclear swords into nuclear ploughshares. In Eisenhower's words in a speech to the United Nations on December 8, 1953, "The United States would seek more than the mere reduction or elimination of atomic materials for military purposes." For "it is not enough to take this weapon out of the hands of the soldiers. It must be put into the hands of those who will know how to strip its military casing and adapt it to the arts of peace." At the time, the good faith of the proposal was widely accepted, and the press in the United States hailed the administration for taking a bold step in pursuit of peace, even for seeking disarmament. For example, *Newsweek* wrote, "It was at least a great psychological victory; at best it would set the world on the road to atomic disarmament."[30]

But building up nuclear power and cutting back on nuclear weapons were not the same, of course. Nor was building up atomic power and building up nuclear arsenals an either/or proposition. It was quite possible to build both, and that is what happened. Eisenhower delivered his "more"—the global spread of nuclear power technology—but had no intention of delivering the "mere" arms reduction than which nuclear power was supposedly more.[31] Quite the contrary, he was planning to build an additional and very different "more"—an immense expansion of the American nuclear arsenal in support of his massive retaliation policy.*

Atoms for Peace also turned out to have another hidden cost attached. Even as it was used to mask the accelerated American arms buildup of the 1950s, it would lay the technical foundations for accelerated nuclear proliferation. The seeds sown by Eisenhower's proposal would bear poisonous fruit in the negotiations for the Nuclear Non-Proliferation Treaty (NPT) in the late 1960s. The treaty, which divided its signatories into two classes—nonnuclear weapon states, which agreed to forgo nuclear weapons, and nuclear weapon states, which were permitted for the time being to continue to possess the nuclear weapons they already had—created a need to compensate the deprived class. (The possessors then were the United States, the Soviet Union, Britain, France, and China.) The treaty's Article IV, ratifying and extending the Atoms for Peace program, filled the need by guaranteeing the nonnuclear weapon states a right to full nuclear power technology, including the fuel cycle, on condition that they submit the facilities to international inspections. The nuclear powers bought the right to keep their nuclear arsenals, at least temporarily (the treaty's Article VI required that they surrender them eventually), by institutionalizing the spread of nuclear technology to other countries. Or, to put the matter differently, the nonnuclear states won full access to nuclear power technology as

---

*In the "Atoms for Peace" speech, the product of months of drafting by Eisenhower's speechwriters, we can watch Eisenhower's sleight of hand in action. Having first acknowledged that nuclear weapons are a dread thing, he notes that the UN General Assembly once called for "an acceptable solution" to the armaments race "which overshadows not only the peace but the very life of the world," and avows that the United States is "instantly prepared to meet" to seek this solution. It might seem at this point that he will unfold a disarmament proposal, but instead, in the crucial twist, he states that it is into these "talks" (which were not occurring and which he was trying to avoid) that the U.S. would introduce a "new conception"— the Atoms for Peace program, quite falsely packaged as a kind of atomic swords for ploughshares scheme. Then follow the sentences quoted above about needing to go beyond "mere" disarmament to make positive use of nuclear technology.

the reward for renouncing nuclear weapons in a world in which the five possessors were permitted to keep theirs.

That deal was a Trojan horse written into the text of the treaty. Continued possession by the five assured that in many other countries the desire to obtain nuclear weapons would be strong, while the Article IV provisions assured that they would legally be able to acquire nine-tenths of the wherewithal to fulfill their ambitions. The stage was being set for the collision between nuclear possessors and nuclear proliferators that is now occurring.

Sacrificing the commonweal for unilateral advantage, Eisenhower bought public acceptance for an American nuclear buildup by sponsoring a plan whose declared intention was peace but whose actual consequences would be to broaden and deepen the nuclear predicament in the future. Atoms for Peace, while providing cover for an immense increase in existing superpower arsenals, sowed the dragon's teeth of nuclear proliferation that future generations have wrestled with in vain. Once again, the arena of nuclear disarmament had been reduced, this time quite cynically, to a playground of false hopes, bad faith, posturing, and grandiloquence deliberately drained of any connection (other than concealment) to real decisions.*

---

*The less grounded a proposal was in fact, it seemed, the higher the rhetoric soared. To give just one characteristic example of this "let-them-eat-fine-words" genre, Eisenhower said in his "Atoms for Peace" speech, "So my country's purpose is to help us move out of the dark chamber of horrors into the light, to find a way by which the minds of men, the hopes of men, the souls of men everywhere, can move forward toward peace and happiness and well-being."

CHAPTER 3

NUCLEAR REALISTS, NUCLEAR ROMANTICS

The failure of international control in 1946, Russia's acquisition of the bomb, and the implementation of Eisenhower's Atoms for Peace created the framework in which a basic question of the nuclear age would thereafter be asked and answered: why do states want the bomb? One reason has stood out: Since Hiroshima, almost all states that have acquired the bomb, starting with the Soviet Union, have pointed to an existing arsenal or arsenals as their motive. They have fallen into the Rooseveltian tradition of "responding," later called deterrence. Thereafter, one bomb would give birth to the next.

These early events of the nuclear age displayed another of the ingrained features of the nuclear dilemma that binds its seemingly disparate parts into a whole: deterrence and proliferation are two sides of the same coin. After all, proliferators are only those governments that have taken to heart the central tenet of deterrence, taught by the words and deeds of all nuclear powers over the last sixty years: safety from nuclear weapons depends on possessing some yourself. Or, to put the belief negatively, countries that lack nuclear arms will be helpless before those that have them. There is scarcely anything surprising about these simple, even primeval reactions. They are merely an extension into the nuclear age of elementary principles of political realism. Simply put, its main tenets are that nations, like people, are bent above all on survival, and that in the anarchic international sphere, force is the final arbiter of survival. An "ultimate weapon" had been found. In such a world, what country capable of acquiring it would decide, in the face of danger, to do without it, or at least fail to seek an ally that possessed it? What country would leave its survival to the mercy of its enemies?

The theorists of proliferation later spoke of the problem of "$n+1$," in which the number "n" stands for the existing nuclear powers and "1" stands for the additional country—the "proliferator"—that seeks to join the "club." In the understanding proposed here, the "nth" country in 1939, when Albert Einstein and Leo Szilard informed Roosevelt that an atomic bomb was feasible, was the Republic of Science (Sciencestan, if you will, or perhaps Laboratorystan), possessor of the bomb in the mind, and the "1" stands for the next acquirer, the first actualizer, the United States. Seen thus, the United States was not the true originator of the bomb but the first proliferator.

That is why Roosevelt, fearful of German prowess in nuclear physics, was already in a sense in the deterrence business. And so it has gone ever since. Every deterrer was once a proliferator, and every proliferator has become a deterrer. Stalin, seeking to restore the "equilibrium" shattered by the American attempt to nationalize the bomb, broke the American monopoly by developing his own bomb. Britain, fearing the Soviet Union, and not wanting to rely wholly on the United States for its national survival, joined the nuclear club in 1952. France followed suit in 1960, and China, to the chagrin of all of the above, did likewise in 1964. (No one has ever been *invited* into this "club." All have entered by breaking down the door.) The critical events in the Chinese decision appear to have been crises with the Eisenhower administration in 1954 and 1958 over Quemoy and Matsu, two islands just off the China coast that remained under the control of the Nationalist Chinese government then ruling Taiwan. China noticed that when the United States brandished the bomb to prevent a Chinese takeover of the islands, the Soviet Union was in no hurry to brandish *its* bomb on China's behalf. Soviet First Secretary Nikita Khrushchev prudently issued a nuclear threat against the United States only after the 1958 crisis was on its way to resolution. It was then that Chinese party chairman Mao Zedong decided that the remedy was for China to acquire the bomb.

India, in a slow-motion response to China, conducted its first test, a "peaceful" explosion, in 1974, then waited until 1998 to set off its series of five explicitly warlike tests. To this, Pakistan, which had received nuclear assistance from China, responded immediately with five tests. Meanwhile North Korea, following in the footsteps of China, reacted to its loss of Soviet support (owing to the collapse of the Soviet Union in 1991) and to increasing tensions with the United States by withdrawing from the Nuclear Non-Proliferation Treaty, building its own small arsenal, and, in 2006, conducting its first test. Israel, the odd man out in this story, followed the Roosevelt model. It practiced preemptive regional deterrence by building a nuclear arsenal to safeguard against some future nuclear arsenal that might be developed by a hostile neighbor (such as Iraq, Iran, or Egypt), or to compensate for possible future conventional inferiority in the face of powerful Arab armies that it might one day face. Prime Minister David Ben-Gurion, the initiator of Israel's bomb, who cited the holocaust of Europe's Jews as his motivation, may in a manner of speaking have been targeting not just any current or future foe but also a previous one, Hitler. In a very real sense, the "bomb" that Israel was "responding" to was the Nazi attempt to annihilate the Jewish people. In this way, one kind of holocaust prepared the ground for another kind.

Thus, to the underlying unity of nuclear danger dictated by the universal availability of scientific findings was added a layer of strategic unity composed of an ever-lengthening chain reaction of nuclear threats and counterthreats. It is above all fear—or, to use the proper word in this context, terror—that links one arsenal to another, creating the chain that connects them all. Even as the know-how was seeping outward, from the greater powers to the

lesser, and in our own time threatening to seep down to the terrorist cell or even, perhaps, to the individual, the waves of terror were
also radiating outward in multiplying spheres, drawing ever-more
actors into the game. In 1985, undersecretary of state for political
affairs Michael Armacost paid tribute to the strength of this chain
while on a diplomatic mission to Pakistan to discourage it from going nuclear. He later recalled, "We were unlikely to make much
progress in stopping the Pakistani program if we did not deal with
their motivating regional factors, which meant India. But we en-
countered the old problem: the Indians said their concern was not
only Pakistan, but also China. We would have to bring China into
the process. But this would then lead to Russia's nuclear policies
and on up to ours. So it was impossible to find a way to begin in the
region."[1] Ultimately, you could not deal with Pakistan's arsenal
without dealing with the American arsenal. Here was a task judged
by Armacost—and so many others in the American government—
to be "impossible."

The Atomic Archipelago

The middle term between the scientific unity and the strategic unity
of the nuclear dilemma was its technical unity. Eisenhower's attempt to draw a sharp line between peaceful and warlike atoms
proved untenable. The connections between one national nuclear
program and another, whether for energy or weapons, soon were as
fully internationalized as any of the other technical or commercial
transactions of our day.

Consider India's search in the 1980s for heavy water, which is a
moderator for chain reactions in nuclear reactors. To avoid the im-
position of the sorts of international inspections of its nuclear program that any open purchase of heavy water would have required,
India wished to use heavy water of its own manufacture. However,
the supply was insufficient, so India arranged to buy Chinese heavy
water on the sly through one Alfred Hempel, a German middleman.

Hempel, in turn, diverted Norwegian heavy water meant for Germany, mixed it not only with the Chinese supply but with some Soviet heavy water he had obtained, and shipped the mixture off to Bombay.[2] India's store of Chinese-Norwegian-German-Soviet-Indian heavy water can stand as a symbol of the irreversible internationalization of nuclear technology and of the hopelessness of any attempt to restrict it, absent central international controls, to any one nation or privileged group of nations.

The most spectacular exploitation of the inherent technical unity of the nuclear dilemma, however, was certainly the global supply network for nuclear weapon technology created by A. Q. Khan, the "father" of Pakistan's bomb. Within Pakistan, his nuclear project became a virtual state within the state, controlled less by prime ministers than by the country's military and security services. Repeatedly, American intelligence, which tried to keep abreast of developments, startled Pakistani heads of state by informing them of the progress—largely unknown to them—of their own nuclear program. In 1989, for example, the director of the CIA, William H. Webster, gave Prime Minister Benazir Bhutto a briefing that included a mockup of the Pakistani bomb. She had never seen the real article.[3] When she was ejected from power in 1990, she called what had happened a "nuclear coup" by forces intent on resisting her attempts to gain control over their bomb program.

At the same time, this nuclear state within the Pakistani state was a state beyond the state—a truly international enterprise—for it was born as a network of companies in many countries that were to supply Pakistan with materials for uranium enrichment, and then, after that goal was achieved, it became the reverse: a network for supplying everything necessary for nuclear weapons *to* other countries.

A question that remains unanswered is how much knowledge of and control over the network the Pakistani government ever exercised. Either Khan and his accomplices enjoyed a shocking independence from the state in peddling its most dangerous technical secrets around the world, or else the Pakistani state was itself engaged in a global yard sale of those secrets to the highest bidder. It's difficult to decide which of these situations would be more alarming.

A metallurgist by training, Khan was working for a subsidiary of the European uranium enrichment company Urenco, located in Almelo, Holland, when, in 1971, India intervened in the rebellion against the Pakistani government in the nation's eastern territories. Its armies crushed the Pakistani military in a mere three days, and the independent nation of Bangladesh was born. The proud and patriotic Khan felt humiliated and became enraged. However, it was not only India that roused his fury. He was steeped in resentment of the West in general and of the United States in particular. He gave voice to his feelings in a letter to the German magazine *Der Spiegel* in 1979. "I want to question the bloody holier-than-thou attitudes of the Americans and the British. Those bastards are God-appointed guardians of the world to stockpile hundreds of thousands of nuclear warheads [*sic*] and have the God-given authority of carrying out explosions every month. But if we start a modest program, we are the Satans, the devils."[4]

Around this time, Khan conceived the idea of equipping Pakistan with the wherewithal to take the uranium route to acquiring the bomb. As an employee of a Urenco subsidiary with security clearance, he was well positioned to do so, and, in 1974, he wrote Pakistani prime minister Zulfikar Ali Bhutto a letter offering his services to accomplish the task. Over the next few years, he stole technical components for centrifuges, while secretly copying blueprints for making this uranium-enriching technology as well as the contact information that would allow him to be in touch with the key suppliers of all necessary technology. (Later, Khan would brag that these contacts were as important for his later work in Pakistan as the technical blueprints.) Not since Klaus Fuchs delivered the design for the Manhattan Project's plutonium bomb to the Russians had there been such extensive and consequential spying in the nuclear arena. By the time the Dutch authorities began to catch up with him, he had everything he needed, and in 1975 he fled to Pakistan, where Bhutto appointed him to run a uranium-enrichment effort called Project 706.[5]

Khan immediately put his stolen secrets and contacts to work, sending agents around the world to obtain what he needed to build the cascades of thousands of centrifuges required to enrich uranium for the bomb. His technique was to scatter his purchases, ordering only bits and pieces of the necessary technology from any one supplier, in order to allay suspicion. He and his helpers then assembled these fragments into the finished centrifuges.

The suppliers were willing. From South Africa, Switzerland, and Dubai came specialized pipes and valves; from Dubai and Malaysia, end caps and baffles. Rotors originated in South Korea, South Africa, and Switzerland. From Turkey and elsewhere came maraging steel.[6] A British company provided high-frequency inverters.[7] Even before Khan became involved, Bhutto had talked China into providing help—including a design for a nuclear bomb and partially or wholly processed uranium.[8] German companies were especially eager for the business and became suppliers of, among other things, a plant for handling uranium hexafluoride. A former Israeli living in South Africa contrived to ship American oscilloscopes to Pakistan.[9] In this system, a product could be "designed in one country, manufactured in a second, shipped through a third, assembled in a fourth, and put to use in a fifth."[10]

Khan did not slacken his pace after he had succeeded in getting the centrifuges up and running in Pakistan. Rather, he stepped up the pace, now turning his attention to supplying other countries with the same technology. Considered a hero in Pakistan for his role in its bomb program, he began to enrich himself from his illicit commerce. Brochures—one reportedly adorned with a drawing of a mushroom cloud—were produced to advertise his wares.[11] The known buyers were Iran, North Korea, and Libya, but others are suspected. His network expanded to include production facilities in Malaysia and an extensive shipping network run out of Dubai. The designs of the centrifuges now under construction in Iran were almost certainly provided by Khan, at a reported cost of tens of millions or perhaps a hundred million dollars.

Khan visited North Korea at least thirteen times, and a brisk exchange of nuclear-related goods ensued, with North Korea receiving centrifuges and Pakistan much-desired missile technology. But the network's most ambitious endeavor was its attempt to supply Libya with the entire panoply of nuclear-weapon-producing materials, from centrifuges to bomb designs—a kind of do-it-yourself kit for joining the nuclear club. It was exposure of this immense project that led to international pressure on Pakistan's self-appointed president, Pervez Musharraf, to place Khan under house arrest in February of 2004.

Though we speak of "A. Q. Khan's network," the label may be misleading. Enterprising as Khan undoubtedly was, the network consisted chiefly of a global array of scientists, businessmen, corporations, intelligence and military services, and states at whose center Khan placed himself. Founding what was in effect a clandestine, state-supported multinational corporation for supplying nuclear weapon technology (the head of the International Atomic Energy Agency called it a "Wal-Mart of private sector proliferation"),[12] he brought to light one more universal pressure that fuels the spread of nuclear know-how—the all-pervading circulation of goods and services by the market system in our globalized globe.

Because the relationships among nuclear rivals are hostile, it can seem at first that the sources of nuclear danger are independent from one another. But when it comes to nuclear arms, hostilities are the ties that bind, forming what we can call—borrowing from Aleksandr Solzhenitsyn, who coined the phrase "gulag archipelago" for Stalin's system of concentration camps—the atomic archipelago. As in many literal archipelagos, the islands of this one are joined beneath the surface by a mountain range of which they are merely the visible peaks. We might say that the energy stored in atoms is like

permitted nuclear weapons while others were forbidden them was inequitable—"nuclear apartheid," a de facto continuation of imperial rule, against which India had rebelled when it won independence. This view at least left the door open to nuclear realism, for it implied a belief that countries were unwise to do without nuclear weapons in a world in which others had them—the central tenet of deterrence.

In the first decades of the nuclear age, the two themes—that nuclear weapons were immoral and that a two-tiered world of nuclear haves and have-nots was discriminatory—seemed consonant, but over time they began to clash. In 1970 and thereafter, India refused to sign the Nuclear Non-Proliferation Treaty, on the ground that it froze in place a nuclear double standard. For the same reason, India also refused to sign the Comprehensive Nuclear Test Ban Treaty. The idealist view that nuclear weapons were inherently repugnant in all circumstances yielded steadily to the realist view that if some nations had them India should as well. Official and popular opinion were both strongly opposed to the NPT's indefinite extension in 1995. The demand for equity gradually eclipsed moral condemnation of the bomb.

India had always advocated abolition of nuclear arms, and that is still its formal position. In 1988, Prime Minister Rajiv Gandhi dramatically proposed a third world version of the Baruch Plan, in which India and other potential proliferators would permanently forswear the bomb if the nuclear weapon states agreed to eliminate their nuclear arsenals by 2010. When the proposal fell on deaf ears, he stepped up India's nuclear weapon program. Once again, a rejected disarmament program had become the springboard for a realist policy of pursuing nuclear arms. From then on, India increasingly took the position that if there were going to be two classes of nations in the world, India was going to be in the first class. As the nuclear scientist Homi J. Bhabha, the scientific founder of India's nuclear program, had warned, "We will stand on the brink of a dangerous era sharply dividing the world into atomic 'haves' and 'have nots.'" The historian of India's nuclear bomb project George Perkovich comments, "This morally and politically charged argument proved difficult to rebut and has remained central to India's nuclear diplomacy to this day. India was determined to repudiate all vestiges of colonialism in relations with the leading global powers."[17]

While these shifts in sentiment were occurring, India was gradually acquiring the wherewithal for building a nuclear arsenal. The strictly technological momentum of the bomb was especially notable in India, where constant pressure to move forward was exerted by a well-funded, secretive, politically unaccountable "strategic enclave" for nuclear weapon development created by Bhabha. Even as Prime Minister Nehru was unequivocally denouncing nuclear arms in public, he was quietly working with Bhabha to create the capacity to build them. It was this program, growing behind a veil of secrecy for almost thirty years, that enabled Indira Gandhi to conduct the 1974 dress rehearsal for 1998. That the interval between the two was twenty-four years was perhaps a testament to the resilience of the traditional Indian loathing of the bomb, which temporarily reasserted itself.

Indira Gandhi, of course, claimed no strategic justification for the "peaceful" explosion of 1974. Nevertheless, it produced an immediate wave of support for her government, enabling her to overcome the political consequences of an economic crisis caused in part by a national railroad strike. The reaction of the *Hindu* was typical of press reports: "no more thrilling news could have come to lift the drooping . . . spirits of the people than the Atomic Energy Commission's announcement yesterday."[18] The *Indian Express* discerned that "India's nuclear blast has catapulted her into the front rank of nations. No longer is she dismissed as a 'pitiful giant.'"[19] "Monopoly of Big Five Broken," the *Sunday Standard* announced. A man on a bicycle interviewed by a reporter summed up the general mood when he said, "Now we're the same as America and Russia and China."[20]

Notwithstanding this history, the realist explanation of India's decision to become a nuclear power has been challenged. Some observers have forcefully argued that India's real motives for becoming a nuclear power had little to do with countering Chinese or Pakistani threats but were instead largely "domestic," "political," and "psychological." Such reasons for acquiring the bomb may be called "romantic," as distinct from realist, in that, like a Napoleonic hero's longing for greatness, they pertain less to any specific urgent threats that must be met than to the general self-image of the leaders and country in question. The observers point out that the Chinese invasion of India cited by Vajpayee had occurred thirty-six years earlier. Could the 1998 tests really be considered a "response" to such a remote event? In fact, as Vajpayee himself admitted in his letter to Clinton, Sino-Indian relations had improved since 1962.

It was true that Pakistan, technically assisted by China, had become a covert weapons state, but so had India, which in 1998 possessed an estimated twenty-five ready-to-assemble bombs.[21] Moreover, Pakistan's program had been initiated only after Indian forces had helped separate Bangladesh from Pakistan in 1971. (Pakistan's alleged ally China had stayed out of that war.) Then India had further goaded Pakistan by setting off the 1974 nuclear explosion. (Pakistan's president, Ali Bhutto, was not persuaded when India's prime minister, Indira Gandhi, declared at the time, "There are no political or foreign policy implications of this test.")[22]

Moreover, according to realist thinking, it is the party inferior in conventional arms that is most likely to resort to nuclear demonstrations, to compensate for its weakness, but India enjoyed conventional superiority over Pakistan. Hence, the true question for India in 1998 was not whether anyone needed to "respond" to any move by a hostile neighbor but whether India and Pakistan, as a pair of antagonists, were better off remaining "covert" nuclear powers or turning themselves into overt ones. It was India's decision, not Pakistan's, to embark on a full-scale, overt nuclear competition.

However, as the Indian writers Praful Bidwai and Achin Vanaik

observe, there was one dramatic event that unquestionably did precipitate the tests—not anything that China or Pakistan had done
but the victory, just two months before the first test, of Vajpayee's
Hindu fundamentalist Bharatiya Janata Party (BJP) over the Congress Party, which had guided India to independence. The BJP and
its political predecessors had championed an Indian bomb since the
1950s, and upon arriving in power implemented its long-advocated
policy. To be sure, during the campaign, the party had partially dis-
guised its intention, promising only to "re-evaluate the nuclear policy
and exercise the policy to *induct* nuclear weapons"—a formulation
that, if it did not point directly to a decision to test, did suggest that
somehow or other India's nuclear explosive capacity, hitherto deemed
peaceful, would be peaceful no more.[23] Induction, after all, is the way
a person is enlisted in an army.

After winning power, the BJP promised to conduct a strategic
review before any decision on testing was taken but then rushed the
tests through without one. Only afterward did it order the review—
a sequence hardly suggesting that gathering external threats had
precipitated the decision. In fact, the government's public statements as well as the Indian public's reaction struck quite a different
note. For instance, Vajpayee bragged that India now had "a big
bomb."[24] The BJP supporter Bal Thackeray put India's weakness in
the prenuclear past, declaring, "We have proved that we are not
eunuchs any more."[25] One newspaper's headline was "Megatons of
Prestige." Another celebrated an "Explosion of Self-Esteem."

When Pakistan responded with its series of tests, another Indian
paper mocked it as a "Copy-cat." Vajpayee curiously declared that
Pakistan's tests had "vindicated" his decision to test,[26] and Defense
Minister George Fernandes boasted, "We have superior strength
and potency."[27] And in the days between India's tests and Pakistan's,
Home Minister L. K. Advani announced that in the improved
"geostrategic" environment, India would adopt a "pro-active" policy
regarding the contested border region of Kashmir.[28] The leadership
of the Congress Party, notwithstanding its long history of reviling

nuclear weapons, fell nearly silent in the face of a wave of popular approval. Although some of the enthusiasm later faded, no serious consideration was ever given by either the BJP or the Congress Party to reverting to nonnuclear status. The international community, including the United States, also acquiesced before long. In one more demonstration of the powerful inertia resident in the nuclear establishment, the 1998 fait accompli created an unchallenged new international reality.

Bidwai and Vanaik carry their argument a step further, holding that of three possible motivations for the tests—threats from without, indignation at the great-power double standard in regard to nuclear arms, and domestic political pride—the third was clearly dominant. They hold that the BJP's accession to power in 1998 confirmed a revolution in nothing less than the "soul of Indian nationalism." The previous, Nehruvian orthodoxy, embraced by the Congress Party, had combined socialism in economics, democracy in politics, secularism in the spiritual field, and nonalignment in the international sphere. The Gandhian wing of the Congress Party had also embraced nonviolence. The BJP offered a model that differed at every point. In economics, its orientation was capitalist; in politics, it displayed an authoritarian streak; in the religious sphere, it was Hindu fundamentalist, with a strong element of antipathy to Islam (in a country comprising a large Muslim majority); and in the international sphere it was the unashamed exponent of might in pursuit of great-power status. As for nonviolence, the BJP rejected it in principle. Indeed, Gandhi's assassin in 1948, Naturam Godse, was a follower of a predecessor organization to the party's youth wing.

In sum, in 1998, Indians seemed less interested in delivering a message to their enemies, as realist theory specifies (and as Vajpayee's letter to Clinton purported), than in delivering one to themselves. No new foreign threats can explain the 1998 test because the reasons for it do not lie there. They are to be sought in a broader shift in Indian self-understanding—in, that is, psychology. The bomb was indeed less a strategic than a "political" object—another sort of bomb in the mind—both in the narrow sense that it generated a wave of support for the government in power and in the broader sense that it assuaged a profound sense of national humiliation harking back to colonial days. In 1998, not self-defense but the "romantic" pursuit of national greatness, defined in terms of military might, was the BJP's reason for turning India into a nuclear power.

However, even if we accept this interpretation, it is important to guard against a misunderstanding that may arise. Some analysts have suggested that because India's reasons for becoming a nuclear power were "domestic"—or at most "regional"—the decision is unrelated to the persistence of existing nuclear powers in holding on to their nuclear arsenals after the end of the Cold War.[29] In this view, each regional case of proliferation is a more or less independent story, having little to do with American or Russian nuclear policies, not to speak of the whole evolution of the nuclear dilemma since 1945. Yet even if it is true that India's tests were political in timing and played more to a domestic audience hungry for greatness than to hostile powers that urgently needed to be deterred, we must go on to ask why it was that the bomb served to buttress the Indian nationalist image of greatness. After all, whatever else nuclear weapons are, they are first and foremost instruments of foreign policy. Political parties do not literally aim them at one another. And if they do so metaphorically, and find the exercise politically advantageous, the reason is that the bomb is widely seen as a shortcut to great-power status. And that belief in turn is inseparable from the fact that the world's greatest powers do in fact possess the bomb and insist on holding on to it. The key word is "prestige," a two-sided idol that faces outward to other nations even as it faces inward toward the domestic public. The chain of cause and effect in such cases is not terror but emulation, but the chain is still there, linking one arsenal to another and all to the domestic publics in each nation.

Our Place Above the Salt

These "political" yearnings for the bomb in India are less surprising if we consider the nuclear programs of two long-established nuclear powers, Britain and France. Both invoked classical realist motives for obtaining the bomb: like the United States, they feared Soviet power. Both also relied for their defense on the United States, which, for its part, was unenthusiastic about British and French assistance in the nuclear field and intermittently sought to prevent both from acquiring the bomb. Indeed, as early as 1943, the Roosevelt administration shocked the British by restricting the flow of nuclear know-how from the Manhattan Project to Britain, even though it had been the British Maud report that had prompted the project in the first place. In a kind of rehearsal for India's rejection of the Nuclear Non-Proliferation Treaty and the Comprehensive Test Ban Treaty, Britain joined the Soviet Union in resisting the United States' Baruch Plan in 1946, fearing, as Stalin did, that such a treaty would bar all national bomb programs but the existing one in the United States, freezing its atomic monopoly in place. (The Soviet opposition is often recalled, the British opposition rarely.) Of course, arguments were made that the modest arsenals Britain and France could hope to build would add something to the defense of the West afforded by the stupendous American arsenal. Yet the argument that seemed to carry the most weight in the two countries' national counsels was quite different: Britain and France, used to thinking of themselves as great powers, wanted to keep up with the new great power—the "superpower" (the H-bomb was initially called "the super")—of the Western world.

In 1946, after a bruising meeting with the American secretary of state James Byrnes, the British foreign minister Ernest Bevin remonstrated with Prime Minister Clement Atlee when he intimated that perhaps Britain didn't need the bomb. "No Prime Minister, that won't do at all," Bevin said. "We've *got* to have this. I don't mind for myself, but I don't want any other Foreign Secretary of this country to be talked at, or to, by the Secretary of State in the United States as I just have in my discussions with Mr. Byrnes. We've got to have this thing over here, whatever it costs. We've got to have the bloody Union Jack on top of it."[30] Harold Macmillan, who became prime minister in 1957, also thought that the relationship with the United States was the critical consideration. For him, Britain's "independent nuclear capability" would assure its right "to retain our special relation with the United States and, through it, our influence in world affairs, and especially our right to have a voice in the final issue of peace and war."[31] For Macmillan's successor, Prime Minister Alec Douglas-Home, the reason Britain needed the hydrogen bomb was "to secure our place above the salt at the negotiating table."[32] These are all sentiments that the Indian cyclist who was so proud of his country's bomb would have readily understood.

The character of France's interest in the bomb was remarkably similar. In January 1946, France formally renounced any ambition to build the bomb, but after the failure of the Baruch Plan, it reconsidered and renounced its renunciation.[33] The French prime minister who first formally made the decision to launch a crash program was Pierre Mendès-France. In the summer of 1954, a debate was joined. In November, Mendès-France visited Washington and made a speech at the United Nations proposing an atmospheric test ban. Washington rejected his proposal. It was on the plane on the way home that he made his decision. (Yet again, a failed arms control initiative had become the starting point for a new local chapter of the arms race.)

Mendès-France's adviser Francis Perrin later reported on a conversation with the prime minister during the flight. "During our return trip from the United States after your initiative at the U.N.," he wrote to Mendès-France, "I believed I understood that your decision [to make the bomb] had to do not so much with giving France a militarily significant nuclear capacity but had to do basically with the political significance for France of taking the first qualitative step."[34] Charles de Gaulle, who returned to office in 1958, agreed.

"The *force de frappe* [nuclear strike force]," he avowed, "is a political weapon, and technical precision is not essential."[35]

Like India and England, France spoke less of specific threats from enemies and more of a generalized ascension, by means of the bomb, to great power status. In keeping with this objective, France's strategy was to aim its modest arsenal at no country in particular but to target *tout azimuth*—all points of the compass—which is to say everyone (theoretically including the United States) and no one. France's *having* the bomb, you might say, was more important than any particular use envisioned for it. In the words of Prime Minister Michel Debré, nuclear weapons were necessary for "all influence in international life."[36] If Britain refused to yield exclusive great-power status (or, now, superpower status) to the United States, France refused to yield it to Britain and the United States. Believing that if it did otherwise, then, in the words of a note from the Quai d'Orsay (Ministry of Foreign Affairs), France's "security will be entirely in the hands of the Anglo-Saxons." Or as de Gaulle would put it, with the bomb in France's possession, "We'll take back our status as a great power at the negotiating table."[37] The bomb in his view was an equalizer, permitting France, otherwise a middling power, to rise to the first rank, for "world developments have created a weapon that permits us to be feared and respected regardless of differences in the quantity [of weapons]." De Gaulle also once said, "France must continue to behave as a great power precisely because she no longer is one."[38] Nuclear weapons were ideally suited for such purposes. When France conducted its first test, in 1960, de Gaulle cried out, "Hurray for France!"

The timing of the French and English decisions was important. Both nations were embattled imperial powers well on the way to losing their empires in a series of humiliations. In the summer of 1954, the French military base at Dien Bien Phu in French-occupied Vietnam fell to the Communist Viet Minh revolutionary forces after a long siege, sealing the end of French rule in Indo-China. In the words of the historian of the bomb, Gerard DeGroot, "Like a jilted lover, France turned from Empire to the Bomb."[39] It was, in a sense, compensation for the lost colony.

England had already quit India and was in full imperial retreat elsewhere in the world. Prime Minister Winston Churchill's science adviser, Lord Cherwell, even feared that if, in the American-dominated world order, Britain failed to get the bomb, it would not only lose its own empire but become a colony in a new American empire. "If we are unable to make bombs ourselves and have to rely entirely on the United States army for this vital weapon," he said, "we shall sink to the rank of second-class nation, only permitted to supply auxiliary troops, like the native levies who were allowed small arms but not artillery."[40] Having very recently imposed just this status on India, among other colonies, Britain had vivid impressions of what it meant to be under the imperial boot: sans the bomb, the empire might find itself imperialized.

While France in the era of de Gaulle was bent on independence and would soon leave NATO, Britain was hoping to secure its place at the table above the salt through the "special relationship" that Churchill had hoped to establish with the United States during the Second World War. Opposite as these reactions to American super-powerdom were, both countries turned to the bomb to compensate for imperial decline. Indeed, there appears to be a profound connection between empire and the bomb. Every phase of imperial operations—reaching for one (the United States), rebelling against one (India), and losing one (Britain and France)—has fueled yearning for nuclear arms.

The Bomb in the Mind, 3—Deterrence Revisited

Are there perhaps two classes of nuclear powers—those who obtain the bomb in response to distinct threats, as the realist school holds, and the nuclear romantics, who acquire the bomb for vaguer "psychological" or "political" reasons? The distinction is real but masks a deeper, underlying commonality; for in practice, the realist's policy of deterrence, too, has turned out to be a psychological operation through and through.

The doctrine of deterrence seems to start off as a strictly realist proposition: any nation facing a foe in possession of a terrible weapon must acquire it for itself, perhaps even preemptively, as Roosevelt sought to do. Such behavior is as old as warfare. Conventional (prenuclear) realism requires that any nation that has fallen behind in weaponry must seek to catch up. But once any two or more nations have, in obedience to this rule, protected themselves by building nuclear arsenals, the picture changes. A new situation is born in which realism offers no further guidance. In prenuclear times, military buildups were useful for deterrence *and* for winning wars. In the nuclear age, however, with great-power victory or defeat taken off the table, only "mutually assured destruction" is left. Now survival depends not on military superiority and winning wars but on not fighting them. For this, equality is better than superiority, because equality is more "stable."

Though born of realism, nuclear deterrence bursts its bounds, not because nations or morals have changed but because the chemistry of power, helpless to escape the implications of the formula $E = mc^2$, has changed. Success in war, formerly the path to survival, has now become the path to annihilation. Deterrence is the attempt to square this circle. It emerges, you might say, as half-sane and half-crazy. The sane, properly realist part consists in matching the nuclear threats of your foe in order to forestall his attack. The crazy part, lying outside the realist scheme, consists of actually waging the war you must threaten, for in that event the result is suicide all around—hardly a result that can be applauded by realism, which values survival above all else. In short, to threaten seems wise, but to act is deranged.

Unfortunately, the sane half and the crazy half cannot easily be pried apart. For the sane end of protecting yourself depends on the crazy means of getting ready for national suicide. For how can you forestall attack without threatening suicide? Yet how, on the other hand, can it make sense to threaten an action whose execution would be crazy? Why should you actually fight a war whose prevention is the only sane goal of your policy? Decades of ratiocination in think tanks and among government officials and strategists have failed to solve this incongruity, which, fortunately, has never been put to the test in action.

In practice, governments trapped in the contradiction have resorted to a surprising makeshift. They have supplanted real battles waged by real weapons with shadow battles waged by posturing and words. A duel of threats replaced the duel of arms. In short, military strategy at the nuclear level became entirely "psychological." The phrase "balance of terror," popular in the Cold War era, is not an accidental one. Terror is a state of the psyche. Its creation is the only rational purpose for possessing nuclear arms under the deterrence doctrine. Hence, the battles that could not be fought in reality were displaced to a realm of appearances, and the actual substance of nuclear strategy became the making of threats—threats issued precisely in order to avoid launching the war they threatened. The bomb of deterrence is thus one more bomb in the mind.

That is why, at the famed "brink" of the bipolar superpower face-off of the Cold War, the leaders of the two sides were, like their counterparts in India, Britain, and France, speaking incessantly of nuclear weapons as "political" and "psychological." We find further, also as in India, Britain, and France, that the psychology in question cannot be confined, as realists might like, to specific enemies. Rather it is projected outward in all directions, profoundly and deliberately influencing domestic publics, allies, and world opinion generally. And the reactions of each of these "audiences" (to use a word favored by Cold War strategists) is as important to "the outcome" as any reaction in any enemy capital. In this respect, nuclear strategy remains in the tradition of the Hiroshima and Nagasaki bombings, whose ends were also avowedly "psychological" and directed at multiple audiences, including the Japanese people and the Soviet leadership. In 1957, Eisenhower portrayed intercontinental missiles in the same light. They are not "much military weapons," he said, "but have great psychological importance."[41] Eisenhower's whole massive retaliation policy has been interpreted as an attempt to create such a convincing *picture* of readiness to use nuclear weapons that the need for use would never arise. The doctrine of "mutual assured destruction" is indeed nothing but a codification of that hope. In truth, exactly that peculiar formula, in one version or another, would prove to be at the core of every American president's or Soviet leader's practice of the nuclear game. In the peculiar world of deterrence, the less you could actually make sensible use of the weapons, the more important it became to project the impression that you could and would.

Soviet General Secretary Nikita Khrushchev was perhaps the boldest practitioner of the art. Possessing, in the late 1950s, only four missiles capable of hitting the United States, he let Eisenhower and Kennedy believe that the USSR was turning out missiles "like sausages," producing a "missile gap" in his favor—when in reality the gap was overwhelmingly in the United States' favor. Or consider John F. Kennedy's reaction when, in October 1962, he discovered that the Soviet Union was placing nuclear-armed missiles in Cuba. He and most of his advisers quickly came to the conclusion that those missiles would do nothing to concretely alter the military balance. Nevertheless, they felt compelled to take Khrushchev's move seriously because of the "political" consequences, as Secretary of Defense Robert McNamara put it. As in India, the "political" encompassed both domestic political repercussions (Robert Kennedy said that his brother would be impeached if he did nothing, and the president agreed) and international considerations of "credibility." In McNamara's words:

> And, speaking strictly in military terms, really in terms of weapons, it doesn't change it [the military balance] at all, in my personal opinion. . . . It's not a military problem that we're facing. It's a political problem.

And in that political zone, international and domestic considerations were all but indistinguishable. As McNamara continued to say:

> The problem of holding the [NATO] alliance together, and the problem of conditioning Khrushchev for our future moves, the problem of dealing with our domestic public, all require action that, in my opinion, the shift in military balance does not require.[42]

At the height of the crisis, the president engaged in a short exchange with Assistant Secretary of State for Inter-American Affairs Edward Martin. National Security Adviser McGeorge Bundy had just asked McNamara what effect the deployment of the Soviet missiles might have on the strategic balance, and he had answered, "None at all." Martin then said, "Well it's a psychological factor that we have sat back and let them do it to us. That is more important than the direct threat. . . ."

Kennedy agreed: the problem, he said, wasn't military, since the Soviets have "got enough to blow us up now anyway." But "this is a political struggle just as much as military."[43]

The problem wasn't the numbers of missiles flying back and forth. Once that happened, all was lost. The problem was the play of perceptions before that happened. Only there could anyone gain anything.

It is true that the meaning of the "political" and the "psychological" are different for the nuclear romantics and the nuclear realists. For India, Britain, and France, a generalized glow of prestige, somehow conferring great-power status, was reason enough to acquire nuclear arsenals. For the United States, the Soviet Union, and perhaps China, meeting specific threats from specific enemies was still the principal motive; yet when we look at their deliberations, we find them entangled in concepts involving prestige and "credibility" of their nations as great powers that are not so easy to distinguish from the Indo-Anglo-Gallic motives. And, as it happened, the gap between the two was only to narrow until, today, it has become almost impossible to detect.

The Bomb in the Parlor

The primacy of the psychological in nuclear strategy also emerges, if in somewhat different form, in the outlying zones of the nuclear archipelago, where small powers have developed their small arsenals. One of the most interesting and ingenious policies has been Israel's. It is an unquestioned fact that Israel is the possessor of a nuclear arsenal numbering perhaps 170 warheads as well as rockets and planes capable of delivering nuclear payloads upon its foes, giving it the capacity to effectively eliminate the human population of the Middle East and more. There is no indication that Israel plans to do such a thing, but neither has Israel given any indication of what, in a showdown, it *would* do with such a large number of weapons. Israel's arsenal is an open secret. Its strategic planning remains a closed secret.

However, Israel, alone among the nuclear powers, has never openly tested a nuclear bomb. (There is debate about whether, with the connivance of the white regime of South Africa during the apartheid era, it may have tested one secretly in the Indian Ocean in 1979.) Nor has Israel ever officially admitted to the existence of its arsenal.[44] Israel's declaratory policy is that it "will not introduce" nuclear weapons into the Middle East—a phrase curiously reminiscent of the BJP's choice of the word "induct" to describe its intentions before the tests of 1998. The question for both countries was not whether to possess nuclear weapons (both of course do); it was whether to admit that they possessed them. And this not admitting, in one more remarkable demonstration of the power of appearances in the nuclear arena, has been considered by most observers to be as important as the possessing. India's innovation in 1998 was not its tests—it had, after all, tested already, in 1974. Rather, the novelty was the accompanying declaration that India was a nuclear

weapon state. Prime Minister Indira Gandhi had once said that India's nuclear "explosives" were not "bombs." Now they were. They
had been militarized—"inducted."

Israel has so far taken the opposite tack. While possessing a far
larger arsenal than India's, it has persisted in declining to declare its
bombs—that is, "introduce" them. Like a crazy relative living in the
attic or the basement ("bomb in the basement" is a phrase often
used for undeclared arsenals), the Israeli bomb is never invited up-
stairs to meet the guests in the parlor. ("Mr. Mubarak, permit me to
present Mr. Thermonuclear Warhead.") A policy of declining to ac-
knowledge publicly a fact that the whole world knows might seem
the height of absurdity—if we did not already understand that,
in matters of the bomb, appearances and psychology have been
trumping realities across the board for more than half a century.

In actuality, Israel's nondeclaration policy has played at least
some role in slowing nuclear proliferation in the region. Strange to
say, some of Israel's Arab neighbors have expressed a kind of support for Israel's policy—or, least, have warned vociferously against
declaration. They do not care to be introduced to the crazy relative.
Amre Moussa, the former foreign minister of Egypt, has said that if
Israel declared or tested its arsenal, "Egypt would have to take drastic action." There would be "immeasurable pressure" on "certain
Arab countries to go nuclear. . . . It would change the entire equa-
tion in the region. Israel would be saying, 'I am the dominant
power.' Membership in the NPT for Arabs would become humiliating." Foreign Minister Ahmed Maher said, "An Israeli declaration
would be seen as throwing down the gauntlet. It would have a profound psychological impact in Egypt. We would have to react."[45]
Israel's bomb has been acceptable. A *declaration* of Israel's bomb
would not be. Maher's use of the phrase "profound psychological
impact," so close to the formulation of the Interim Committee's goal
for the Hiroshima bombing (to create a "profound psychological
impression"), is an arresting indication of the persistence of the psychological theme in the nuclear dilemma.[46]

A variation on these themes is supplied by North Korea. In 2005, North Korea declared that it was a nuclear power. For the next year, it noisily repeated the claim, but it had not tested a weapon. In 2006, when it did test, producing what likely was a fizzle, it announced the deed several days in advance and gave it maximum publicity. Israel, surrounded by hostile neighbors that have not (yet) gone nuclear, maintains what the historian Avner Cohen calls an "opaque" arsenal. North Korea, facing a nuclear-armed superpower, wants even its fizzle to be klieg lit. In both cases, the lighting is as important as the show.

In any division of countries into nuclear realists and nuclear romantics, Israel and North Korea, both of which face specific threats that they wish to deter with nuclear arms, belong in the realist camp. Yet even they have discovered that the bomb in the mind—the bomb whose terror they project outward to the world—is as important as the physical object in the basement, and have, in response to their different needs, crafted their policies accordingly.

CHAPTER 4

NUCLEAR WILSONIANS

The displacement of the bomb, at all levels of strategy and in all nations, from the battlefield to the psyche is a result, in part, of the most fortunate fact of the nuclear age so far: since Nagasaki, no nuclear weapon has been exploded in anger. This happy development is the product of a healthy respect for one of the bomb's intrinsic, "genetic" features, its unlimited destructive power. It's demanding enough to ask historians to tell us why something happened without also asking them to explain why something didn't happen, and it is especially difficult, or perhaps impossible, to judge why the nuclear arsenals, though primed for launch for sixty years, have not been used. It would require a volume, and probably several, to make headway with the subject. Such an investigation would have to analyze the reasons for restraint in each nuclear crisis and look for common features.

Yet whatever those reasons might be, the fact of nonuse remains, defying many contrary anxieties and predictions, and has even been seized upon as a doctrine, the tradition of nonuse, a phrase coined by McGeorge Bundy. After serving as President Kennedy's national security adviser during the Berlin and Cuban missile crises, Bundy turned himself into a historian of the bomb. Thus, he became one of the very few people who had both significant direct experience and scholarly, as distinct from theoretical, knowledge of nuclear crises. What impressed him was the distance between experience and theory. Noting that although in strategic planning, attacks and counterattacks of all descriptions involving thousands of nuclear warheads and tens of millions of casualties were commonplace, he observed, "In the real world of real political leaders . . . to bring even one hydrogen bomb on one city of one's own country would be recognized in advance as a catastrophic blunder; ten bombs on ten cities would be a disaster beyond history; and a hundred bombs on a hundred cities are unthinkable."[1] (There are some twenty-seven thousand bombs in the world's nuclear arsenals today.)

Bundy coined another, related phrase, "existential deterrence." It suggests that the bare existence of nuclear arsenals can produce their restraining effects irrespective of complicated strategizing, posturing, or threat making. An arsenal's mere mute, dread presence is enough to send a fully adequate message. Bundy's phrase might be understood in another sense as well. Nuclear arms, of course, are the only means invented so far that threaten human existence and so are "existential" in that way, too. Putting together the two meanings of what, elaborating on Bundy, we might call nuclear existentialism, we arrive at an existence (of the bomb) that protects existence (of human life) by perpetually threatening to unmake that existence—all of which is the paradoxical essence of deterrence.

The Bomb in the Mind, 4: The Nuclear Wilsonians

The belief of many analysts and policy makers, who might be called nuclear Wilsonians, that nuclear armaments will spell the end of war has never been the prime motive in any nation's acquisition of nuclear arms, but it was seldom entirely absent, either, and therefore belongs on the list of reasons why people have wanted the bomb. To the nuclear realist's hope for security and the nuclear romantic's longing for greatness, we must add the nuclear Wilsonian's dream of peace based on nuclear terror. President Woodrow Wilson believed that the rule of law, embodied in international institutions, could take the place of war. The nuclear Wilsonians believe that the presence of nuclear arsenals can play the same role. In the psychological calculus that envelops the bomb, the hope for peace has its place.

Like the other fundamental reasons for wanting the bomb, this one has a long pedigree and appears in many forms. Its birth is coeval with the bomb's advent. The earliest form was a hope that the mere invention of the bomb would lead to the international control of all nuclear technology (as in the Baruch Plan) and to peace. The physicist Niels Bohr, for instance, believed that the nuclear dilemma forced the world to choose between a new pair of alternatives: annihilation (something far worse than the cost of any war) and the end of war, a goal that rose as high above the evils of a warring world as nuclear annihilation sank below it. That is, the bomb might contain the seeds of a kind of salvation. As Bohr explained to the Manhattan Project scientist Victor Weisskopf in 1944, "Every great and deep difficulty bears in itself its own solution."[2]

Bohr, by then acknowledged to be one of the greatest physicists of his age, sought in 1945 to convey his understanding of the new situation, which he called the "complementarity" of the bomb, to Roosevelt and Churchill in meetings he had with both, but his initiative was repulsed, especially by Churchill, who thought Bohr should perhaps be locked up.[3] Other nuclear scientists, both within the Manhattan Project and outside it, held views close to Bohr's. They knew the contours of the bomb in the mind as no one else could—they had brought it into being—and so were able in thought to project its influence, for good and ill, deep into the future. They, too, hoped that the long shadow of their discovery, if understood properly and felt deeply enough, might not only forestall a dangerous and futile arms race but supply a foundation for world peace.

A group of scientists in the Manhattan Project expressed this view in a document called the Franck Report, which they tried to send up the chain of command to the decision makers in June 1945.

However, it was intercepted by General Groves, who saw to it that the report never reached President Truman. Its authors believed that the decision regarding use of the bomb against Japan could be decisive for the entire shape of the nuclear future. In their words, "The way in which nuclear weapons, now secretly developed in this country, will first be revealed to the world appears of great, perhaps fateful importance." One way, which they opposed, was the sudden use without warning against Japan that was about to occur. Another way, which they preferred, was "a demonstration of the new weapon . . . before the eyes of representatives of all United Nations, on the desert or a barren island." Then, "America would be able to say to the world, 'You see what weapon we had but did not use. We are ready to renounce its use in the future and to join other nations in working out adequate supervision of the use of this nuclear weapon.' "[4] In their words, we hear the longing for nonuse that was so notably lacking in the president's decision making on Hiroshima. Like the Interim Committee, they wanted to use the bomb to make a "profound psychological impression," but the impression they had in mind was a different one. In contrast to the committee, which tried to create terror through an act of annihilation, they wished to produce reassurance through an act of restraint. Their advice, as we know, was not taken, and the arms race ensued, as they had foreseen.

There was another school of nuclear Wilsonians who believed that the use of the bomb on Japan, rather than spoiling any chance for international control, was just the thing that would make it possible. J. Robert Oppenheimer was in this camp. Speaking in June 1945, for the Scientific Panel, which gave policy makers scientific advice on the bomb, he reported that many colleagues, with whom he agreed, thought that use might "improve the international prospects, in that they are more concerned with the prevention of war than with the elimination of this specific weapon. We find ourselves closer to these latter views; we see no acceptable alternative to direct military use."[5] James Conant, the president of Harvard, who, as chairman of the National Defense Research Committee, played a major role in overseeing the Manhattan Project, recalled that he, too, supported using the bomb "on the grounds that 1), I believed it would shorten the war against the Japanese and 2) that unless used in battle there was no chance of convincing the American public and the world that it should be controlled by international agreement."[6] In a union of the most idealistic ends and the most horrifying means that would prove long lasting, all these men argued that the corpses of Hiroshima would so disgust the world that it would ban the bomb.

In this prescription, the poles of Bohr's complementarity, kept distinct by Bohr, were fused. It seems not to have occurred to Oppenheimer or Conant that the act of deciding to drop the bomb might be as much an example to future decision makers as the suffering of Japanese victims would be a deterrent to possible future victims. If you use a bomb in full knowledge of its awful consequences, you have not demonstrated that it is too horrible to be used; you have demonstrated that notwithstanding the horribleness it can be used. U.S. policy thereafter was predicated on this example but not in the way Conant had hoped. The bombing of Japan was not often brandished by future American officials, but on occasion it was. For example, in 1980, when a State Department official was asked if the United States was really ready to use nuclear weapons to counter Soviet influence in the Persian Gulf, as the "Carter doctrine" required, he answered, "We make no comment on that whatsoever, but the Soviets know that this terrible weapon has been dropped on human beings twice in history and it was an American president who dropped it both times."[7]

In the scientific community, opponents and proponents of using the bomb shared common goals: the elimination of both nuclear weapons and war. But the means they proposed to secure these ends placed them in separate strategic and moral universes. For Bohr, Szilard, and the other signatories of the Franck Report, the bomb in the mind (perhaps reinforced by a highly publicized test that harmed no one) would be enough to frighten the world into its senses. "We are in a completely new situation," Bohr said, "that cannot be resolved by war."[8] For Oppenheimer, Teller, and Conant, the influence of the mental object was not enough. They required that the physical thing be used to kill hundreds of thousands of people. War was exactly the means by which they proposed to resolve the new situation—albeit in a kind of moral jujitsu in which the example of the horrors of nuclear war would produce a U-turn toward peace.

Their hopes were disappointed. Hiroshima and Nagasaki did not lead to international control or a world without war. But neither did a third world war, involving the use of nuclear weapons, break out. Instead, something unexpected happened—the Cold War, theoretically kept cold by the balance of nuclear terror. For after the Second World War, a third variation on nuclear Wilsonianism was discovered. This was of course the classic doctrine of deterrence, the main strategic doctrine of the age. To stave off use of the bomb and prevent war, it proposed a middle ground: the bomb in hand without use, which is to say possession in order to prevent use.

In deterrence's early incarnations, the Wilsonian ambitions were purged. The previous hopes for a radical and permanent transformation of world affairs fell away. The aim of ending all war was forgotten. So was the international control of nuclear technology that had inspired Conant and Oppenheimer. So of course was the abolition of nuclear arms. No longer a panacea for global problems, deterrence was to be only an adjunct to a specific conflict, the Cold War. Keeping the Soviet Union at bay would be enough for the United States, and vice versa. Cold War deterrence was to be a mere finger in the dike, a necessity adopted only for the duration of the conflict or until some better arrangement was somehow discovered. For example, the nuclear strategist Hermann Kahn declared in the early 1960s that the goal of his policies was merely "getting to 1979."

The main competition to this school (one that remained vital throughout the Cold War) did not come from nuclear Wilsonians but from advocates of "nuclear war fighting," who persisted in believing that nuclear war was winnable. Yet over time, some of the more ambitious Wilsonian aims that had been left behind with the defeat of the Baruch Plan began to reemerge in new forms. As the deterrence theorists reflected on their handiwork, they began to believe that what they had invented perhaps was not a mere stopgap after all but a broad solution to the problem of nuclear danger and war. As the nuclear theorist James May argued, "Nuclear weapons are not all that is needed to make war obsolete, but they have no real substitute."[9] A conclusion followed. If two hostile countries wanted to find security, one way to do it might be, however paradoxically, to aim nuclear arsenals at one another. And if that were so, then weren't nuclear arms a solution to the problem of war?

Accompanying this intellectual evolution was a moral reevaluation of nuclear weapons, which came to be seen as a positive good—or if not actually a good, then at least a normal fixture of international arrangements, undeserving of special attention, not to speak of indignation, horror, outrage, or protest. In any case, it was argued, eliminating them was impossible, so what choice was there but to accept, refine, systematize, and extend the deterrence system?

For the early nuclear Wilsonians, such as Bohr and Szilard, the bomb had potentially been the foundation for both abolition and the end of the war. The new generation of nuclear Wilsonians adopted the second goal while rejecting the first. To them, the bomb's existence, not its abolition, was what made world peace possible. The longer the Cold War continued without accident, the warmer this embrace of nuclear weapons became. If, when the Cold War ended, there was no corresponding reconsideration of deterrence—and certainly no return to Baruch Plan–like schemes for full nuclear disarmament—one reason was that deterrence had been so thoroughly accepted by the nuclear establishment. If the bomb was a boon, then justification for possessing it no longer required particular threats or hostilities of the Cold War kind. Even friends, such as the United States and the Soviet Union's successor Russia, might actually prefer to aim nuclear arsenals at one another, in a sort of good-fences-make-good-neighbors spirit. "Deterrence worked" for the United States and the Soviet Union, people said. Nuclear bombs had kept them from war. Why throw away the instrument of proven value?

Among American strategic thinkers, a few were even ready to take the logical next step. If the bomb was good, then its spread— proliferation—must also be good. According to Kenneth Waltz, a prime exponent of this particular realist school, the deterrence that kept the peace during the Cold War could, if extended through proliferation, perform the same service for a world of potentially warring powers. "Those who dread a world with more nuclear states," he argued, "do little more than assert that more is worse and claim without substantiation that new nuclear states will be less responsible and less capable of self-control than the old ones have been. . . . The gradual spread of nuclear weapons is more to be welcomed than feared."[10] Proliferation should not be prevented—probably an impossible task anyway—it should be "managed" by the existing nuclear powers. In such prescriptions, the modern-day nuclear Wilsonian reevaluation of the bomb reached a culmination. But most American policy makers rejected this solution and were left to wonder how, as devotees of a doctrine of deterrence that logically led to universal nuclear armament, they could head such a development off.

A New Nuclear World Order?

The evolution in deterrence thinking in the last years of the Cold War brought the United States surprisingly close to the justifications given by the nuclear romantics. Whereas they dreamed of global stature, the nuclear Wilsonians dreamed of global peace, but neither required, as the nuclear realists did, specification of any particular foe that was being "deterred." This new view proved especially serviceable when the end of the Cold War deprived its antagonists of the specific enemies whose threats had, in the heyday of deterrence, constituted the justification for nuclear arsenals. Now, in a grand post–Cold War convergence arrived at along different paths, many of the most important nuclear powers seemed to agree that nuclear weapons, no longer a nightmare to be dreaded, were a positive good, not only for their possessors but for the world. They were a sine qua non for a great power—in the words of the Russian writer Vasily Grossman, they were "the scepter of the state"—just as de Gaulle and Macmillan had said, and their existence in the hands of responsible nations was a foundation of world peace.

Several recent events have put this convergence on display. France opposed the Bush administration's invasion of Iraq, yet in a speech in January 2006 to personnel of the French strategic forces, President Jacques Chirac articulated a distinctly Bushian justification for France's nuclear arsenal, which consists of about 350 warheads. He threatened nuclear destruction of any state that supported terrorism or that used any weapons of mass destruction against France. "The leaders of States who would use terrorist means against us," he said, "as well as those who would consider using, in one way or another, weapons of mass destruction, must understand that they would lay themselves open to a firm and adapted response on our part. And this response could be a conventional one. Or it could also be of a different kind." In addition, Chirac revived France's Cold War policy of aiming its missiles at "all points of the compass." He named only broad categories of threats as targets. One was a generic "regional power," against which "our choice would not be between inaction or annihilation," for "the flexibility and reactivity of our strategic forces would enable us to exercise our response directly against its centers of power and its capacity to act. All our nuclear forces are configured accordingly."[11] And, just like the United States, France found that the post–Cold War period required new weapons to meet the "new situations." A new nuclear-capable bomber, the Rafale, was to be deployed; a new aircraft carrier to launch it was being commissioned and was scheduled to enter service in 2014; a new submarine, *Le Terrible*, of the Triomphant class was in the works, as was a new submarine-launched ballistic missile, the M51, to place on it.

Chirac explained that France's existing weapons, which were "of very limited range," were now inadequate. Not so the M51, which "thanks to its intercontinental range, and improved Air-to-Ground Medium Range Missiles system (ASMPA) will, in a volatile world, give us the means to cover threats wherever they arise and whatever their nature." For were not nuclear weapons "the ultimate guarantor of our security?"[12]

India was thinking along related lines. On July 18, 2005, India and the United States issued a joint statement announcing an agreement whereby the United States would give India nuclear materials and other assistance for its nuclear power program, and in return India would agree to place fifteen of its twenty-four reactors under international inspection and devote them exclusively to peaceful uses. The other nine would remain available to produce fissile materials for nuclear bombs. By acquiring the American fuel and other technology for its nuclear power program, India would be able to divert enough of its existing supplies of nuclear material to its military program to increase its production of nuclear weapons from an estimated dozen per year to fifty per year.[13] In a practical fulfillment of the two governments' underlying common philosophy regarding nuclear strategy, eclipsing both India's former resistance to the bomb and the United States' resistance to proliferation in South Asia, Americans and Indians were now proposing to engage in de facto cooperation on India's nuclear buildup. The United States, eager for an Asian ally in its rivalry with China, would actively support India's strategic ambitions. As Robert Blackwill, an American ambassador to India in George W. Bush's first term and a principal advocate of the deal, commented, there were "no two [other] countries which share equally the challenge of trying to shape the rise of Chinese power."[14] Undersecretary of State R. Nicholas Burns explained that "the civil nuclear agreement is in our eyes the symbolic center of the new strategic partnership between India and the United States."[15] (The word "strategic" signaled the underlying anti-Chinese motive.) In a recapitulation of Eisenhower's Atoms for Peace, an agreement fostering nuclear power would fuel an arms race. Now as then, nonproliferation took a back seat to strategic advantage. (On April 13, 2007, India test-fired an Agni III missile, which, with a range of 1,900 miles, can strike Beijing and Shanghai.)[16]

But perhaps the most notable expression of the new convergence was a phrase, as striking for its implications as it was little noted, used by Prime Minister Vajpayee's successor, Manmohan Singh, of the Congress Party, who announced that by signing the agreement India had now joined a "new nuclear world order." Here, evidently, spoke a new voice for nuclear Wilsonianism. For most of its independent existence, India had decried nuclear arms, but now a prime minister belonging to the formerly antinuclear Congress Party was speaking of nuclear arms as a foundation of a new global order.

What did he mean? Was there in fact a new world order? And what did nuclear weapons have to do with it? In a speech given shortly after India's 1998 tests, Jaswant Singh, Prime Minister Vajpayee's minister for external affairs, pointed out that "large parts of the world today, enjoy the benefit of the extended deterrence of nuclear weapons powers. . . ."[17] He proceeded to outline the perceived threats to India from China and Pakistan. In an interview with the *New York Times*, he further explained that most of the world had the good fortune to be covered by nuclear targeting:

> If you examine the stretch from roughly Vancouver to Vladivostok, you have a kind of a nuclear security paradigm that has come into existence through the dissolution of the Warsaw Pact. The Asia Pacific is covered in part. China is an independent nuclear power in its own right. It is only Southern Asia and Africa that are out of this protective pattern of security arrangements. . . . If we have the kind of neighborhood that India has, which is extremely troubled, and if we have two

declared nuclear weapons powers in our neighborhood, the basic requirement is to acquire a balancing deterrent capability.[18]

President Bill Clinton, on the other hand, had responded to the Indian tests in this way: "To think that you have to manifest your greatness by behavior that recalls the very worst events of the twentieth century on the edge of the twenty-first century, when everybody else is trying to leave the nuclear age behind, is just wrong. It is just wrong. And they clearly don't need it to maintain their security, vis-à-vis China, Pakistan, or anybody else. So I just think they made a terrible mistake. And I think that we, all of us, have a responsibility to say that, and to say that their best days are ahead of them, but they can't—they have to define the greatness of India in twenty-first century terms, not in terms that everybody else has already decided to reject."[19] But Indian spokesmen like Singh, noticing that Clinton had by no means ordered the United States to leave the nuclear age behind, turned these sentiments on their head: no "mistake" of the twentieth century, the bomb would become a gift to the twenty-first, the foundation of a "new security paradigm," a global "protective pattern of security arrangements." Although some areas unfortunately had been deprived of its "benefits"—subjected to "nuclear apartheid"—the defect had been remedied. Indians and Pakistanis were now targeted by nuclear weapons, too. To be sure, India did not yet join France and the United States in targeting the whole world with its arsenal. But it believed itself to be joining a global system that gave the world full nuclear "coverage." Rarely had the dreams of nuclear Wilsonianism been given clearer expression. Indeed, in the comments of the two Singhs, one from the Congress Party, the other from its chief rival, the BJP, the post–Cold War revaluation of the bomb reached a high point.

Britain was also revising its nuclear strategy. In the late 1990s, it consolidated its arsenal of some two hundred deployed nuclear warheads on a single weapon system, a quartet of Trident submarines. By the early 2020s, the system will have to be either retired or replaced.

Britain's entire nuclear arsenal was thus at stake in a single decision regarding a single program. In December 2006, Prime Minister Tony Blair made his choice. He would seek to renew the Trident system, and he won a vote in Parliament in favor of the program. The Trident D-5 missile, a U.S. program in which Britain participates, would be extended until the 2040s. At that point, Britain would work with the United States to build still another missile,[20] perpetuating the age of nuclear weapons into the second half of the twenty-first century.

In a speech in the House of Commons announcing his decision, Blair raised a large question. "The world has changed dramatically, not least in the collapse of the Soviet Union, the original context in which the deterrent was acquired. . . . The question is whether it is wise to maintain the deterrent in the very different times of today." In his answer, he recapitulated each and every one of the rationales cited in the American, French, and Indian answers. Nuclear Wilsonianism appears in a claim that "the whole point about the deterrent is not to create the circumstance in which it [the bomb] can be used but on the contrary to try to create the circumstances in which it is never used." In short, the British bomb is an instrument not of war but of peace. He cited the need to target states that support terrorists. He targeted proliferation—"a distinct and novel reason for Britain not to give up its capacity to deter." And, in phrases reminiscent of Chirac, Blair invoked the broadest of the new reasons for needing nuclear arms: the very unpredictability of history. In his words, "In the early 21st century, the world may have changed beyond recognition, since the decision taken by the Atlee government over half a century ago. But it is precisely because we could not have recognized then, the world we live in now, that it would not be wise to predict the unpredictable in the times to come."[21]

In these justifications for nuclear arsenals put forward by a quartet of nations, the case for the bomb, after more than a half century of evolution, seemed to reach full maturity. In the psychological field of action at the center of all nuclear strategy, the realist's fear, the romantic's ambition for greatness, and the Wilsonian's yearning for peace flowed together to provide a flexible, new, encompassing rationale for possessing nuclear arsenals in the twenty-first century.

Such was the view, anyway, from the precincts of some of the self-appointed guardians of the new nuclear world order, from the heart of the nuclear archipelago. From any other angle of vision, the picture looked very different. The great majority of nations, 183 of whom adhere to the Nuclear Non-Proliferation Treaty as sworn nuclear-weapon-free nations, perceived no benefit from the nuclear powers' rededication to their nuclear arsenals. In their view, nuclear weapons had not undergone any transvaluation into agents of peace and harmony. Rather, they had remained what they had always been: a hideous, limitless threat posed by the most deadly devices ever invented. They were not valued "insurance" but a hated menace. India's accession to the nuclear club therefore did not look to these countries like the fortunate completion of a "new paradigm," extending the "benefit" of nuclear "protection" to a previously deprived area; it looked like one more island in the explosive and expansionary nuclear archipelago breaking the surface of the sea. Worse, it looked like the herald of further eruptions.

Since in this vision of a new nuclear world order, not *all* countries were considered worthy of nuclear arms, the emerging consensus among nuclear powers was in practice a tacit embrace of a new version of the two-tier world, in which a few "responsible" states would deploy their nuclear forces to safeguard against nuclear proliferation by "rogue" states and terrorist groups. But which countries belonged in which category? If the bomb is good for you, a lengthening list of nuclear-weapon-free countries were asking the nuclear powers, why is it bad for us? Are you to live but we to die, you to be "super" but we puny, you to enjoy peace but we to be condemned to war? Those considered "rogues" by the great powers did not consider themselves such; nor were the self-designated responsible powers seen as responsible by the putative rogues or, for that matter, by most other nations. Moreover, neither India, Britain, nor France had even a suggestion of an answer to the insistent question of who can and who cannot be in the nuclear club—a question that, if left unanswered, was bound to break up the whole system. The same, however, was not true of the fourth member of the quartet, the United States, to whose bid to answer this question we now must turn.

PART II

THE EMPIRE AND THE BOMB: RISE AND FALL OF THE BUSH DOCTRINE

CHAPTER 5

RISE OF THE IMPERIAL IDEA

Like the other nuclear powers, the United States found its way to new justifications for its nuclear arsenal in the post–Cold War period. But the road to this destination was long and characterized as much by concealment, evasion, and abdication as by disclosure, forthright facing of facts, and decision. Today, basic elements of the nuclear policies of the United States are still concealed in a miasma of official obfuscation and, insofar as they can be understood at all, must be deduced from a combination of leaked classified documents, obscure testimony, and inference from public policy statements. Even then, nothing as definite as the Cold War's doctrine of deterrence (itself an enigma never fully grasped by most of the public) emerges.

Although the Cold War's end gave every appearance of being a moment of truth for nuclear policy, no truth emerged from it. If a miracle is a wonderful event that defies all expectation, then the end of the Cold War was a miracle. The unexpected miracle seemed to invite a planned miracle—some policy initiative fashioned to secure the peace that had fallen into the world's lap—and in no area did the invitation seem more appropriate or promising than in the nuclear domain. For more than forty years, nuclear arsenals had been sustained by the proposition that each party to the conflict needed them because the other party possessed them. In the United States, the judgment had been that it was better to be "dead" (annihilated in a nuclear holocaust) than "red" (subjugated by Communism).

But now the conflict was over, the Soviet Union had actually disappeared, and Russia and the United States were on friendly terms. An opportunity without precedent in the nuclear age seemed to have opened up. The questions that history had put on the table went to the core of the nuclear dilemma. Was it still necessary for Moscow and Washington to threaten each other with mutual assured destruction? What of other nations? Were there now perhaps pairs of countries that needed nuclear weapons for purposes unrelated to the United States and Russia? If so, what degree of hostility between nations warranted the establishment or continuation of a nuclear standoff—that is, a balance of terror backed by nuclear arms? If there were no such countries, then could nuclear weapons be abolished altogether? If not, what stood in the way? In a silence that was as loud as the Cold War debates over nuclear arms had been, those questions somehow went not just unanswered but largely unasked.

It is true that the first two post–Cold War administrations took several significant steps in response to the new realities. In 1991, George H. W. Bush unilaterally took American strategic bombers off alert and withdrew most tactical weapons from overseas and naval deployment, and General Secretary Mikhail Gorbachev responded with comparable measures. After the Soviet downfall, Clinton helped negotiate the transfer into Russian hands of nuclear arms in Ukraine, Kazakhstan, and Belarus, assuring that those newborn countries would not become nuclear powers. The Strategic Arms Limitation Treaty (START) I, which had been negotiated mainly by President Ronald Reagan and Mikhail Gorbachev, and mandated reductions of warheads to six thousand on each side, was signed in 1991, and START II, mandating reductions to thirty-five hundred per side, was signed in 1993 (though the latter would never be ratified by the Russian Duma).

However, neglect of the larger questions of strategic policy was made almost official through the results of the *Nuclear Posture Review* launched by the Clinton administration in 1993. Its advertised purpose was to address the question, Why do we need nuclear weapons? But it did no such thing.[1] Continuing in the tradition of nondecision begun by Truman at the time of the Hiroshima bombing, the administration sidestepped its own question. Probably any chance that it would do otherwise was removed when the review's initiator, Secretary of Defense Les Aspin, who had once written an article called "From Deterrence to De-nuking"[2] and said, "a world without nuclear weapons would actually be better,"[3] left office in January 1994. At no point did President Clinton, Secretary of State Warren Christopher, or National Security Adviser Anthony Lake become heavily involved in the review, which was left to second- and third-tier bureaucrats and military officers at the Pentagon.

They included Assistant Secretary of Defense Ashton Carter, who put forward several modest arms control proposals. One was to agree with Russia to stand down the two arsenals from their Cold War condition of hair-trigger alert. Another was to make alterations in the plans for launching a retaliation in the event of a nuclear first strike by Russia. Both addressed unexpected perils that had grown out of the balance of terror during the Cold War. The declared posture of the United States had been that it would retaliate only after Soviet bombs had begun to explode on American soil; yet in reality American military commanders had judged that the command and control system of their nuclear forces, which was supposed to assure the capacity to retaliate, could not survive a Soviet first strike. Therefore, in practice, they adopted a posture of "launch on warning," which meant that the president would order "retaliation" merely upon receiving reports that Soviet missiles had been launched.[4] This posture severely compressed the interval available for the president's decision. The flight time of missiles between the United States and Russia was only about twenty-five to thirty minutes. Confirmation of the warning of launch took ten minutes, and another ten was required for the execution of any presidential order to retaliate, leaving only ten minutes for the president to inform himself, weigh his options, and make his decision. Only thirty seconds was allotted for the Strategic Air commander's briefing to the president on the nature of the attack underway.[5] Soviet commanders had drawn similar conclusions and adopted the same remedy. The extraordinary pressures of the system sharply increased the danger of misjudgments or accidental launch in a crisis.

Now Ashton Carter was proposing to reduce that danger by bringing post–Cold War operational policy in line with declaratory Cold War policy—that is, by planning for launch only after a first strike had arrived, thereby indefinitely increasing the president's time to make his decision regarding retaliation. But even these minimal proposals were chewed up in the Pentagon bureaucracy, and the two Cold War arsenals sailed on undisturbed into the post–Cold War era—still made up of a triad of submarines, aircraft, and land-based missiles, still on hair-trigger alert, still ready to fire at an instant's notice after mere warning of attack, still prone to accidental use, and still capable of destroying the United States and the Soviet Union dozens of times over.

The formal answer eventually given by the Nuclear Posture Review was that the United States would "lead but hedge," meaning that it would pursue gradual arms control as before (lead) but hold on to a big arsenal in the meantime in case Russia became an enemy again (hedge). This formulation in effect erased the collapse of the Soviet Union as an event worthy of major response in the nuclear field. With or without a global antagonist, nuclear policy and the arsenal that supported it would remain essentially unchanged. Somehow, no one addressed the question of whether, if the feared regression by Russia occurred, the United States would prefer to face a fully nuclear-armed backslider, still capable of annihilating the United States, or face one with just a few nuclear weapons or none. However one interpreted the new formulation, it seemed a makeshift, a vestige of Cold War thinking resurrected to disguise the review's failure to respond to the geopolitical revolution that had just occurred.

Fantastically, these nuclear arrangements *between friends* for instant annihilation still persist—outside history, outside discussion, outside reason. Even today, almost no one asks why the United States and Russia should still threaten one another with obliteration. The very absurdity of the situation seems to block any challenge to it. How can one rebut a policy when none has been articulated? As at earlier points of decision in the nuclear age, the danger seems to flow not so much from the victory of one view over another as from sheer nuclear momentum over all views.

The Threat Blank

The arsenals' bureaucratic defenders had effortlessly shrugged off the feeble grip of the arms controllers. The number of nuclear weapons continued to drop, but the essential features of the mutual-annihilation machine remained intact. The question of why the former Cold War rivals wanted nuclear weapons was forgotten, and their arsenals drifted into a kind of policy-free zone. Unsustained by Cold War rationales but not yet assigned any new ones, they seemed to exist for their own sakes, leaving a strong feeling that in the new era, missions would be sought for nuclear weapons rather than the other way around.

Elementary information regarding the American arsenals dissolved into ambiguity. Were the missiles still targeted at Russia? No one could quite say. In 1992, General Lee Butler, the head of the U.S. Strategic Command (STRATCOM), stated that "as early as October 1989, we abandoned global war with the Soviet Union as the principal planning and programming paradigm for the U.S. armed forces."[6] The practical consequence, Butler added, was that targets in the Soviet Union were being reduced from ten thousand to around twenty-five hundred—giving a rare glimpse at concrete targeting arrangements in the new era.[7] In 1994, Russia and the United

States reached a formal detargeting agreement, which seemed to suggest that the two countries no longer targeted one another at all. In reality, the practical consequences were nil, as the target sets were kept in computers in both countries, allowing retargeting to take place in hours or even minutes. Yet the two countries had no bone of contention between them that could justify any hostilities whatsoever, not to speak of nuclear war. Were the missiles targeted elsewhere? In 1995, Ambassador Thomas Graham, the head of the U.S. delegation to the NPT Review Conference, mysteriously announced that "as of May 31, 1994, no country is targeted by the strategic forces of the United States"—a statement that, if true, seemed to cry out for a follow-up question: in that case, why does the United States still require nuclear weapons in the thousands?

In the midst of all these half-true or contradictory or merely puzzling statements, there remained, as Senator Sam Nunn put it, a "threat blank."[8] No new strategic guidance was provided for the U.S. arsenal. As for Russian policy, it was widely reported that owing to the radical decline of its conventional forces, not to speak of its shrunken economy as well as geographical extent, it wished to hold on to a large nuclear arsenal as the last vestige of its former superpowerdom. Though notably standing apart from the alliance of Britain, France, the United States, and, increasingly, India, Moscow, formerly a practitioner of the coldest realism, now seemed to tilt to the romantic school of nuclear enthusiasts. For both the United States and the Soviet Union, it seemed, the lingering balance of nuclear terror, rhetorically repudiated yet not abandoned in fact, had been granted a ghostly afterlife as a kind of holding pen for still-huge arsenals that might be—or would soon be—assigned some new purpose. But if that were so, what was it?

A Momentous Question

It is important to underscore the magnitude of this question in the context of the entire nuclear story. For the United States, the end of the

Cold War was the fourth time that the issue of the fundamental purpose for having nuclear weapons had arisen. President Roosevelt had first ordered work on the bomb with Hitler's Germany in mind, but as Germany approached defeat, targeting shifted half a world away to Japan. The change in target carried with it a change in rationale for developing the bomb. Germany was believed to have the scientific resources to build nuclear arms, and the American project had been launched more to head off a possible German nuclear monopoly than to actually use the bomb to defeat Germany. (No specific German target for the bomb was ever chosen.) Expressed in terms of later jargon, the aim was as much deterrence as first strike or "first use"—that is, nuclear attack. Indeed, one reason for detargeting Germany was fear that if the bomb were a dud, German scientists would recover and reverse engineer it to make a bomb themselves. Japan, on the other hand, was rightly believed to have no prospect of building the bomb, and so the question of prospective deterrence did not arise. Targeted on Japan, the bomb could only be used as a first-strike weapon.

Within the government, the shift from Germany to Japan occurred smoothly, with little recorded discussion. For the scientists in the labs of the Manhattan Project, it was another matter. Many of them, as we have seen, were refugees from countries occupied or dominated by Hitler, and the belief that they were heading off a possible Hitlerian nuclear monopoly had served to trump serious moral objections they had about building such a terrible weapon. Nevertheless, when, thanks to American intelligence reports, they learned that Hitler was nowhere near having a bomb, and nuclear-incapable Japan had become the target, all but one of the scientists— the Polish émigré Joseph Rotblat, who then quit the Manhattan Project—suppressed their qualms and stuck to their work. The physicist Richard Feynman later described this collective act of nonresponse. He noted, "We *started* for a good reason," but soon the work—the drive "to do something, to accomplish it"—took over. So although "After you thought at the beginning," later "you just stop."[9] It was not the last time the bomb would stop thought.

The third round of targeting, shifting from Japan to the Soviet Union, which began in the last days of the war, was more complicated. Even before Hiroshima, officials of the Truman administration were looking forward to the advantage the bomb would afford in controlling the Soviet threat. Secretary of War Henry Stimson called the bomb a "master card," and successfully advised Truman not to go to the summit meeting in Potsdam to meet Stalin in the summer of 1945 until he had the weapon in his hands. Yet the enlistment of the bomb in the Cold War and the subsequent arms race were not undertaken lightly or without reflection. After Hiroshima, the bomb, having been built in secrecy, for the first time became an open fact. The public grasped its apocalyptic potential with astonishing rapidity. During 1946, when John Hersey's book *Hiroshima* and other important writings were published, the crushing moral weight and existential dread imposed by this instrument of unlimited and indiscriminate destruction received a considerable airing.

American presidents as well as Soviet chiefs explicitly acknowledged from the first days of the nuclear age that civilization, even the continued existence of human beings, was at stake. To justify such a risk, immense political and moral stakes—the survival of the United States, of freedom worldwide—were invoked. The American posture since the rejection of the Baruch Plan had been that the United States was eager to live in a world free of nuclear arms but was prevented from doing so by the Soviet Union, which, owing to its totalitarian system, rejected the sorts of inspection that would be necessary for any abolition agreement to work.

Such was the background to the momentous question that arose once more when America's third target of the nuclear age, the Soviet Union, liquidated itself, and the old issue of whom, if anyone, to target was put on the table again. By now, the Soviet Union's successor and nuclear legatee, Russia, was ready to accept inspections at least as intrusive as any the United States would tolerate, removing the greatest specific technical obstacle to full disarmament.

It was this question that Presidents George H. W. Bush and Bill

Clinton evaded, in a top-level abdication that left the policy vacuum represented by the threat blank. The failure even to coherently address the issue, however, carried a highly consequential message to the rest of the world: in the view of the sole superpower as well as its former rival, possession of nuclear arms no longer required any large, deeply considered, publicly salable political or moral justification. Once seen as a drastic recourse, these weapons had become normalized. Their possession was acceptable even with no enemy in the field. It was a lesson attended to closely by India, Pakistan, Iran, North Korea, and other nations who did not want to be without nuclear weapons in a nuclear-armed world. For as McGeorge Bundy had pointed out, nuclear arsenals, even when unaccompanied by specific threats, have a language all their own. They say: We are here. We are not going away. We may not be targeting you right now, but we may in the future. Beware.

A Living SIOP

Into the high-level explanatory void in Washington, lower-level officials, especially in the Pentagon, began to advance the beginnings of answers. Most had something to do with preventing the proliferation of nuclear arms and other weapons of mass destruction. Classical strategic policy and nonproliferation policy began to merge. In 1990, the first Gulf War was waged to reverse Iraq's conquest of Kuwait, but it inadvertently revealed Saddam Hussein's nuclear weapon program, which was perhaps a year away from creating an atomic bomb. It was in those years that the phrase "rogue states," meaning irresponsible governments that might acquire weapons of mass destruction, became fashionable.

The first seeds of a new policy were sewn in the early 1990s by Dick Cheney, who was secretary of defense during the Gulf War. He issued a secret "Nuclear Weapons Employment Policy," which ordered the military to plan for the use of nuclear weapons against proliferators. In 1991, a Joint Military Net Assessment stated that nuclear weapons "could assume a broader role globally in response to the proliferation of nuclear capability among Third World nations."[10] That same year, the public got a brief glimpse of Pentagon thinking when a commission set up by the Strategic Command suggested an "expeditionary force with low-yield portable [nuclear] weapons."[11] In the light of later events, it's striking to note that the commission commented, "It is not difficult to entertain nightmarish visions in which a future Saddam Hussein threatens U.S. forces abroad, U.S. allies or friends, and perhaps even the United States itself with nuclear, biological, or chemical weapons. If that were to happen, U.S. nuclear weapons may well be a resource for seeking to deter execution of the threat."[12]

The idea that new targets for nuclear weapons might be discovered in the third world began to take root. In 1992, the Defense Department's annual report officially declared that nuclear strategy "must now also encompass potential instabilities that could arise when states perceive they have little to lose from employing weapons of mass destruction."[13] Largely out of sight, operational changes ensued. The military discovered that its targeting system "had no capability south of the equator," in the words of a 1992 STRATCOM report, which, in a key passage, foretold the direction of policy.[14] The United States was now the world's "sole superpower," as people began to say, yet fully one half of the planet remained untargeted by its nuclear arsenal.

To remedy the omission, STRATCOM recommended the creation of a "global capability." A Strategic Planning Study Group recommended a "living SIOP." The SIOP, or Single Integrated Operational Plan, established in 1960, was the United States' order of battle for waging nuclear war. During the Cold War, it had been, so to speak, "dead"—that is, inflexible. Its option 1A, the only one truly available to the president, called for annihilation of all Communist-ruled nations between East Germany and Beijing, with an estimated three hundred million immediate fatalities. Now the "living" SIOP would permit the generation of new groups of targets, on a less sweeping scale, within twenty-four hours.[15] In another shift, as important as it was little noticed, chemical and biological weapon sites were added to the nuclear target list, placing the full range of weapons of mass destruction—a term that, along with "rogue states," was rapidly gaining currency—in the crosshairs and multiplying the number of targets. Detailed planning and hardware to match followed. In 1993, so-called SILVER Books were created, containing plans for attacking specific nations, including Iran, Iraq, Libya, and North Korea. (SILVER was an acronym for the equally uncommunicative full title of the project: "Strategic Installation List of Vulnerability Effects and Results.")[16] The new targets were assigned to a "reserve" nuclear force of about a thousand warheads. The change prompted SAC commander Butler to propose renaming the SIOP. As he pointed out, the plan was no longer a "single" or "integrated" plan; rather, it had fractured into a "family" of many plans.

The targets of the United States' nuclear arms now fell into two broad categories: those in Russia and those outside Russia. The shift away from Russian targets to others around the world—the first specific, concrete move in assigning nuclear weapons a new, post–Cold War mission—went largely unnoticed. It's not clear, for instance, whether President Clinton was aware of it. The identity of the newly targeted countries and the number of nuclear weapons assigned to them is still unknown. (Remarkably, if the current Bush administration has its way, this ignorance will only deepen. Its apparatchiks have been reclassifying figures on the size of American arsenals as far back as the 1950s, even though these have already been released.)

Meanwhile, planning began to design new nuclear weapons. In late 1991, the air force formally established a nuclear weapons program—the Project on Precision Low-Yield Weapons Design—to investigate, among other possibilities, "a credible option to counter the employment of nuclear weapons by Third World nations."[17] One result was the B61-11 bomb, a bunker buster that entered the arsenal in 1997. A second was a new targeting system for the nuclear-armed Trident submarines allowing them to "quickly, accurately and reliably retarget" missiles. A third was planning for a new generation of low-yield "mini-nukes," for battlefield use in the Third World.

The Osirak Option

In 1993, at just the time that the *Nuclear Posture Review* was under way, a serious crisis over North Korea's nuclear program erupted, carrying the United States and North Korea to the brink of war. It naturally concentrated the Clinton administration's mind on proliferation policy—and perhaps distracted it from the strategic policies under consideration in the *Nuclear Posture Review*. What is clear is that it was the North Korean crisis, not the *Nuclear Posture Review*, that got the lion's share of high-level attention.

From the American point of view, the crisis began to brew in 1992, when the International Atomic Energy Agency, acting under the auspices of the Nuclear Non-Proliferation Treaty, signed by North Korea in 1985, announced that it had found evidence that North Korea might have diverted plutonium from its supposedly strictly civilian nuclear program. Construction on the reactor had begun in the 1980s. North Korea responded by refusing further inspections and stating its intention to withdraw from the NPT. With plutonium in hand, North Korea would face few obstacles to building an atomic bomb. At stake was the emergence of a nuclear-armed North Korea.

In May, the United States secured a resolution by the United Nations Security Council imposing sanctions on North Korea if it did not permit the inspections. North Korea responded that sanctions would constitute a declaration of war, whereupon the United States began a military buildup in South Korea. A war, it was estimated, could cost hundreds of thousands of lives. Since the administration surmised that North Korea might already have diverted enough plutonium for one or two bombs, it might possess them and be ready to use them. In that case, the United States might retaliate, leading to history's first two-sided nuclear war.

At this moment of high tension, the Clinton administration gave serious consideration to a preemptive attack, called the Osirak option (after Israel's attack on Iraq's nuclear reactor at Osirak in 1981), on North Korea's nuclear facilities. At a meeting of the principal American officials involved, on June 14, 1993, three military options were presented. One was an attack on North Korea's reactor at Yongbyon; a second was an attack on the reactor and its spent fuel-storage pond; and the third would assault not only both of these but also North Korea's entire military establishment. Strategies to remove the existing regime from power were also discussed.[18]

However, the crisis was temporarily resolved when, with help from a diplomatic mission by former president Jimmy Carter, the two countries signed an Agreed Framework, requiring North Korea to accept the inspectors back and forswear plutonium production and diversion, in return for which the United States and other nations would supply aid, including two light-water reactors (which are not as well suited for plutonium production as heavy-water reactors) and shipments of oil. Unfortunately, the framework did not address the possible diversion of plutonium that might already have occurred, leaving North Korea with a possible capacity to build an estimated one or two bombs.

There is no current evidence that any of the versions of the Osirak option included plans for using nuclear weapons, although a definitive judgment on this point awaits full declassification of the relevant papers. However, at the Pentagon, including STRAT-COM, generalized planning along exactly these lines continued throughout the Clinton years. In 1995, not long after the *Nuclear Posture Review* had failed to give any new impetus to disarmament, a STRATCOM review called "Essentials of Post–Cold War Deterrence" explored ways to "expand deterrence" to the Third World. Borrowing an idea of Cold War vintage, it even argued that "rogues" (including, of course, North Korea) should be encouraged to see the United States as " 'out of control,' " and liable to inflict "national extinction" on enemies.[19]

However, outside the Pentagon, resistance to the new targeting trend developed. Congress, still in the hands of a Democratic majority, staged a modest rebellion. Displaying a pattern that would continue, it concentrated opposition not on the dramatic policy changes that were almost covertly under way but on specific pieces of new hardware. In November 1993, Congress passed the Spratt-Furse Amendment, which banned "research and development which could lead to the production by the United States of a new low-yield nuclear weapon."[20] That is, it voted against making nuclear weapons more usable in regional crises.

Closer attention was being paid abroad. The 1995 Review Conference for the Nuclear Non-Proliferation Treaty was approaching, and the Clinton administration was seeking an indefinite extension of the treaty. To achieve this, it had renewed a promise, first made by Jimmy Carter in 1978, that the United States would not attack countries that did not possess nuclear weapons and were not allied with countries that did. If honored, this pledge of "negative security assurances" would forbid most of the strategic planning for preventing proliferation with nuclear attacks that had steadily and stealthily been going forward at the Pentagon since Defense Secretary Dick Cheney had initiated it in the early 1990s. The pledge was made, yet the policies it forbade continued on their seemingly unstoppable path to realization.

The issue arose again in the midnineties, when African nations were negotiating the Pelindaba Treaty, which renders Africa a nuclear-weapon-free zone. To take effect, the treaty required that the nuclear powers agree not to launch any nuclear attacks on the signatories. In the administration, a debate broke out between the State Department, which wanted to sign the treaty, and the Pentagon, which seemed simply to be averse to formal acknowledgment of any limitation whatsoever on its right to use nuclear arms, even against African nations who possessed none. The United States signed the treaty but accompanied the deed with a cryptic declaration that it would not "limit options available to the U.S. if attacked by an African country with weapons of mass destruction."[21]

This bureaucratic skirmish touched on a fundamental unresolved issue that had always haunted the Nuclear Non-Proliferation Treaty: would the existing nuclear double standard be made permanent or would the treaty's provision requiring nuclear powers to give up their nuclear weapons be honored? If the former, was it conceivable that the nonnuclear powers would accept enforcement of the double standard by the very means the treaty sought to eliminate, namely nuclear arms?

The Cold War had to a certain extent kept these questions on hold. Whatever the answers should have been in principle, everyone could see that the Cold War antagonists had especially deep-seated reasons to possess nuclear weapons. Historically, the greatest conflicts among the greatest powers had summoned the most powerful weapons into existence, and the Cold War superpowers, tensed for global conflict, were no exception to this rule. But now it was much less acceptable to nuclear-weapon-free countries to accord these nations, lacking any quarrel among themselves, the special privilege of keeping their nuclear arsenals. On the contrary, if intense, entrenched hostilities were the qualification for having nuclear arsenals, then other pairs of powers, such as India and Pakistan, not to speak of Iran and Iraq, or Iran and Israel, or North Korea and Japan, had more to boast of. If this were the standard, the Cold War powers should have lost their nuclear licenses, while the rogues, by stepping up their enmities, should have acquired them. Thus, when the Cold War ended, a long, slow-motion collision between the existing nuclear powers and the nuclear hopefuls became unavoidable.

It was in this context that the question of negative security assurances acquired its importance. If some countries not only retained the right to possess nuclear weapons but were free to use them against their nonnuclear former colonies, then, in the eyes of the latter, the NPT became nothing more than a new system of global domination. The worry that the NPT might sanction a new system of global inequity was at least as old as the treaty. For example, Germany's chancellor Willy Brandt had said during the treaty's negotiation in the 1960s, "The moral and political justification of a nonproliferation treaty follows only if the nuclear states regard it as a step toward restrictions of their own armaments and toward disarmament and clearly state they are willing to act accordingly."[22] Or as Mao Zedong put it in 1963, just before China joined the nuclear club, "It is absolutely impermissible for two or three countries to brandish their nuclear weapons at will, issue orders and commands, and lord it over the world as self-ordained nuclear overlords, while the overwhelming majority of countries are expected to kneel and obey orders meekly, as if they were nuclear slaves. The time of power politics has gone forever, and major questions of the world can no longer decided by a few big powers."[23] Two basic policies were now in direct conflict: the traditional American assertion of a right to use nuclear weapons first, and its newer resolve, shared by most of the world, to contain nuclear proliferation. In the years ahead, the tension between them would increase until, on September 11, 2001, a breaking point was reached, and a clear choice was made.

Disarmament Wars

President George W. Bush arrived at the nuclear question, as he did at so much else, indirectly, through his reaction to September 11, less than one year into his presidency. Before that day, he displayed no more interest in America's nuclear arsenal than Clinton had. (His administration's principal initiative in the nuclear field was deployment of ballistic missile defenses.) But after September 11, he embarked on a series of initiatives that would constitute a full-scale transformation of the nation's nuclear policies.

The resulting vision was comprehensive. It proffered an answer to the most urgent question of the nuclear age at the beginning of the twenty-first century: who, if anyone, should possess nuclear arms, who should not, and who should decide which was to be which, and make the decision stick?

It may be helpful to see the transformation of Bush's proliferation policies as the consequence of a series of expanding concentric rings racing like a shock wave outward from the site of the fallen World Trade Center towers, soon called Ground Zero (a zero being itself a ring), in unspoken acknowledgment of the new nuclear dangers to which the atrocity pointed. (Originally, "ground zero" was of course the name given to the aim points of nuclear weapons.)

Bush's phrase "the war on terror," adopted immediately after the attacks, described the first of these expanding rings. The choice of the word "war" meant that the stupendous machinery of the American military would be summoned instantly into action. The choice of a generic activity, "terror," rather than any particular foe, such as Al Qaeda, guaranteed that the war would be global and of unlimited duration. (In the president's words: "The enemy is not a single political regime or person or religion or ideology. The enemy is terrorism. . . .")[24] The second concentric ring was traced by the president in an address to Congress on September 20, 2001, when he added to the list of enemies states that supported terror as targets of the war. "From this day forward," he proclaimed, "any nation that continues to harbor or support terrorism will be regarded by the United States as a hostile regime." Since Vice President Cheney soon claimed that terrorists were operating in no fewer than sixty countries, the list of potential targets in the war on terror had widened exponentially.

It is, however, the third concentric ring that commands our special attention here, for it suddenly turned nuclear nonproliferation policy into a subdepartment of the war on terror. In his State of the Union address for 2002, Bush declared the existence of an "axis of evil" consisting of Iraq, North Korea, and Iran, whose only common features were that they were judged to be among the world's worst regimes and were said to be seeking weapons of mass destruction, allegedly including, in all three cases, nuclear arms. The WMD programs of the three countries represented, as the administration put it later that year in a seminal document, the *National Security Strategy of the United States of America (NSSUSA)*, the "crossroads of radicalism and technology" and the "nexus of terror and weapons of mass destruction"—a formulation that was to be repeated often. (Although the phrase "axis of evil" was dropped, these other phrases were not and became mainstays of Bush's policy.)

Once war had been chosen as the way to address proliferation, it followed that it would not do to wait until the target regimes succeeded in building the feared weapons and could retaliate with them; rather, as the president began to insist, America must resolve to destroy the nuclear larvae in their nests—that is, "preventively." (The National Security Strategy document stated, "We must deter and defend against the threat [of WMD] before it is unleashed.") The policy of overthrowing rather than merely defeating the offending governments—of "regime change," as it quickly came to be known—was another corollary of the militarization of nonproliferation. For it was quite true that when the worst regimes were laying hands on the worst weapons it would not be enough merely to bomb their weapon facilities, which could soon be rebuilt. (The point had been driven home by history's only previous attempt to stop proliferation by force—Israel's attack in 1981 on Iraq's reactor complex at Osirak. The Iraqis had been using the reactor to obtain plutonium to make an atomic bomb. After the attack, they turned to uranium enrichment, a quicker path to the bomb.) Nuclear disarmament—once the province of diplomacy and international cooperation—was for the first time to be pursued by military force, including the overthrow of regimes, in a projected series of what can be called disarmament wars.

The widest of the rings spreading outward from Ground Zero—one that encompassed another round object, the earth itself—was the assertion of global military dominance by the United States. In a speech given at West Point in 2002, the president said, "America has, and intends to keep, military strengths beyond challenge, thereby making the destabilizing arms races of other eras pointless, and limiting rivalries to trade and other pursuits of peace." Did he really mean that America would become so strong that all nations but the United States would, for the first time in history, simply retire from military competition and confine themselves to barter and entertainment? The *NSSUSA*, published two months later, made it clear that he did. Repeating that the United States must "build and maintain our defenses beyond challenge," it listed, as one of the goals of the policy, to "dissuade future military competition." In this vision, sometime in the near future neither preemption nor prevention, not to speak of traditional self-defense, would be necessary. Americans could dictate terms to the world through the mere display of American power on a global scale, which would cause every other sword to drop from every other hand.

Such ambitions were correctly seen as imperial. It became commonplace among administration supporters to refer to the United States as a globe-straddling empire, a new Rome. Although the administration itself shunned the word "imperial," it did not hesitate to lay down rules for the economic, political, and even moral and spiritual development of all peoples that only a global empire could sustain. Asserting again the "unparalleled military strength and great economic and political influence" of the United States, the *NSSUSA* went on to claim that the "struggles of the twentieth century" had left the world with "a single sustainable model for national success: freedom, democracy, and free enterprise"—in short, the American model.

A Revolution in Nonproliferation Policy

The subsumption of proliferation policy by the war on terror brought to completion a 180-degree reversal of traditional American nonproliferation policy. Bush was proposing to stop proliferation through the unilateral, preventive use of force to overthrow offending regimes. Never before had the United States—or any country—proposed that military action should be the means for solving the world's proliferation problem. Yet seen in the context of the global evolution of the nuclear dilemma since the Cold War, the new policy possessed a decided logic. If in the new era the nuclear powers were insisting that the world continue to be two-tiered, then Bush's policy constituted the final missing piece to the puzzle: the method by which the membership rules were to be enforced. The United States would do it, and do it with military power.

In keeping with the new policy, the administration definitively renounced negative security assurances. In March 2002, Undersecretary of State John R. Bolton said that such assurances represented "an unrealistic view of the international situation" and that, in case of an attack, "we would have to do what is appropriate under the circumstances. . . ."[25] Clinton had taken some steps in the same direction. He had permitted the Pentagon to develop plans for dealing with proliferation by force. He had threatened the use of force (but apparently not nuclear force) against North Korea in 1994. Most important, he had, if more by default than commission, recommitted the United States to holding on to its Cold War arsenal. But he had never drawn these elements together to form a new doctrine of global scope. Bush did. He spelled out the American commitment in the grave language of ultimatums in his axis of evil speech: "The United States of America will not permit the world's most dangerous regimes to threaten us with the world's most destructive weapons." And soon he took the first step toward fulfilling his vow by invading Iraq.

The Rejected Tradition

The distance of Bush's policies from previous American nonproliferation policy is hard to overstate. Every previous American president in the nuclear age had relied on peaceful means to stop proliferation. Clinton's consideration of the Osirak option is the closest thing to an exception. Preventive war had on occasion been proposed by presidential advisers but was always rejected. For example, in 1946, when the United States' atomic monopoly was new, General Leslie Groves, the military overseer of the Manhattan Project, recommended that if any nonallied country "started to make or possess atomic weapons we would destroy its capacity to make them before it has progressed far enough to threaten us."[26] There is no evidence that Truman ever gave the idea serious consideration. Neither Eisenhower nor Kennedy was presented with an episode of proliferation that might have tempted a preventive attack.

President Lyndon Johnson was. In 1964, American intelligence reported that China was preparing its first nuclear test, and the idea of prevention was proposed. Johnson went as far as to send Ambassador Averill Harriman to Moscow to sound out the Soviets on their possible readiness either to join the United States in a preventive attack on China's facilities or else to stand by while the United States alone attacked. The Soviets rejected both suggestions, and the idea, which, as far as we know, had never in any case been advocated by any high-level administration official, died.[27]

The Chinese test, which occurred in October 1964, was a turning point. What happened next was decisive for nonproliferation policy for the balance of the twentieth century, both for the United States and the world. Preventive war and nonproliferation agreements are functional equivalents: two ways of achieving the same end. Having rejected the first, Johnson swung to the second. He ordered a thorough review of the United States' entire nuclear nonproliferation policy. Should the United States favor proliferation in some cases and not others? For example, should it permit India, Japan, or even Germany to obtain the bomb? (At the time, Germany was keenly interested in acquiring access to the bomb in one way or another, and a former chancellor, Konrad Adenauer, even declared that signing the Nuclear Non-Proliferation Treaty would be Germany's death warrant.) Should it oppose proliferation in all cases? If so, what obligations should the existing nuclear powers undertake in this regard? These, of course, were the very questions the Bush administration would face again after September 11.

The Johnson administration's decision was to oppose *all* proliferation, and to do so by negotiation. Thereafter, the United States threw its full diplomatic weight behind the creation of the Nuclear Non-Proliferation Treaty, which entered into force in 1970 and still provides the legal framework in which all questions of proliferation, including the crises that now surround the nuclear programs of Iran and North Korea, are addressed. The treaty's Article I and II forbade nuclear weapons to all signatories but the five who already possessed them (the United States, the Soviet Union, Britain, France, and—just under the wire—China) were permitted under the treaty's Article VI to join as nuclear weapon states on condition that they give up their arsenals over time. In the treaty's words, they must "pursue negotiations in good faith on effective measures relating to cessation of the nuclear arms race at an early date and to nuclear disarmament, and on a treaty on general and complete disarmament under strict and effective international control." This commitment, which the nonnuclear weapon states took seriously but the nuclear weapon states did not, meant that, formally speaking, the NPT was a slow-motion nuclear abolition agreement. As already noted, under the treaty's Article IV, the nonnuclear states were guaranteed, in exchange for accepting their temporary second-class status in the weapon area, access to all the technology needed for nuclear power, including the nuclear fuel cycle, and the nuclear weapon states obliged themselves to take positive efforts to provide this support. Article X permitted signatories to withdraw on three months' notice if "extraordinary events" jeopardized their "supreme interests."

The treaty is widely credited with drastically slowing the rate of proliferation globally. Today, the number of nonnuclear weapon states under the treaty stands at 183. Three states—Israel, India, and Pakistan—never joined the NPT, and all have since become nuclear powers, while one, North Korea, joined, withdrew, and then conducted its 2006 test. However, the treaty left open the final settlement of the nuclear question. While requiring the possessors to eliminate their arsenals, it committed them to no timetable for fulfilling the vow. On the other hand, the obligations of the nonnuclear weapon states were immediate and strict.

As the scholar Francis J. Gavin has pointed out, the United States described the Chinese government of that time in terms very similar to those used later by George W. Bush to describe the "axis" governments. Soviet leaders, American observers were already saying, were ruthless but rational. They wanted to stay in power and stay alive, not die in a universal conflagration. They could be deterred. Mao Zedong was said to be different. He was a proven fanatic. He could not be counted on to make rational decisions. He had displayed a remarkable insouciance regarding nuclear devastation. In comments that unnerved the Soviet leader Nikita Khrushchev, he once proclaimed, "We shouldn't be afraid of atomic bombs and missiles. No matter what kind of war breaks out, conventional or thermonuclear—we'll win. As for China, if the imperialists unleash war on us, we may lose more than three hundred million people. So what?"[28] The choice for the American government, then as now, was between relying chiefly on diplomacy or chiefly on force. Johnson, like every other president but the current one, chose diplomacy, and the Nuclear Non-Proliferation Treaty was born.

In 1968, Johnson also initiated the Strategic Arms Limitations Talks (SALT), which led to a long procession of Soviet-American arms control treaties in the final decades of the Cold War. The United States and the Soviet Union touted these treaties as steps toward fulfilling their promise to pursue nuclear disarmament under the NPT's Article VI. Although the NPT and SALT negotiations were formally separate, they were manifestations of the same underlying turn toward treaties as the United States' chosen means of reducing nuclear danger across the board. However, it is also true that in this period neither the United States nor the Soviet Union expressed the slightest serious interest in actually fulfilling the terms of Article VI by surrendering their own nuclear arms. On the contrary, they rejected abolition as utopian. In practical terms, the question of whether the NPT would lead to a permanent two-tier nuclear order or to a nuclear-weapon-free world was left in abeyance. The great powers staked out the middle ground defined by the deterrence doctrine. For the duration of the Cold War, nuclear weapons were accepted, indeed highly valued, but the final shape of the world's nuclear order was left undetermined.

By contrast, President Bush's demotion of diplomacy and treaties across the board was as clear as his elevation of force. In decision after decision, his administration tore at the web of arms control treaties that had grown up over four decades. Upon coming into office, he declined to revive the Comprehensive Test-Ban Treaty, which his fellow party members in the Republican-controlled Senate had voted down in 1999. In December 2001, over Russian protests, he announced the United States' withdrawal from the Anti-Ballistic Missile (ABM) Treaty, which had been a cornerstone of arms control agreements with the Soviet Union since its signing in 1972 by Richard Nixon. (The signers had reasoned that a balance in offensive arms would be stable only if antinuclear defenses were formally banned.) Bush asserted that the treaty "hinders our government's ability to develop ways to protect our people from future terrorist or rogue state missile attacks."[29] He also took a number of steps that weakened the Nuclear Non-Proliferation Treaty, which had been renewed indefinitely in 1995. In a Treaty Review Conference in 2000, the United States had joined other countries in affirming that thirteen steps should be taken to strengthen the treaty. These included early entry into force of the Comprehensive Test Ban Treaty, conclusion within five years of a ban on the production of new fissile materials, preservation of the ABM Treaty, and an "unequivocal commitment" by the nuclear weapon states to "accomplish the total elimination of their nuclear arsenals." But at the 2004 Review Conference, the American representative declared these commitments merely "historical," and that same year Undersecretary of State John Bolton declared that obligations of the nuclear powers to fulfill their disarmament commitments under Article VI were "issues that do not exist."[30]

The administration did sign one arms control treaty, the Russian-American Strategic Offensive Reductions Treaty (SORT) of 2002, otherwise known as the Moscow Treaty, requiring the two nations to reduce their deployed strategic arms to between 1,700 and 2,200 by 2012. A successor to the bilateral Washington-Moscow Strategic Arms Limitation Talks of the 1970s and the Strategic Arms Reduction Talks of the eighties and nineties, the Moscow Treaty was negotiated in a manner that devalued arms control treaties. Less than a single page in length, it failed to specify any timetable for the agreed-upon reductions; permitted undeployed warheads, in any number, to be kept in storage; imposed no new restrictions on delivery vehicles; established no inspection procedures; and permitted withdrawal from the treaty and all its obligations on three months' notice.

Because the treaty specifies no timetable for the mandated reductions yet permits quick withdrawal, the signatories can, if they choose, easily escape any obligation imposed by the document. A National Resources Defense Council report is therefore correct in concluding that it had "no binding provisions dictating what either nation is permitted to do."[31] Although compliance with the reductions of deployed warheads required in 2012 nevertheless seems likely (unless something happens to change minds in either Moscow or the United States), this will not be because the terms of the treaty require it. Is a treaty without obligations still a treaty? The Moscow agreement, which neither contemplated nor called for any sequel, emerged less as an arms control agreement than as an exit from all arms control by means of a treaty. "Just keep in mind," Secretary of State Powell testified, "what we are doing in this treaty, we were going to do anyway."[32]

Law and Empire

Like the administration's predilection for force, its aversion to treaties and other forms of international law was part of a broader pattern, which, as a great many observers have noted, was also demonstrated in a refusal to join in a long list of treaties outside the nuclear sphere, including the Landmine Convention, the Kyoto Protocol on climate change, and the Rome Statute establishing the International Criminal Court. The latter, signed by President Bill Clinton, was "unsigned" by Bush, who proceeded to mount a global campaign of arm-twisting to pressure other countries to stay out of the treaty. The administration proposed and Congress passed legislation called the American Service-members Protection Act authorizing the president to invade any country holding American soldiers who might be brought to justice before the International Criminal Court.

The troops of the empire were not to be subject to legal sanction by the subject nations. For international law and global empire are not merely different; they are, like nonproliferation by treaty and counterproliferation by force, opposite and contradictory means of attempting the same thing, in this case nothing less than bringing some order to planet Earth. The president's representative to the UN, John Bolton (a man of unvarnished candor who once said of the institution to which he would be the United States' representative, "There is no such thing as the United Nations"), spoke to this point: "It is a big mistake for us to grant any validity to international law even when it may seem in our short-term interest to do so—because, over the long term, the goal of those who think that international law really means anything are those who want to constrict the United States."[33]

An even more startling expression of the same view came in a Defense Department document of 2005 called the *National Defense Strategy of the United States of America,* which stated, "Our strength as a nation state will continue to be challenged by those who employ a strategy of the weak using international fora, judicial processes, and terrorism."[34] So strange at first reading, this conflation of judicial proceedings and terrorism as threats to American power in fact accurately reflected the fundamental logic of the Bush doctrine. It's in the nature of the rule of law that it establishes a single standard for all parties. It is in the nature of imperial rule that it establishes two standards, one for the ruling imperial power (which must possess "unchallengeable" might) and another for the ruled (those restricted to "trade and other pursuits of peace"). Indeed, a double standard is required by any form of rule by force: those who hold the sword prescribe the law but are not under it, whereas those against whom the sword is wielded must obey the law but can have no part in making it.

On March 21, 2003, the very eve of the invasion of Iraq, Richard Perle, a member of the Pentagon's Defense Advisory Board and an intellectual forerunner of the Bush doctrine, expounded its revolutionary essence, prospectively reveling in the triumph he had long believed was to come. He wrote, "Saddam Hussein's reign of terror is about to end. He will go quickly, but not alone: in a parting irony, he will take the UN down with him. Well, not the whole UN. The 'good works' part will survive, the low-risk peacekeeping bureaucracies will remain, the chatterbox on the Hudson [sic] will continue to bleat. What will die is the fantasy of the UN as the foundation of a new world order. As we sift the debris, it will be important to preserve, the better to understand, the intellectual wreckage of the liberal conceit of safety through international law administered by international institutions."[35]

The choice between the force of law and the law of force is always a fundamental one in politics, and in the wake of September 11, the Bush administration opted for the latter as its organizing principle for international affairs in general and for nonproliferation policy in particular.

Return to Nuclear Primacy

The Bush administration's nonproliferation policies were widely covered, not least because they were invoked to justify the Iraq war. However, its strategic nuclear policies—its guidance for the United States' own arsenals—received almost no attention. The American stockpile remained in the shadows that had shrouded it since the end of the Cold War. (Curiously joining it in obscurity was the Russian arsenal, whose continuing capacity to annihilate the United States in a few minutes was rarely mentioned, either by government officials or the news media.) But changes were soon quietly under way. Taken in their totality, they constituted, at least on paper, as thoroughgoing a transformation of the strategic policies of the United States as any in the nuclear age.

This transformation is not easy to either characterize or describe. Even in the context of the nuclear dilemma, the layers of concealment and confusion are unusually dense. First, the transformation included policies that were radically new by any standard. Second, it incorporated half-hidden innovations that went back to the administration of the elder Bush, and especially to the changes made by then secretary of defense Dick Cheney. Third, it included policies that remained unchanged since the Cold War but were radical for just that reason—because they survived deep into the new era in the absence of their former political referents. Fourth, the transformation included startling reversals of other Cold War policies that might well have been preserved—for example, the long-standing framework of arms control, which Bush overthrew. Fifth, major elements of the shift were fundamentally and sometimes deliberately misrepresented in the administration's public explanations. Sixth, many of the most important documents related to the entire transformation have been classified, partially classified, or otherwise withheld from circulation, though some have been unearthed by intrepid researchers. Seventh, even in the documents we do have, the changes are couched in a strategic jargon so

vague, euphemistic, and abstract that it repels ordinary understanding.

Let us start with the administration's deceptive rhetoric. According to its declared policies, it has been *reducing* the role of nuclear weapons in military policy. In particular, it claims to have
ended the practice of deterring Russia with nuclear arms. In his first
presidential campaign, Bush had even accused Clinton of being
"locked in a Cold War mentality."[36] Repeatedly, Bush and others
have claimed that because the Cold War is over, the policy of mutual
assured destruction (MAD) has been abandoned. For example,
upon signing the Moscow Treaty, the president declared that it "liq-
uidates the legacy of the cold war." Asked at a Senate hearing how
that could be if, under the treaty, the two nations would still retain
from seventeen hundred to two thousand two hundred deployed
nuclear warheads in the year 2012, Secretary of Defense Rumsfeld
answered, "I think it would be a mistake to leave the impression
that . . . either the SIOP or the 1,700 to 2,200 is premised on Russia."[37] And Undersecretary of Defense for Policy Douglas J. Feith
testified before the Senate that the administration had "moved away
from this MAD policy framework. . . . We no longer consider a
MAD relationship with Russia the appropriate basis for calculating
our nuclear requirements."[38]

If so, however, the word had not reached the operational planners. As Chief Admiral Richard A. Mies explained to Congress in
June 2001, the American triad of bombers, submarines, and land-
based missiles remained necessary "to complicate any adversary's
offensive and defense planning calculation while simultaneously
providing protection against the failure of a single leg of the triad."
The only country on earth that conceivably could threaten even one
leg of the triad was, of course, the United States' sole nuclear peer,
Russia.

The situation was stranger still. Even as the Bush administration
was disavowing competition with Russia, it seemed to be taking
steps to give itself what the experts on nuclear policy Keir A. Lieber

and Daryl G. Press have called "nuclear primacy" in an article in *Foreign Affairs*. The authors observed that although on paper Russian forces were equivalent to American ones, they were in fact eroding and declining rapidly. For example, the Russian nuclear submarine force was mostly dysfunctional, while Russia's satellite early warning system has been badly degraded. Meanwhile, American missile forces have been steadily improving in accuracy, giving them a potential that they previously lacked to eliminate the Russian missile force before it could be launched in retaliation. The authors wrote, "The weight of the evidence suggests that Washington is, in fact, deliberately seeking nuclear primacy."[39] While this conclusion remains under debate, there can be no doubt that the gap between American and Russian nuclear capacities has been steadily growing. In addition, the United States' ability to conduct a successful first strike against China's much smaller and more vulnerable nuclear force has also increased and will grow as the United States deploys highly accurate Tomahawk 4 missiles in the Pacific.

A situation quite new in the history of American nuclear targeting had now arisen. The United States was dedicating most of its nuclear arsenal to a country, Russia, with whom it declared a warm friendship. At the same time, it was denying that it was doing so. Or, to describe the situation differently, the United States was willing to endure being targeted by thousands of poorly maintained Russian nuclear warheads in exchange for the privilege of aiming its own warheads at its new friend. These arrangements, though not the most dangerous of the nuclear age, were probably the most peculiar—and the most devious and convoluted (an honor for which there is a great deal of competition in the annals of nuclear policy).

What, in fact, was going on? Three indisputable facts should guide our understanding. First, through the Moscow Treaty, the United States had found a means of holding on to an arsenal of thousands of nuclear warheads indefinitely while claiming to reduce the salience of nuclear arms. (The Cold War arsenals were so fantastically large that they could be impressively and repeatedly reduced while still leaving huge margins of overkill.) The trope "the Cold War is over," though shopworn more than a decade after the fact, lent the proceedings a pacific air. (A wit in Moscow commented, "I am tired of attending funerals for the Cold War.")

Second, also through the treaty, the Bush administration had extricated the United States from the Strategic Arms Limitation Talks, and, indeed, from any expectation of further arms control. Those talks had been a machine for producing bilateral reductions. The new belief was, in the words of Undersecretary of Defense Douglas J. Feith, that "a highly dynamic security environment such as we now confront ultimately cannot be tamed by rigid, legal constructs, however sincerely entered into."[40] In other words, the day of treaties was ending. The administration had already cast off all constraints on antinuclear defenses by withdrawing from the ABM Treaty. The Moscow Treaty accomplished the same thing for offensive arms. The seventeen hundred to twenty-two hundred warhead ceiling was also therefore a floor, and this second fact was more important for the future than the first, because it set a global benchmark of high levels of nuclear arms for the indefinite future.

Third, even as the Bush administration reduced the United States arsenal, it was continuing to improve the quality of its nuclear delivery systems, possibly in order to achieve the nuclear primacy that Lieber and Press describe. Certainly, if the administration's stated goal of overall global military supremacy was any guide, it would be unlikely to object to extending it to the nuclear field. The fiction that the United States was liquidating mutual assured destruction was in effect one more mask worn while these other aims were pursued. Just as its policy of preventive attack revolutionized nonproliferation policy, so its strategic nuclear policies swept aside forty years of superpower arms control. By a deft sleight of hand, the administration had, in the nuclear sphere, unobtrusively given itself what it perhaps valued most in every area of foreign policy, a completely free hand, unconstrained by alliances or treaty obligations.

A Momentous Answer

Yet all these maneuverings comprised only a part of the shift in the administration's strategic policies—the arms control portion. There remained the guidance to be given to the post–Cold War arsenal— the very core of traditional nuclear strategy. As early as March 2001, C. Paul Robinson, the president and director of Sandia National Laboratories, had distinguished between two nuclear capabilities— Capability One, or Central Deterrence, dealing with targets in Russia, "the only nation that we can conceive of with the potential to threaten the U.S. national existence"—and Capability Two, which he called the "To Whom It May Concern Force," dealing with everything else, the "non-Russian context."[41] (He craftily recommended that the targets of Capability Two should be "country and leadership specific," but that the particulars should be kept "confidential.")

Though it was untrue that MAD had been dissolved, it does appear that the administration was not much interested in Russia. The whole misleading discussion of the relationship with Russia appeared to be a corollary to what did profoundly concern the administration, namely the To Whom It May Concern targets. Of course, it was this domain of nuclear targeting that, though not anointed with any publicized name, had most interested Dick Cheney as secretary of defense in the early 1990s, when he presided over the "living SIOP," with its concentration on the third world, and its targeting of rogue states. Now, under President George W. Bush, Cheney was a vice president wielding unprecedented influence, and in no arena more than national security policy. His role in framing the nuclear policies of the second President Bush is still veiled in the secrecy that has surrounded so much of his immense power. What is clear is that his ideas, which had stayed alive in the Pentagon bureaucracy even in the Clinton years, had now resurfaced and become the building blocks for far more radical developments.

The most important documents setting forth the Bush administration's strategic revolution have been the *Nuclear Posture Review* of December 2001 (a successor to the feeble Clinton effort), the *National Strategy to Counter Weapons of Mass Destruction,* made public by the White House in December 2002, and a draft of a *Doctrine for Joint Nuclear Operations* produced in the fall of 2005. Neither the review nor the doctrine were meant for public viewing. Though mandated by Congress, the full review was classified. A public version was released, then parts of the classified version were soon leaked. The Doctrine for Joint Nuclear Operations was scheduled for completion in the fall of 2005 and then canceled, but before that happened, the enterprising researcher Hans Kristensen, of the Federation of Atomic Scientists, obtained a copy of a nearly final draft and published it on the Internet. Other leaks, congressional testimony, and public comments by officials have enriched this record.

The changes in nuclear doctrine outlined in these documents were made during the period of the Iraq war, when there was little public discussion of the Cold War arsenals, American or Russian, or of the strategies now guiding them. None of the changes, even when brought to public attention, occasioned significant debate, and they went unmentioned in political campaigns. The omission was the more surprising because the facts were available, had anyone bothered to examine them. Most important was the work of a trio of analysts, made up of Robert S. Norris and Christopher E. Paine, both of the Natural Resources Defense Council, and Kristensen. At the *Washington Post* Web site, William Arkin, drawing on his own original reporting, followed developments in his blog, "Early Warning." From time to time, other reporters at the *Post,* notably Walter Pincus, also chronicled these events. Every now and then a strange or anomalous-seeming development—such as the idea of building "mini-nukes" in order to make nuclear threats easier to carry out or the expansion of the U.S. target list to a new array of countries—would cause a minor stir, but then the silence would return. Nevertheless, the changes were dramatic and brought to completion a strategic revolution that had begun in 1990.

In February 2001, a month after the Bush administration took office, Dr. Stephen Cambone, the deputy undersecretary of defense for policy, set up a group to prepare for the *Nuclear Posture Review,* which, by law, had to be delivered to Congress by the end of the year. It was issued at the last minute, on December 31,[42] less than three months after September 11, and reflected the sudden adoption of the Global War on Terror as the framework in which virtually all security issues were now being analyzed. But what could the United States' colossal arsenal of thermonuclear weapons contribute to a fight against terrorists, with their box cutters on commercial jets and their ammonium-nitrate-laced fertilizer in commercial delivery vans? What use was it to threaten someone ready to give up his life in his own explosion, as the September 11 hijackers had done? Nuclear weapons were for deterring nations, and it quickly become a cliché of the new era that terrorists, who had no countries to lose, were undeterrable.

Nevertheless, links between the apocalyptic weapons and the terrorist threat were found. Once again, we can speak of expanding concentric rings, and once again the central point, the Ground Zero (and here the term is restored to its original, nuclear context), is the "crossroads of radicalism and technology," including but not restricted to the "nexus of terror and weapons of mass destruction." Terrorism and proliferation were conjoined in the "axis" country that acquires nuclear weapons and then possibly supplies one to a terrorist group. It was the prospect of such a transfer that President Bush invoked when, rallying support for the Iraq war, he said, "Facing clear evidence of peril, we cannot wait for the final proof—the smoking gun—that could come in the form of a mushroom cloud."

With states thus brought into the picture, might not nuclear weapons be used against them as counterproliferation weapons? This was, of course, not a new idea; it had originated a decade before, when the bunker-busting B61-11 was built with exactly this mission in mind. The Bush administration's *Nuclear Posture Review (NPR)* embraced the idea firmly, declaring that more than seventy countries now employed over ten thousand buried facilities for military purposes (suggesting a very large number of new nuclear targets indeed), and calling for a new, even more effective bunker busting weapon, the obscenely named Robust Nuclear Earth Penetrator. North Korea, Iraq, Iran, Syria, and Libya were mentioned as possible targets, but how threats from these sources might require an arsenal of some two thousand deployed nuclear weapons and thousands more in reserve was left unexplained. Instead, the familiar two-step evasion occurred. The refrain about desisting from competition with Russia was repeated. According to Secretary of Defense Donald Rumsfeld's letter accompanying the transfer of the review to Congress, "The U.S. will no longer plan, size or sustain its forces as though Russia presented merely a smaller version of the threat posed by the former Soviet Union."[43] But when it came to describing what mission the still-immense arsenal *would* serve, the document withdrew into extreme generalities.

One idea it elaborated was the old claim that the United States had withdrawn from the targeting business altogether. The review announced that the administration was ending the "threat-based approach of the Cold War" and inaugurating an entirely new concept, "capabilities-based" planning. Now, instead of aiming at particular targets in particular countries, the United States would ready itself to attack certain kinds of targets in certain kinds of countries. "This new approach," Rumsfeld wrote, "should provide, over the coming decades, a credible deterrent at the lowest level of nuclear weapons consistent with U.S. and allied security," but he never actually said who was being deterred or why.[44] And indeed when Secretary of State Colin Powell was asked by CBS News whom the United States now targeted, he replied, with a small show of indignation, "Right now, today, not a single nation on the face of the Earth is being targeted by an American nuclear weapon on a day-to-day basis. We just don't do that."[45] But of course if none are targeted, yet large nuclear arsenals are maintained, then in a sense all are targeted, or quickly can be. If the need for specific threats to justify specific weapons is rejected (as being part of the discarded "threat-based"

system) yet the rockets still sit in their silos, then anyone and everyone can be threatened.

With this development included, the chronicle of American targeting in the nuclear age would run thus: first, the target was Germany, then Japan, then the Soviet Union and its allies, and now it
is . . . "capabilities." Which capabilities? With the familiar exception
of the proliferation of weapons of mass destruction (the core of the
"nexus"), the NPR maintains a studied agnosticism. It's in giving
the answers to questions like these that abstraction and euphemism
are pressed into maximum service. In the section of the review on
the first of four goals listed under the heading "Contributions of the
New Triad to Defense Policy Goals," for instance, it is simply impossible to tell any longer who might threaten the United States or why.
We read:

> U.S. nuclear forces will continue to provide assurance to security
> partners, particularly in the presence of known or suspected threats
> of nuclear, biological, or chemical attacks or in the event of surprising
> military developments. This assurance can serve to reduce the incen-
> tives for friendly countries to acquire nuclear weapons of their own
> to deter such threats and circumstances. Nuclear capabilities also as-
> sure the U.S. public that the United States will not be subject to coer-
> cion based on a false perception of U.S. weakness among potential
> adversaries.[46]

The NPR supplied a reason for using such sweepingly indetermi-
nate phrases as "surprising military developments": the world has
become too unpredictable to foresee the origins of threats. "In a
fluid security environment, the precise nuclear force level for the
future cannot be predicted with certainty," Rumsfeld wrote in his
letter.

Here and elsewhere, administration officials become almost
rhapsodic in their presentations of the uncertainty of affairs. For instance, in testimony supporting the review before the Senate Armed
Services Committee, Undersecretary of Defense for Policy Douglas

J. Feith explained that Cold War certainties had been replaced by "the unpredictability of potential opponents who are motivated by goals and values we often do not share nor well understand, and who move in directions we may not anticipate." Do we know what threats they might pose? We do not: "What we can predict today is that we will face unanticipated challenges, a range of opponents— some familiar, some not." (On the other hand, the classified version of the *NPR* did mention some of the countries that the administration might have in mind for targeting. It stated, "North Korea, Iraq, Iran, Syria, and Libya are among the countries that could be involved in immediate, potential, or unexpected contingencies.")[47] Can we guess at least what will inspire them? Again, no. We can only say they will have "varying goals and military capabilities, and a spectrum of potential contingencies involving very different stakes for the United States and its foes."[48] Rumsfeld's most famous articulation of this new strategic uncertainty principle was that you must plan not only for the "known unknowns" but for "the unknown unknowns." In the last analysis, the target of the U.S. nuclear arsenal became history and whatever it might produce—not a foe but a tense, the future itself.

The family resemblance of these new justifications for immense post–Cold War nuclear arsenals to those articulated by such countries as France, Britain, and even Russia is obvious. None of these countries is fazed by the loss of its Cold War enemies. All justify their nuclear arsenals in hazy, generic terms. All seem to await a future enemy who might, somewhere, someplace, sometime, rise up to pose a challenge. All also see *their* arsenals as instruments of peace and global order, while arsenals in other hands are sources of danger and disorder. Whether the policies of these nations have influenced one another is hard to say. Rumsfeld invoked uncertainty as the new enemy before Chirac or Blair did. On the other hand, it was the French who, even during the Cold War, pioneered a generalized non-specific rationale for nuclear arsenals, targeting them at "all points of the compass." And of course, the Indian specialty, the invocation of a new nuclear world order, was soon shared by the Bush doctrine, with the two important differences that it made no mention of any role for positive contributions by other nuclear powers in that order and pledged the United States to use its military—nuclear and conventional—to stop proliferation.

But which deployments were required to cover such unknowable and undefinable targets? Here the review suddenly became very specific, as well as ambitious. It called for a full-scale regeneration and modernization of the whole nuclear strategic infrastructure over the long term. To begin with, the old strategic triad, of missiles, long-range bombers, and submarines was to be scrapped and a new one established in its place. It would consist, first, of the old triad of submarines, missiles, and bombers lumped together; second, of antinuclear defenses (once banned by the ABM Treaty); and, third—stretching the idea of the triad to the limits—of the industrial infrastructure needed for the first two.

What President Dwight Eisenhower once warned against as the military-industrial complex, now renamed a "capability," was hereby built into the very core of military doctrine. However, this oddly matched grouping of two weapon systems and a bureaucratic-corporate base makes sense if we keep in mind that the target of American nuclear forces was now to be nothing less than any of the adverse events that the future might produce, in all their unpredictability. The days of specific foes posing specific threats with specific weapons were over. The days of "potential" (a word much in evidence in the review) foes posing unspecifiable threats with unguessable weapons was upon us. What better "capacity" to meet this "challenge" than the sum total of the military-industrial complex?

Having identified the new capacities needed, the *Nuclear Posture Review* became even more specific about what hardware was needed, and once again the long-range future came into view. It turned out that there were a very large number of specific "shortfalls in current infrastructure sustainment programs for nuclear platforms." The United States must fund and plan: a temporary plutonium "pit" manufacturing facility (a plutonium pit is at the core of most nuclear weapons), then a permanent new facility; a new facility for producing tritium, which boosts the yield of thermonuclear weapons; an expansion of the capacity to build or dismantle nuclear warheads; a new intercontinental ballistic missile, to be operational in the year 2018; a new strategic submarine and a new ballistic missile to go with it, for 2029; a new nuclear-capable bomber for 2040; infrastructure to prepare for possible new nuclear testing; an "initiative in the design and development of new nuclear weapons," including the new bunker buster and new low-yield nuclear weapons (mini-nukes); and upgrades of various kinds in the accuracy of targeting systems.

A large new array of other "capacities" must, the review insisted, be created, including (to pick just a few) the ability to hit "Mobile and Relocatable Targets," equipment for "Defeating hard and Deeply-Buried targets," "Guided missile Submarines," and a "new strike system that might arm . . . converted" submarines. Antinuclear defense systems required an equal number of new programs, capacities, and "initiatives," such as an airborne laser, a "ground-based midcourse system," "4 sea-based midcourse ships," and so forth. The same went for command and control systems and intelligence, where "exquisite" capacities were recommended.

In sum, the 2001 *Nuclear Posture Review* was like a design for a building whose massive foundations were articulated in the finest detail but whose upper stories were only lightly sketched in. A new bomber would be ready in 2040, but whom would it bomb? Targets would be strikable with greater accuracy but where would those targets be? The *NPR* declined to say.

One section of the document, however, did offer some suggestive hints. Throughout the review, the distinction between nuclear and conventional strikes, a cornerstone of American policy during most of the Cold War, was erased. In the section on the "Contributions" of the new triad, there was language in which the shapes of future battles dimly emerge. For example, under the heading "DEFEAT," the review states, "Non-nuclear capabilities may be particularly useful to limit collateral damage and conflict escalation." The document then added ominously, "Nuclear weapons could be employed against targets able to withstand non-nuclear attack."[49] And in the fall of 2006, the administration would indeed propose adapting some submarine-launched ballistic missiles, previously reserved for nuclear warheads, to carry conventional payloads instead.

Although the review consistently suggested that by mingling conventional and nuclear resources, it would be possible to replace nuclear missions with conventional ones, the obverse clearly became equally possible: nuclear strikes could, when needed, be introduced into conventional wars. By blurring the distinction between conventional and nuclear war, the decision to use nuclear weapons had come to depend, at least theoretically, on such technical factors as the depth of an underground target. Indeed, the argument for the new, deeper-digging, more powerful, more accurate bunker buster, which tied the entire strategy to the larger policy objectives of Bush's Global War on Terror, was justified on just these grounds.

By speaking vaguely, as the review does, of "enemies" and "aggressors," an impression of continuity with past strategy was created. But such language concealed the world of difference that exists between a nuclear threat to deter conventional Soviet superiority in the heart of Europe and introducing a nuclear weapon into a conventional war in—let's say—the Middle East.

A second passage pointed to a related and equally wide extension of the aims of the new nuclear strategy. Under the heading "DISSUADE," the review stated, "Systems capable of striking a wide range of targets throughout an adversary's territory may dissuade a potential adversary from pursuing threatening capabilities." As we saw, suppressing any military rivalry with the United States through the sheer presence of its might was a major principle of American policy laid out in the National Security Strategy of the United States of America, and this passage of the review was clearly the nuclear application of that principle. The Cold War policy of threatening to use nuclear weapons against the Soviet Union, and then, if deterrence failed, of using them, had now been widened without limit to send messages of nuclear destruction To Whom It May Concern.

Global Strike

Out of the verbal mist of the *Nuclear Posture Review*, an answer emerged to our momentous question concerning the purpose of the American nuclear arsenal in the post–Cold War era. Its purpose was to dissuade, deter, defeat, or annihilate—preventively, preemptively, or in retaliation—any nation or other grouping of people on the face of the earth, large or small, that militarily opposed, or dreamed of opposing, the United States. The potential range of targets proposed was as wide as the Earth itself. In short, the story of nuclear doctrine recapitulated in the nuclear sphere the extraordinary assertion, made with such admirable frankness in the National Security Strategy of the United States of America, of global American military hegemony. That document had stated, "We must be prepared to stop rogue states and their terrorist clients before they are able to threaten or use weapons of mass destruction," and "to forestall or prevent such hostile acts . . . the United States will, if necessary, act preemptively." These words applied as much to the nuclear as to the conventional arsenals of the United States.

The creation of a new military command, Global Strike, made the policy operational. In "Global Strike: A Chronology of the Pentagon's New Offensive Strike Plan," a tour de force of independent research, its author Hans Kristensen comments, "Although promoted as a way of increasing the President's options for deterring lesser adversaries, Global Strike is first and foremost offensive and preemptive in nature and deeply rooted in the expectation that deterrence *will* fail sooner or later. Rather than waiting for the mushroom cloud to appear . . . the Global Strike seeks to create near-invulnerability for the United States by forcing utter vulnerability upon any potential adversary. As a result, Global Strike is principally about war-fighting rather than deterrence."[50]

In February 2001, the second month of Bush's term, General John Jumper, the head of the Air Combat Command, proposed the "concept" of Global Strike for Air Force Operations. The targets he had in view were weapons of mass destruction in Iran.[51] In October, a month after September 11, as war in Iraq first entered public discussion, he described Global Strike as a mostly conventional "kick down the door" capacity to swiftly respond to "anti-access threats"—in other words, to destroy opposition to invading American forces.[52] But by March 2002, air force major general Franklin J. Blaisdell spoke of the concept for the first time as providing "full spectrum deterrence"—Pentagonese for nuclear as well as conventional weapons.[53] In September 2002, Admiral James O. Ellis established a Global Strike division in STRATCOM, traditionally the command center for nuclear operations but now also including conventional operations. Its location there suggested the addition of nuclear arms to the plan, which Ellis confirmed in the customary coded language, announcing that the force would include "kinetic and non-kinetic capabilities spanning the entire spectrum of force employment."[54]

In January 2003, the president signed a proposed "Change 2," assigning STRATCOM four new missions, including Global Strike. This was described as "providing integrated global strike planning and command and control support to deliver rapid, extended range, precision kinetic (nuclear and conventional) . . . effects in support of theater and national objectives"—thus for the first time explicitly naming (if only parenthetically) nuclear arms as a component of the Global Strike mission.[55] In unnoticed testimony before the House Armed Services Committee on February 5, 2003, Chairman of the Joint Chiefs of Staff Richard B. Myers made the change official. "With its global strike responsibilities," he stated, "the Command will provide a core cadre to plan and execute nuclear, conventional and information operations anywhere in the world."[56] And in a speech at an Air Force Association meeting later in the month, Admiral Ellis, the commander of STRATCOM, stated plainly, "It is full spectrum, global strike. That means just what it says, full spectrum. It is not just nuclear. It is not just conventional. And it includes all of the capabilities that are out there."[57]

Soon Global Strike was supported by the creation of Operational Plan (OPLAN) no. 8022, which in turn was succeeded by OPLAN 8022-02. Already in existence was OPLAN 8044, a successor to the old, solitary SIOP. Although details are unavailable, it is likely that while OPLAN 8044 chiefly supports Capability One, aiming at the supposedly forgotten Russian arsenal, OPLAN 8022-02 is focused on the To Whom It May Concern arsenal covering the rest of the globe. When Ellis retired in July 2005, General Myer congratulated him by saying, "The president charged you to be ready to strike at any moment's notice in any dark corner of the world [and] that's exactly what you've done."[58] On November 18, 2005, the Pentagon announced that the Global Strike Command had achieved "Initial Operational Capability" at Offutt Air Force Base in Nebraska.[59]

Global Strike and its associated documents permit a fuller picture of the role of nuclear weapons in American military policy. They show that Senator Nunn's threat blank has at last been filled in—with planet Earth. Nuclear weapons, ready for use at any instant and without warning, are deployed to undergird each and every military operation undertaken or merely threatened by the United States, from general war to a strike against a terrorist group.

At the same time, in these "non-Russian" theaters, at least, the Cold War balance of terror, dictated by fear of retaliation, has been thrown off, and, in a grand return of the nuclear-war-fighting doctrine, superiority has been declared over all adversaries and even all conceivable future adversaries. (If Lieber and Press are right, this does include Russia.) The Cold War principles of nuclear stalemate and comparative inaction have been superseded by principles of superiority and action. Global Strike has provided the United States with a universal (if grammatically garbled) "Freedom to attack and to be free from attack," in the words of a special notice delivered by the air force to contractors inviting them to attend a "Global Strike Task Force Industry Day."[60] At this most general and abstract level, Global Strike's very existence is meant to pervade the atmosphere, even in peacetime, and, according to the official documents that describe it, stop "adversaries" not only from attacking the United States but even from acquiring any ability to do so: it must "dissuade military competition, and deter aggression and coercion." In plain English, nuclear terror operates everywhere and at all times, even when nuclear weapons are not specifically employed as a threat or going off somewhere.

If necessary, however, nuclear weapons can also be launched, and all targets are open, including not only such specific ones as "WMD production, storage, and delivery systems"[61] but also broad and vague ones like "adversary decision-makers, critical command and control facilities, and various adversary leadership power bases." Above all, the Global Strike force can be used in relation to a specific state for the purpose of "changing its regime and occupying its territory."[62]

Surprise is of the essence of such planning. In the words of Admiral Ellis, "If you can find that time-critical, key terrorist target or that weapons-of-mass-destruction stockpile, and you have minutes rather than hours or days to deal with it, how do you reach out and negate that threat to our nation half a world away?"[63] The new principle, according to Linton Brooks, the administrator of the National Nuclear Security Administration, is that it is "unwise for there to be anything that's beyond the reach of US power."[64] "In the future," Secretary of the Air Force James Roche commented, "we expect adversaries with advanced technologies to try to deny the US military access to a region."[65] However, these pretensions of local people to keep American forces out of their lands in some corner of the Earth will be thwarted by Global Strike.

Nor are nuclear weapons confined to general nuclear wars and combating weapons of mass destruction; they are also available for the middle range of military activities: theater wars. The Doctrine for Joint Nuclear Operations (or DJNO—a document that was developed in late 2005 and then withdrawn when the leaking of a draft stirred protests) fills in this important remaining zone of the threat blank. In a classified directive in January 2004, the president had assigned "theater" objectives to Global Strike. In April 2005, the new STRATCOM commander, General James E. Cartright, stated that Global Strike "allows us to provide effect for a regional combatant commander. . . ."

In October 2002, STRATCOM and the Space Command were merged. By presidential order, antimissile defenses and space operations were added to the Global Strike command. In public rhetoric, both were presented as ways to defend the American people. However, in Pentagon documents, they are also revealed to be adjuncts to regional attacks launched by Global Strike. In the DJNO's opaque prose, "In an operational application, defenses allow a geographic combatant commander to consider employing offensive counterforce strikes while enhancing security from catastrophic results if an adversary launches a retaliatory strike while under attack."[66] That is to say, when American forces are invading other countries, defenses can knock down missiles aimed at them.

Rounding out the picture are space operations and Special Operations Forces. According to General Lance Lord, head of the Air Force Space Command, "Space superiority is not our birthright, but it is our destiny."[67] The Command's "Master Plan for 2004 and Beyond" states, "Our vision calls for prompt global strike space systems with the capability to directly apply force from space against terrestrial targets."[68] Or, in the words of Pete Teets, then secretary of the air force, "We haven't reached the point of strafing and bombing from space, but we are thinking about the possibilities." Meanwhile, on the ground, Special Forces will be a component of Global Strike.

"Terminal Fury"

A profusion of military exercises have been conducted to test the new policies—"the new deterrence" of enemies ranging from "the former Soviet Union" to a "terrorist," in the words of STRATCOM commander General James Cartwright.[69] The names of the exercises suggest the tenor of the proceedings: Terminal Fury, Global Lightning, Global Thunder, Global Storm. For example, in the exercises Vigilant Shield, Global Lightning, and Global Storm, all run concurrently in late 2005, a scenario posits that Russia ("Slomonia" in the scenarios) is on its way to losing Ukraine ("Ublame"), because of a "domestically-driven political realignment." The aim of the exercises was to provide "A Bridging Exercise between Nuclear and Non-Nuclear Forces" and also for "nuclear combat readiness, proficiency and training."[70] In the scenario, Russia/Slomonia's relations with the United States deteriorate, and NATO masses troops on the Ukraine border; Russia responds with its own mobilization. To "punish" the West, Russia starts supporting North Korea ("Purple"). The Russia–North Korean axis gets ready to launch a nuclear attack on the United States, and soon Russia does attack Alaska with bombers. But the United States wins and Moscow decides to "Sue for Peace."[71]

In the Vigilant Shield exercise a year later, Russia (still Slomonia) teams up with North Korea (now "Nemazee") and Iran ("Irmingham") and attacks the United States. The crisis begins when Iran steps up its uranium enrichment program and Russia secretly supports it. Meanwhile, North Korea starts readying missiles to attack the United States. For some reason, China ("Churya") and Russia conduct a round of cyberwar against each other. Then Russia and Iran conduct joint military exercises. A terrorist nuclear attack on the Pentagon is thrown into the mix. North Korea and Russia launch a "limited" nuclear attack on the United States, which retaliates against these countries. Again, Russia gives up.

Reality in the Nuclear Age

Seen in the long sweep of the history of the nuclear age, the transformation of nuclear doctrine represented by Global Strike and its associated policy documents constitutes a startling development. It represents a regression to some of the earliest impulses and recommendations of the nuclear age—and to thoroughly and consistently rejected ones at that. Sixty years after General Leslie Groves recommended that the United States promptly attack and preventively disarm any unfriendly country about to acquire nuclear weapons, his counsel has become the policy of the United States.

Specifically, in the new theater of operations—namely the planet Earth (or at least the non-Russian portions of it)—the doctrine of deterrence has been repealed. During the Cold War, policy was ranged along a spectrum at the ends of which were two poles—mere nuclear threats, designed to prevent nuclear use, and nuclear use itself. Like a needle on a gauge, policy swung between these extremes. The Mutual Assured Destruction pushed toward the pole of nonuse, and the nuclear war fighting school pushed toward use.* By the Cold War's last years, when Reagan and Gorbachev made their statement that a nuclear war could not be won and should not be fought, the needle seemed to have moved decisively in the direction of nonuse.

Under Bush, the needle has swung sharply in the direction of use. The prevention strategy is the lynchpin. It is not just an alternative to mutual assured destruction, which Bush has specifically dismissed as anachronistic; it is a prophylactic against the situation of deterrence ever arising. Regimes whose arms have been taken away or precluded cannot deter. And if prevention's corollary regime change has been carried out, then not even the regime is left to make any threats. In the

---

*Yet neither school abandoned the opposite pole altogether. Even in mutual assured destruction, there is a place for use, without which the threats would fall flat. Even in nuclear war fighting, there was a place for deterrence. For deterrence would be effective, they said, only if the foe believed you were ready to fight nuclear wars, and the only way to seem to be ready was actually to be ready.

new dispensation, not a balance of nuclear terror but a monopoly of nuclear terror is to be the order of the day. The mission of nuclear weapons is no longer to produce stalemate with a peer; it is to fight and win wars against nations with little or no ability to respond.

The concept of "dissuading" rivals from arising is an extension of the same shift. Dissuasion is to prevention what deterrence is to nuclear war: the threat that obviates the need for fighting, the shadow of power that serves the ends of power without unleashing it. The same thinking is reflected in the shift from "threats" to "capabilities." Universal, unlimited uncertainty held at bay by Global Strike means that *all* contingencies in "every dark corner of the earth" are perpetually covered—all of which is but chapter and verse of the doctrine of American global military dominance outlined in White House public documents.

Yet a cautionary word is in order. Although the portrait presented here is drawn from the guiding documents of nuclear policy insofar as these are available, the policies they describe have not been announced with fanfare to the world or backed up with the extensive think tank papers, not to speak of the public discussion that used to accompany policy shifts. Rather, the change has been a semicovert, almost shame-faced affair, whose disclosure has required brave, dogged, independent detective work of the kind performed by Kristensen and others, and even then has been widely ignored. In a sphere as multileveled and mask ridden as nuclear strategy, such a presentation raises the question whether the documents correspond to reality. To answer it, however, we would have to say what, in the nuclear arena, we mean by "reality"—a very slippery question. One definition would be: decisions that are likely to be taken; things that can actually happen. But this still leaves us in a realm of great uncertainty. Historically, the gap between declared policy and concrete deployments (one kind of "reality") has often been very large. For example, the gap between the Bush administration's declared detargeting of Russia (and even of the whole world) and the reality of the ease of retargeting is wide indeed.

However, even deployments and operational plans are not the whole of nuclear reality. Nuclear reality is also—perhaps, primarily—the decisions that a chief of state (or, it may be, a technical glitch) might make in the fiery crucible of crisis. Here, history offers reassurance. For example, while President Eisenhower's doctrine of massive retaliation prescribed nuclear strikes to defeat regional threats in Asia and elsewhere, in practice he never came close to ordering the use of a nuclear weapon. President Kennedy ran his election campaign on the hawkish and provocative premise that he would close a missile gap that turned out not to exist; yet when he faced the Cuban missile crisis, he was probably more restrained in his responses than any of his advisers. Previous policy or strategy papers would have given almost no clue to his actions.

It may be that long-established strategy and declaratory statements have little weight at the moments of supreme choice, when one human being must make decisions that could result in the deaths of tens of millions of people. In this connection, let us mention a response that Secretary of Defense Rumsfeld gave to a question about whether his policies tended to blur the traditional threshold between conventional and nuclear war. He answered, "Do we—does the department—have an obligation and have they in successive administrations of both political parties had procedures whereby we would conceivably use nuclear weapons? Yes . . . [but] it seems to me that if one looks at our record, we went through the Korean War, we went through the Vietnam War, we've gone through the war on terror and we've not used nuclear weapons. That ought to say something about the threshold with respect to nuclear weapons."[72] Possibly, these words are a better guide to what actually would be done in a crisis than anything in the Doctrine for Joint Nuclear Operations or what the United States *plans* to do to Slomonia in the Terminal Fury scenarios.

On the other hand, nuclear doctrines do have indisputable importance. It would be rash, on the basis of sheer speculation, to assume that in a crisis an administration will not do what its policy documents say it will. The journalist Seymour Hersh has reported that civilian defense officials sought to include an option for a nuclear strike in Pentagon planning for a possible attack on Iran, only to be resisted, successfully, by the uniformed military. Just as important, perhaps, declarations of policy are the basis on which other governments make their decisions regarding nuclear arms. If the United States builds up its nuclear infrastructure, plans the production of new weapons, affirms their necessity for national defense, and sets forth doctrines for using them anywhere in the world, even against nonnuclear powers, other nations are likely to respond accordingly. When it comes to proliferation, peacetime impressions are at least as important as military realities that will reveal themselves only in a showdown. Indeed, in the nuclear realm as in perhaps no other, what people perceive, not what is real—whatever that may be—determines what they do.

CHAPTER 6

A NUCLEAR RENAISSANCE

By the end of 2002, the Bush administration's nuclear policies were substantially in place. Now, five years have passed, and results can be assessed. It is not too early to say that, broadly speaking, they have failed, in their own terms as well as absolutely. The momentum that has been driving the spread of nuclear weapons since 1945 has not been checked; it has gained new force and breadth. Nuclear deterrence still provokes proliferation and vice versa, and now more countries are involved. An even more deadly contest between proliferators and those who would stop proliferation has begun. The global arrangement that has historically contributed to constraint— the Nuclear Non-Proliferation Treaty—has been placed under severe stress and could be near breakdown. New islands are springing up in the nuclear archipelago, and others threaten to emerge, especially in Asia and the Middle East, where no fewer than a dozen countries are now considering nuclear power programs.[1] Nuclear weapon technology, often doubling as nuclear power technology, continues to spread, sometimes clandestinely, sometimes as the result of shortsighted policy decisions. The mirage of nuclear and other weapons of mass destruction programs in Iraq lured the United States into a disaster that has acquired a dangerous and unpredictable life of its own. (A preemptive counterproliferation policy is inherently prone to intelligence misjudgments, inasmuch as it bases military action not on ascertainable, full-blown threats but on reports of the mere beginnings of WMD programs and assessments of the intentions of their possessors.) Existing nuclear powers have not been "dissuaded" from nuclear competition; they have stepped it up. Military dominance of the globe by an imperial United States, whether aimed at counterproliferation or anything else, is a vanished dream. And signs of renewed confrontation between nuclear powers, largely dormant since the end of the Cold War, have reappeared, as China and Russia (not to say Churya and Slomonia) take stock of the renewed aggressiveness of the United States. The reversals have been moral as well as strategic and political: the bomb is more deeply and more complacently accepted as a normal component of military establishments in more parts of the world than ever before.

Atoms for Peace and War (Continued)

The unfolding Iranian and North Korean nuclear crises marked a new stage in the long story of the symbiosis of civilian nuclear energy and nuclear weapons that began with Eisenhower's Atoms for Peace program in the 1950s. An issue raised by both crises was whether any new countries should be permitted to produce fissionable materials, namely, plutonium and enriched uranium. Both are fuels for reactors. Both are also the key materials for making nuclear weapons. Enriching uranium means increasing the proportion of the scarce, more easily fissionable isotope U-235 in natural uranium relative to the abundant and less easily fissioned isotope U-238. Plutonium, a man-made element, is created by bombarding the uranium isotope U-238 in a reactor and then chemically extracting it from spent fuel. The plutonium for a reactor requires no additional improvement to be used in a bomb. The uranium for a reactor, which needs to be enriched to a level of 3.5 to 5 percent U-235, on the other hand, must be further enriched to be used in a bomb, which generally requires a purity of 90 percent or more. However, the most difficult technical challenges in refining occur in the early stages, which are all that are needed for nuclear power. The further stages—the ones needed to make a bomb—are comparatively easy. The paths to nuclear power and to the bomb are therefore the same except for the last stages of producing plutonium and highly enriched, bomb-grade uranium, and throughout the nuclear age bomb programs have grown in tandem with nuclear power programs.

Fortunately, both of these nuclear fuel-production technologies are almost certainly beyond the capacity of terrorist groups, which, if they want a bomb, must first acquire fissile materials (or a ready-made bomb) from a state. Once they have one of the materials in hand, the remaining steps are quite simple. They are especially easy along the uranium path to the bomb, which requires only that two subcritical masses of the substance be slammed together in the barrel of a "gun-type" device fast enough to suddenly create a critical mass. A nuclear explosion of the kind that wiped out Hiroshima will ensue.

A plutonium explosion is a little more difficult. So volatile is this truly infernal substance, an element not found in the storehouse of terrestrial nature, that two masses of plutonium hurled at one another in the gun-type operation will interact before they make contact, spoiling the chain reaction and producing a fizzle. (The low yield of the North Korean test may have been owing to such a fizzle.) A plutonium bomb, of the kind that destroyed Nagasaki, is initiated by setting off a sphere of explosives that surround the plutonium "pit," imploding it to create the needed critical mass, and thus a full-scale explosion.

Because the steps from fuel production to bomb making are so simple and few, nonproliferation is to a very great extent the art of stopping the spread of the fuel cycle. It is true that plutonium or enriched uranium adequate for a bomb can also be acquired by sale or gift or theft but none of these things, though very possible and even likely, is known to have happened in the nuclear age so far. On several occasions, fissile materials have been put on the black market, though not yet in sufficient quantity to make a bomb. The fuel cycle therefore remains the choke point of proliferation. Without the fissile materials that are the products of the fuel cycle, no one can make the bomb. With them, any competent group of physicists probably can. But granting nonnuclear powers access to the fuel cycle and all other civilian nuclear technology was exactly what the Nuclear Non-Proliferation Treaty's Article IV, extending and formalizing the Atoms for Peace program, gave away as part of the price paid by the nuclear powers for holding on to their arsenals in the 1950s, thereby introducing a Trojan horse into the heart of the nonproliferation regime. Now, in Iran and North Korea, the soldiers were pouring out of the belly of the booby-trapped animal.

Faced with this eruption, the nuclear powers were seeking to backpedal—to rescind the right to the fuel cycle they had previously granted. Iran was pressing forward with a program to enrich uranium. Yet since the Non-Proliferation Treaty did guarantee that right, and no repeal was in sight, the approach of other countries and the UN Security Council to the issue had to be oblique. The Iranian program was in fact a quarter-century old. Indeed, from the 1950s to 1979, when the supporters of the Ayatollah Khomeini overthrew the regime of Shah Mohammed Reza Pahlavi, the United States had given assistance to Iran's program, including elements of the fuel cycle.* Then and later, Iran hid its nuclear activities. The charge against Iran in 2003 was not that it was doing things it had no right to do under the treaty but that it was concealing things it was bound to reveal.

---

*A 1975 U.S. National Security Decision Memorandum signed by Henry Kissinger details the U.S. willingness to cooperate with Iran. The document specifies that the United States would: "Permit U.S. material to be fabricated into fuel in Iran for use in its own reactors and for pass-through to third countries with whom we have Agreements. . . . We could inform the Government of Iran that we shall be prepared to provide our approval for reprocessing of U.S. material in a multinational plant in Iran if the country supplying the reprocessing technology is a full and active participant in the plant, and holding open the possibility of U.S. participation." During the Ford administration, a plan by the Shah to build twenty-two nuclear power reactors was supported by Secretary of Defense Donald Rumsfeld, Chief of Staff Dick Cheney, and Chief of the Arms Control and Disarmament Agency Paul Wolfowitz.[2]

Early in Bush's second term, his administration, sinking ever deeper into the Iraq quagmire, perhaps finally realized that regime change in Iran was no longer conceivable for the overextended U.S. ground force. As an alternative, a contact group of European powers was organized to conduct direct negotiations with Iran while the United States, still unwilling to speak directly to the Iranians, applied military pressure from without. (The threat of military action, including a nuclear strike, was left conspicuously open by President Bush, who said, "All options are on the table.") In September 2005, the International Atomic Energy Agency (IAEA) reported after three years of investigation that it was "still not in a position to conclude that there are no undeclared nuclear materials or activities in Iran."[3] The United States argued that because Iran had violated the Non-Proliferation Treaty by hiding uranium enrichment facilities, it had lost its right to the fuel cycle.

In April 2006, Iran nevertheless announced with pomp and circumstance that it had succeeded in refining some uranium to reactor-grade levels, and in July of that year, the UN Security Council voted that Iran must suspend uranium enrichment by the end of August. It did not, and the council then imposed light sanctions, much watered down at the insistence of Russia and China. Iran's consistent position throughout the negotiations had been that it did not seek nuclear weapons and had every right under the NPT to all nuclear power technology, including uranium enrichment.

But if the Bush administration's approach to Iran regarding its claim to the fuel cycle had to be oblique, its approach to the fuel cycle issue as a global danger was direct. It proposed restricting the fuel cycle to those who already had it while offering guarantees of nuclear fuel supplies to nations that did not possess the cycle. That way, they would be able to develop nuclear power without gaining the capacity to make nuclear bombs. In other words, the United States wanted to eject from the Non-Proliferation Treaty the Article IV Trojan horse it had once helped place there. But the proposal was now highly unacceptable to the treaties' nonnuclear parties, for whom full rights to nuclear power technology had been a modest compensation for their provisional agreement to the NPT's double standard.

With this recommendation for inequitable technical rollback, the United States was proposing to deepen the moat between the nuclear haves and have-nots by reserving the fuel cycle, too, for itself and a few other powers. The 115-member Non-Aligned Movement consistently rejected the idea. The group's opposition might have seemed ineffectual and unimportant—until one remembered that it contained a large number of potential proliferators.

The director of the IAEA, Mohammed ElBaradei, sought to cure the inequity with a crucially different proposal: all nuclear fuel production would be placed under the control of an international organization, which in turn would supply nuclear power fuels to nations. He had been led back to a core provision of the Baruch Plan, which had called for international ownership of all nuclear technology. However, the United States and other nuclear powers, unwilling to surrender their own fuel cycle technologies to international managers, demurred—underscoring once again their commitment to double-standard solutions. In this new arena as in others, two tectonic plates were accelerating toward a collision: on the one side was the vision of a world moving toward an exit from the nuclear weapon business and on the other, a vision of a world, to be led by the United States, that was on the way to ratifying a nuclear double standard—a standard to be enforced, when necessary, by war, including nuclear war.

"You are not going to do it to us"

The same deepening impasse was on view in a different form in the confrontation with North Korea, which was continuing its quest for the bomb down the plutonium path. A turning point in that crisis was reached in late 2002. U.S. intelligence had found evidence the year before that North Korea, thwarted in further progress toward the bomb by the Agreed Framework negotiated by the Clinton administration, had secretly acquired equipment from A. Q. Kahn to pursue the uranium option. But the administration postponed a confrontation until October 4, 2002, when Assistant Secretary of State James Kelly challenged North Korea's Deputy Foreign Minister Kang Sok Ju with the intelligence findings.[4] The confrontation occurred at the moment of the administration's maximum self-confidence in its strategic vision. Just two weeks before, on September 17, the seminal document of the Bush doctrine, the *National Security Strategy for the United States of America*, had been issued by the White House. Victory in the vote in Congress on the Authorization to Use Military Force in Iraq, just three days away, was a foregone conclusion. A Republican victory in the congressional elections, run on a platform of Republican strength versus Democratic weakness in the "war on terror," was just a month away and fully expected. The foundational document for the administration's nuclear policies, the *Nuclear Posture Review*, had already been published. Most important, the preparations for attacking Iraq were in full swing. Bush had, of course, linked Iran, Iraq, and North Korea in his State of the Union speech in January as the members of the "axis of evil." He was now fashioning a consistent policy to deal with all three. His administration was contemptuous of the Agreed Framework, regarding it as a "reward" for North Korean "bad behavior," if not outright appeasement. The evidence of a secret uranium project provided an occasion to break out of it. The United States promptly suspended its aid under the Agreed Framework, and North Korea responded by taking the step that Clinton had threatened war to prevent: removal of the spent fuel rods from the Yongbyon reactor pool.

No American attack followed. Asked just before the Iraq war by a visitor to explain why his country was pursuing its nuclear program, a North Korean general answered, "We see what you are getting ready to do with Iraq. And you are not going to do it to us."[5] Soon, the government of Iraq was indeed overthrown, while the regime in North

Korea remained standing. The paradox-filled nuclear age now had one more paradox to deal with. The most pathological of regimes (if judged on the basis of its treatment of its oppressed, hungry people) had been equipped with one of the most rational reasons ever put forward for possessing a nuclear weapon: to protect its very existence against a superpower with a clear intent to overthrow regimes at will. Never had the doctrine of deterrence made more sense.*

As in the Iran crisis later, the administration, floundering in Iraq, turned away to a certain extent from the unilateral, imperial path and began to give more leeway to diplomacy. Internecine struggle between the advocates of regime change and the advocates of negotiation followed. The result was half-hearted diplomacy, able neither to make credible threats nor to promise the economic assistance and security guarantees to North Korea that alone had any chance of progress. Futile negotiations—first with three parties, then with six, sometimes a little more confrontational, sometimes a little less—followed, all the while giving North Korea time to get ready for its nuclear test of October 9, 2006. Like an exclamation point at the end of a sentence, the test proclaimed a triple failure—in Iraq, in Iran, and in North Korea—of the Bush policy of preventive nonproliferation. Bush had tried dominance because, in his view, Clinton's diplomacy had failed, and now dominance had failed.

Bush fell back again. Having been unable to hold the line against a North Korean bomb, he now drew a new one barring transfer of that bomb or its fissile materials to others. Using (or once again abusing) the most menacing words of statecraft, he said

---

*Yet even this apparently clear-cut case may not be as simple as it at first seems. There is a school of thought that holds that the country North Korea most fears is not the United States but China. The model for this interpretation would be another highly nationalistic Asian country, Vietnam, whose leader Ho Chi Minh during the Cold War once commented, "Which would you prefer: to put up with ten years of French occupation or eat Chinese shit for a thousand years?" In 1979, of course, Vietnam did indeed go to war with China. In this view, North Korea is using its bomb to obtain a security guarantee from the United States in order to balance Chinese influence.

on October 9, "The transfer of nuclear weapons or material by North Korea to states or non-state entities would be considered a grave threat to the United States. And we would hold North Korea fully accountable for the consequences of such action."[6]

The administration now made a full return to Clinton-style diplomacy, this time offering the economic rewards that it had shunned in its more belligerent days. As a result, in February 2007, North Korea agreed in principle to dismantle its nuclear program in the long run and suspended operation of its reactor at Yongbyon and readmitted International Atomic Energy Agency inspectors in return for fifty thousand tons of fuel oil.[7] For the time being, its nuclear program seemed to be on its way to being capped—though no one could yet say how long North Korea would remain a nuclear power.

A Cascade of Proliferation

In the aftermath of the Korean test, Secretary of State Condoleezza Rice toured Asia seeking to shore up "extended deterrence." In Japan, she said menacingly, "The United States has the will and the capability to meet the full range—and I underscore full range—of its deterrent and security commitments to Japan."[8] In South Korea, she gave similar assurances. No statement was made about Taiwan, the third nation enjoying de facto protection by American nuclear forces, probably for fear of angering the Chinese, whom the administration was then trying to enlist in putting pressure on North Korea. However, the issue now was not so much whether the United States would protect any of these three beneficiaries of extended deterrence in the event of North Korean attack (something exceedingly unlikely) as whether the three would move to develop nuclear arsenals of their own.

That danger indeed was part of a far larger one that now approached: a full breakdown of the nonproliferation regime based on the NPT, accompanied by a full-scale nuclear renaissance among the current nuclear powers. According to a report by a high-level panel to Secretary-General of the UN Kofi Annan, the Non-Proliferation

Treaty had already eroded to a point at which the process "could become irreversible and result in a cascade of proliferation."[9]

The trio of Asian nations guarded by American extended deterrence had each flirted with a nuclear program in the past. Twice—
once in the mid-1970s, once in the 1980s—South Korea, then under
military rule, had embarked on a nuclear weapons program, and
both times the United States had successfully pressured it to desist.
Since the establishment of democracy in the eighties, South Korean
leaders at the policy level have shown little interest in acquiring the
bomb or in any military confrontation with North Korea. When President Clinton had threatened war to disable North Korea's reactor at
Yongbyon in 1994, President Kim Young Sam had protested in dramatic terms. "As long as I am the president, I would not mobilize any
one of our 600,000 troops," he said, adding, "No war is acceptable. I
cannot afford to commit a crime against our history and people."[10]
Yet in 2005, in a reminder that both Koreas were nuclear capable, it
was revealed that South Korean scientists had secretly produced small
amounts of both plutonium and highly enriched uranium.

Taiwan had also established a nuclear weapons program after
the Chinese test of 1964, and, by the late eighties, was an estimated
two years from getting the bomb. Again the United States, fearful
that a nuclear-armed Taiwan would drag it into a conflict with
China it didn't want, pressured the country into dropping its program.[11] But of the three potential Asian proliferators, the most worrisome was Japan. The only country to have experienced atomic
devastation, Japan has long been deeply imbued with antinuclear
sentiments. Its singular "peace constitution," imposed by the United
States after the Second World War but then embraced by the Japanese, forbids the creation of offensive military forces. The adoption
by the Japanese government in 1967 of the Three Non-Nuclear
Principles, ruling out the production, possession, or "introduction"
of nuclear weapons, has been a further barrier to nuclearization.

Nevertheless, the idea of going nuclear, like an underground
stream that keeps bubbling to the surface, has persisted. In 1964,

after China's test, Prime Minister Eisaku Sato informed President Lyndon Johnson that he thought Japan, too, should have nuclear weapons. In 1968, he subordinated the Three Non-Nuclear Principles to a Four Pillars Nuclear Policy. The third of the pillars was reliance on American nuclear deterrence against nuclear attack, thus conditioning the Three Principles on a continuation of America's extended deterrence. It followed that if the American assurance were ever withdrawn or seemed shaky, Japan might have no choice but to go nuclear. In other words, Japan's leaders left their nuclear option open. Like Germany, Japan had signed the NPT only after it had received assurances from the United States that its right to nuclear power technology, including the full fuel cycle, would be respected. Today, Japan possesses more than two hundred tons of plutonium, enough for more than five thousand weapons. If it chooses to make nuclear weapons, it surely can do so in a matter of months at most.

In 1995, a high-level Foreign Ministry review reaffirmed the country's nonnuclear policy, on the grounds that going nuclear would destroy the military balance in Asia, unleash an arms race with China, precipitate a similar decision by South Korea, and undermine or destroy the NPT. Yet in 1999, Vice Defense Minister Shingo Nishimura stated that the government "should consider the fact that Japan may be better off if it armed itself with nuclear weapons,"[12] and Deputy Chief Cabinet Secretary Shinzo Abe, who became prime minister in September 2006, insisted that the peace constitution "does not necessarily ban the possession of nuclear weapons as long as they are kept at a minimum and are tactical." Chief Cabinet Secretary Yasuo Fukuda expressed similar arguments. When Rice visited Japan after the North Korean test, in October 2006, Abe and Foreign Minister Taro Aso reaffirmed Japan's renunciation of nuclear arms; yet Aso had told the Diet, Japan's legislature, "We can't consider [nuclear arms], we can't talk, we can't do anything and we can't exchange opinions—that's one way of thinking. I believe it is important to have various discussions on it as another way of thinking."[13] In short, Japanese leaders who are at the least strongly interested in acquiring the bomb are now in power, and Japan's nonnuclear status, previously a kind of assumption of the international order, is in question.

Neoconservative opinion in the United States is already favorable to a nuclear Japan. Just as the Bush administration was turning out to be quietly supportive of India's decision to become a nuclear power, so now its supporters find much to recommend in the idea that Japan do likewise. For example, the arch-neoconservative columnist for the *Washington Post*, Charles Krauthammer, a leading proponent of the Iraq war, argued, with a logic that nuclear Wilsonians could only welcome, that Japan "is a true anomaly," for "all the other Great Powers went nuclear decades ago. . . ." Why should Japan be out of step with the happy trend? He continued, "Why are we so intent on denying this stable, reliable, democratic ally the means to help us shoulder the burden in a world where so many other allies—the inveterately appeasing South Koreans most notoriously—insist on the free ride?"[14] David Frum, formerly a speechwriter for Bush and the man who reportedly coined the phrase "axis of evil," also mocked the idea that "the worst possible consequence of nuclear weapons in the hands of one of America's direst enemies would be the acquisition of nuclear weapons by one of America's best friends." He, too, wanted the United States to "encourage Japan to renounce the Nuclear Non-Proliferation Treaty and create its own nuclear deterrent."

Frum foresaw benefits for the Middle East in Japan's nuclearization. As he wrote, "It would show Iran that the United States and its friends will aggressively seek to correct any attempt by rogue states to unsettle any regional nuclear balance. The analogue for Iran, of course, would be the threat of American aid to improve Israel's capacity to hit targets with nuclear weapons."[15]

Like the de facto welcome given the Indian bomb, the friendly noises made by neoconservatives about a Japanese bomb show that in some quarters the reevaluation of national arsenals, transforming

them from something of unspeakable horror to something benefi-
cent, is on its way to being recapitulated on a global basis.

Analyzed in realist terms, the key to Japan's nuclear decision is
its estimation of the American security guarantees recently reaffirmed by Rice. Because a decision to develop the bomb would likely
bring all the evil consequences foreseen in the 1995 Foreign Ministry report, and because antinuclear feeling is still powerful in
Japan, the reasons not to do so remain strong. Yet Japan has seen
that the United States, for all its self-proclaimed might, was unable
to stop North Korea from becoming a nuclear power. Japan sees,
too, that a three-cornered Sino-Indo-Pakistani arms race, in which
stability remains out of reach, is under way. Moreover, Japan's own
understanding of its role in the world, even of its identity as a nation, largely imposed by the United States after the war, has been
undergoing a quiet sea change for some years. Prime Minister
Shinzo Abe of the ruling Liberal Party has upgraded the Japan Defense Agency to a Ministry of Defense. The Liberal Party has also
embarked on nothing less than writing and promulgating a new
draft of Japan's constitution to replace the "peace constitution"
drafted for Japan during the occupation after the Second World
War. One of the appeals of the project for Abe is shedding the foreign product in favor of a native document. In his words, "This [ex-
isting] constitution was drafted while Japan was under occupation.
I believe it is important that we Japanese write a constitution for
ourselves that would reflect the shape of the country we consider de-
sirable in the 21st century."[16] Like Germany, Japan is beginning to
shed the inhibitions left over from its defeat in 1945. But unlike
Germany, Japan has yet to undergo a thorough process of facing up
to its crimes of that era. Indeed, one of the symptoms of its new self-
assertiveness has been the continuing revision of school textbooks
to whitewash Japan's wartime atrocities, much to the dismay of their
prime victims, the Chinese and the Koreans.

In the six decades since the war's end, Germany and France, the
two giants of federated Europe, have buried the hatchet so deep that

it would be hard for anyone to find it again. That is not the case for Japan and China, or even Japan and South Korea. The resentments born of the Second World War still fester in the region. And whereas Germany's new self-assertion points away from nuclear armament, Japan's self-assertion points in the opposite direction. Praful Bidwai and Achin Vanaik's insight that the most important precipitating factor of nuclearization can be domestic—above all, a change of regime, reflecting a deep shift in national identity—could turn out to apply to Japan.

If Japan were to go nuclear, South Korea and perhaps Taiwan would likely follow, creating a region crammed with four jostling nuclear powers. If we enlarge the angle of vision only slightly, then we can see an Asia with nine possible nuclear powers: the Soviet Union, the United States (another Pacific power and for the foreseeable future the greatest Asian nuclear power), China, North Korea, South Korea, Japan, Taiwan, India, and Pakistan, all capable of devastating one or more of the others, all caught in a mind-bogglingly complex cat's cradle of possible threats and counterthreats and an equally complex diplomacy. At that moment, Prime Minister Manmohan Singh's "new nuclear world order" would truly have been achieved, the NPT would be a dead letter, and we would have to stop speaking of a second nuclear era and start speaking of a third.

The unraveling of the nonproliferation regime would be unlikely to stop there. In the event that Iran proceeded to break into the nuclear club, a picture highly similar to the one just painted for Asia might appear in the Middle East. There, the countries that have already flirted with nuclear programs and might now go nuclear are Egypt, which has just announced that it will pour new resources into its nuclear energy program, Turkey, Saudi Arabia, and, for all we know, Iraq. (Having once put together most of the know-how for building the bomb, Iraq could one day call on its scientists to do so again.) Saudi Arabia, in particular, has a long history of flirtation with nuclear capabilities. In the late 1980s, it purchased intercontinental ballistic missiles from China. It provided financing for the Pakistan bomb project. In October 2003, the head of Israeli intelligence asserted that Saudi Arabia had secretly signed a deal with Pakistani to obtain nuclear arms in return for cheap oil.[17]

In such circumstances, still-wider circles of proliferation are possible. Brazil and Argentina, both of which have extensive nuclear programs, jointly chose not to make nuclear weapons. They could reconsider their decisions. It would not happen suddenly. But it's noteworthy that in Brazil, which possesses the uranium fuel cycle, President Lula Ignacio da Silva has expressed his frustration with the double standard embedded in the NPT. "If," he complained to a meeting of military officers, "someone asks me to disarm and keep a slingshot while he comes at me with a cannon, what good does that do?"[18]

In 2004, Brazil announced the construction of a new uranium enrichment facility that, if turned to military purposes, could supply enough material for five or six bombs a year. It also declined for a while to let its fuel cycle facilities be inspected by the IAEA, pending the outcome of negotiations. It has so far failed to sign an "additional protocol" for more intrusive inspections that the IAEA is urging upon nations.[19] These moves hardly represent a decision to make a bomb, but they might represent a decision to keep the option open a little wider than it was before.

Developments in other areas are also fueling a planet-wide nuclear renaissance. The need imposed by global warming to cut back on the use of fossil fuels has revived interest in nuclear power, a prime vector of proliferation. Argentina, Australia, and South Africa—all countries that have large nuclear establishments and have at one time considered building the bomb—are planning to start enriching uranium. Credible studies estimate that the world's current stock of 443 reactors could rise to 5,000 before the end of the century—a development that would hugely increase the availability of nuclear technology and the danger of its diversion into unauthorized hands. "People are positioning themselves" to join the nuclear power boom, according to Hans-Holger Rogner, an economist at the IAEA.[20] The Bush administration in particular is vigorously promoting the technology. Its nuclear deal with India would of course sacrifice nonproliferation concerns for the sake of nuclear power in India (and sale of nuclear technology by U.S. corporations), all in the name of the vague strategic competition with China.

More ambitious by far is Bush's proposed $100 billion Global Nuclear Energy Partnership, which would greatly expand plutonium reprocessing around the world. In a further extension of the two-tier system, the partnership proposes a vast expansion of the fuel cycle at the same time that the United States threatens war against Iran to prevent it from acquiring that cycle. Regarding this plan, a National Resources Defense Council report has commented, "A global partnership that further develops, disseminates, and trains tens of thousands of people in the complex chemical techniques for separating long-lived weapon-usable materials, like plutonium, from self-protecting, intensely radioactive fission byproducts such as cesium and strontium, can hardly be called 'proliferation resistant.' "[21] In a future of this description, can it be long before a terrorist group lays its hands on fissile materials or a bomb?

Meanwhile, the affirmation by the larger nuclear powers of their nuclear arsenals and the dedication of them to post–Cold War purposes with a global range completes the vicious circle. The world's possessors, witnessing proliferation, are retooling their arsenals to counter it, and proliferators, witnessing the nuclear revival among the possessors, are stepping up their efforts to proliferate. The United States is pressing forward with the revival of the nuclear weapon infrastructure outlined in the *Nuclear Posture Review*. At its core is a program called "Complex 2030." The administration is proposing to design a new "Reliable Replacement Warhead." Presented as a plan to increase the safety and reliability of the American arsenal, it will also "improve the capability to design, develop, certify and complete production of new or adapted warheads in the event of new military requirements."[22] Planning for a consolidated plutonium center to produce new plutonium pits, among other things, moves forward. Overall spending on nuclear weapons has risen from a little more than $4 billion in 1998 to $6.5 billion.[23] These developments, together with America's Global Strike, Russia's countermeasures, China's modernization efforts, the South Asian nuclear arms race, Korea's nuclear test, Britain's plans for a new missile for the decades beyond the 2040s, France's nuclear plans to "cover threats wherever they arise and whatever their nature," and India's announcement of a new nuclear world order convey a single, insistent, monotonous message: the world of the twenty-first century will be nuclear armed. That is both the premise and the consequence of the policies of the nuclear powers. For the first time, *the world* has been targeted by several nuclear powers. How will the world respond?

"A Major Nuclear Threat to Our Strategic Interests"

A danger that could become the most important aspect of the nuclear renaissance remains to be mentioned. Among Prime Minister Tony Blair's reasons for renewing Britain's nuclear arsenal was one often left out of the discussion of today's nuclear dangers. He commented, "It is written as fact by many that there is no possibility of nuclear confrontation with any major nuclear power. Except that it isn't a fact." One reason to renew Britain's arsenal, he insisted, was that "we cannot be certain in the decades ahead that a major nuclear threat to our strategic interests will not emerge."* He didn't say whom he had in mind, but the most obvious answer remains Russia, which has declared itself in favor of "multipolar" not a "unipolar" (meaning U.S.-dominated) world.

Neither friend nor foe, Russia exists in a sort of strategic limbo. Its turn toward authoritarian rule under President Vladimir Putin

---

*President Jacques Chirac maintained a studied ambiguity regarding this danger. On the one hand, he said, "It is true that, with the end of the Cold War, we are currently under no direct threat from a major power." Nevertheless, he pointed out that France was "in a position to inflict damage of any kind on a major power that would want to attack interests we would regard as vital."

has cooled its relations with Europe and the United States. It has felt pressured by the expansion eastward of NATO, the United States' deployment of missile defenses, Global Strike, and the other components of the American drive toward possible nuclear "primacy," and has reacted by upgrading its nuclear forces across the board. Discussing a Russian missile test in 2004, Putin proclaimed, "It means that Russia has been and will remain one of the biggest nuclear missile powers in the world. Some people may like it and some may not, but everyone will have to reckon with it."[24] When the United States proposed to build missile defense bases in Czechoslovakia and Poland in 2007, Putin threatened to target them, and Russia warned that it would withdraw from the Intermediate-Range Nuclear Forces Treaty, signed by President Ronald Reagan and Soviet general secretary Mikhail Gorbachev in 1987.

Russia continues work on a new mobile ICBM, the Topol M, and on a new submarine-launched ballistic missile, the Bulava. Overall expenditures on nuclear arms are on the rise. Putin has cryptically announced that Russia has developed "projects which do not exist elsewhere and which other nuclear states will not have in the next few years."[25] Russian scientists have suggested that he may be referring to a maneuverable ballistic missile, designed to elude any possible American missile defense system.[26] The prospect that the Russian arsenal may develop a more "forward-leaning" posture was suggested in a worrisome comment by Colonel General Nikolai Solovtsov, the Commander of Russia's strategic missile forces. He stated that Russia's "nuclear umbrella" now defends all states in the successor organization to the Soviet Union, the Commonwealth of Independent States, including Ukraine. (Let's recall that in the Global Lightning war exercise, Russia's "loss" of Ukraine precipitated a crisis that ended in a U.S.-Soviet nuclear war.) This is protection that Ukraine, which has expressed an interest in joining NATO, may not care to have.[27] The current tensions with the West do not amount to a new Cold War, but they surely underlie Blair's reminder that strategic hostilities are not necessarily a thing of the past.

Another candidate for Blair's strategic foe of the future is China. The point of contention with Western powers is more obvious in its case: Taiwan. The American enlistment of India as a "strategic partner" reminds us that Sino-American nuclear tensions could quickly develop global ramifications. Among the nuclear powers, China has until recently been notable for the slowness of its nuclear buildup and the conservatism of its nuclear policies. It has not undergone any public reassessment of its nuclear doctrine of the kind seen elsewhere. Unlike the United States, it has not discovered any global role for its arsenal. At present, it possesses an estimated two hundred warheads, of which some twenty can, if affixed to China's twenty liquid-fueled Dongfeng 5 missiles, strike the United States. The latter figure has changed little since the 1980s. On the other hand, China has long been at work on a new nuclear-capable submarine and a new, more accurate ICBM, the Dongfeng 31A, capable of striking the United States, and China may choose to respond with still other countermeasures to aggressive or threatening developments in U.S. strategy. The U.S. ballistic missile defense program, on which it spends $9 billion annually, and its prospective deployment of highly accurate Tomahawk 4 missiles in the Pacific give China obvious motives to protect its retaliatory capacity by accelerating this expansion of its forces.

It would be premature to predict that a new nuclear confrontation, perhaps pitting authoritarian China and/or Russia against the United States, Britain, France, and India will develop. (Where Pakistan, an ally both of the United States and China, would wind up should such an eventuality occur is hard to guess.) But wasn't the possibility of a confrontation such as this the underlying reason for the American decision to hold on to so many thousands of nuclear warheads in the post–Cold War period? And doesn't Blair's citation of threats to Britain from "major" nuclear powers send the same message? The great arsenals, you might say, stripped of their international quarrel by the end of the Cold War, have been waiting for the new confrontation that will justify them. It is not yet here, but it has drawn closer.

While it is true that the most salient political divide of the present is between potential nuclear proliferators and the current nuclear possessors in our two-tier world, it is also true that the nations of the top tier are anything but united. If they were, they would not be holding on to large arsenals and pointing them at one another. Insofar as the phrase "nuclear club" (not to speak of "new nuclear order") suggests members that enjoy cordial relations, it is utterly deceptive. Its members tend to look on one another with suspicion, sometimes murderous hatred. They are ready, in a crisis, to blow one another off the face of the earth. It is a community of dread.

The world's preoccupation with proliferation is thus in one sense deeply misleading. Nuclear danger is posed above all by nations that possess nuclear weapons, not by those that don't. Today's nuclear powers are beginning to jostle one another. Depending on political events, these fresh tensions could turn out in a not-so-very-distant future to be as important as anything now happening in North Korea or Iran.

Nevertheless, it would be a mistake to draw too sharp a line between the intensifying nuclear power rivalries and proliferation. The larger point is that they are of a piece. Wherever possession and proliferation occur, they are always two sides of a single process, the nuclearization of the globe, which, in the early twenty-first century, is accelerating across the board.

CHAPTER 7

THE FALL AND ITS USES

The unraveling of the Bush Administration's post–September 11 nuclear policies was coextensive with the fall of its bid for global empire in which those policies formed a central part.

To begin with, the "war on terror" almost immediately proved inappropriate as a framework for either understanding or addressing the nuclear dilemma. The two predicaments intersected only at a single point—the "nexus," at which a terrorist group might one day get hold of a nuclear weapon, perhaps from a reckless state. Such an event would indeed be a milestone in the history of the nuclear age, marking the moment when the spread of nuclear know-how passed out of the control of governments, and President Bush was perfectly correct when he suggested that September 11 could be a harbinger of an incomparably greater tragedy involving nuclear weapons. That danger was new, real, and growing. It was in fact brought clearly into view, as Robert J. Lifton was the first to point out, not by Al Qaeda in 2001 but by the Japanese terrorist cult Aum Shinrikyo,[1] which carried out an attack with homemade sarin gas on the Tokyo subway in 1995, killing twelve people and hospitalizing one thousand. The cult's leader, Shoko Asahara, was enchanted with the idea of the apocalypse, and, well before the Tokyo attack, had taken serious steps to acquire nuclear bomb technology and materials, including uranium. As Lifton notes, there was a decided moral and spiritual—or perhaps one should say immoral and infernal—logic to this development. Terror has always been the coinage of the nuclear realm. A "balance of terror," holding all human life at risk, was the stock-in-trade of Cold War nuclear strategy, and no one should have been surprised that *terrorists* would seek out this supreme instrument of terror.*

Yet for all the undeniable historic importance of the nexus, terrorism and nuclear danger remain for the most part distinct and incommensurable, posing risks of different orders of magnitude and requiring sharply different strategies to deal with them. Terrorism, after all, would remain a threat even if there were no nuclear weapons in the world, and nuclear weapons would remain a threat—an incomparably greater one—even if terrorism disappeared from the face of the Earth. Above all, the danger of nuclear terrorism and proliferation did not replace the nuclear danger still posed by the twenty-seven thousand warheads in the hands of the existing nuclear powers.

The incorporation of the nuclear dilemma into the war on terror thus skewed policy on both. In the first place, it was unrealistic to imagine that the problem of the nuclear-equipped terrorist could be solved by "defeating terrorism." The long experience of many nations (for example, Britain and Ireland in the face of the Irish Republican Army and Protestant terror cells or Sri Lanka in the face of Tamil suicide bombers) has shown that while terrorism can be reduced, mostly by police methods, it can rarely, if ever, be eliminated. It can only be outlasted or gradually dissolved by deep political change, usually occurring over decades. Yet the survival of even a

---

*It is not only the technical but the moral seeds of nuclear terrorism that were planted by the official policies and conventional wisdom of the Cold War era. A great state possessing nuclear weapons is not the same as a fanatical cult seeking them, yet the suicide bomber has a definite kinship with the conventional nuclear strategist. Both hold the civilian population hostage. Both are prepared to endure suicide to achieve their objectives. Both prepare meticulously to commit the act and are ready to commit it. In fairness, of course, one important difference is that even as the nuclear strategist plans for suicide—and has created a "button" to render the deed prompt and easy—he hopes that his foe, terrified by this same deed, will back off at the last minute, at "the brink," giving everyone a reprieve. The suicide bomber, the nemesis of deterrence, is, on the other hand, simply itching to step joyfully over the brink and immolate himself in the flames in which he engulfs others.

small cadre of terrorists would be more than enough to wield a nuclear weapon should one become available. On the other hand, it is entirely imaginable that weapon-grade materials, which so far only states have been able to produce, could be kept out of the hands of terrorists. But to achieve this, nuclear technology would have to be addressed in all its permutations. The nexus, in sum, could have been dealt with far more promisingly by a global effort to secure and reduce fissile materials that might fall into the hands of terrorists than by a full-scale, militarized war on terror.

Both key words in the phrase "war on terror," in fact, misdirected efforts to tackle nuclear danger. Because the Bush agenda has been a war on *terror,* many sensible and achievable antiproliferation efforts have been sacrificed to the hunt for terrorists. The unacknowledged clash between the Bush administration's war on terror and nonproliferation was dramatically (but secretly) manifested immediately after September 11. As it happened, the chief of Pakistan's intelligence service, Lieutenant General Mahmood Ahmed, was in Washington at the time. He was summoned forthwith to meet with Deputy Secretary of State Richard Armitage, who informed him that in the war on terror, "You are either one hundred percent with us or one hundred percent against us." The next day, he was presented with seven demands that Pakistan must meet if it wished to be "with us." The demands centered on Pakistani cooperation in assailing its proxy, the Taliban regime in Afghanistan, which had, of course, harbored Osama bin Laden and his Al Qaeda training camps. No mention was made of A. Q. Khan or his proliferation activities, although these were well known to Washington and had been brought up frequently in previous discussions at the highest levels, including the presidential.[2]

Because the Bush agenda was framed as a *war* on terror, threats from proliferators against whom a military campaign was inconvenient or impossible were played down. Pakistan was only one of the nations in this category. Another was North Korea, which may already have possessed one or two nuclear bombs when Bush arrived in office and definitely possessed a potent conventional army.

North Korea was pushed down the target list. So, at least for the time being, was Iran, also a militarily strong country possessing a vigorous nuclear program and, with a feisty population of some seventy million, a decidedly forbidding target for forcible regime change. That left Iraq, a weak and therefore easily defeatable state, as the most promising candidate for the first of the disarmament wars and a demonstration project of the Bush doctrine.

These disordered priorities were in evidence even before the Iraq war began, when Bush decided to focus all attention on Iraq at the expense of North Korea. In his announcement of the campaign against the "axis of evil" in his 2002 State of the Union Address, Bush had staked the credibility of the United States on the outcome. Crises in relations with the two axis of evil nations happened to occur at the same time, in late 2002. It was on October 4, that the U.S. negotiator with North Korea, James Kelly, reported to Washington that North Korea's Vice Foreign Minister Kang Sok Ju had admitted to possessing a uranium enrichment program, in violation of treaty obligations, and furthermore had asserted his country's perfect right to possess nuclear weapons if it chose to. It was on October 7 that Bush summed up his case for war against Iraq in a speech in Cleveland. And it was on October 10, 2003, that Congress voted for the Authorization for Use of Military Force Against Iraq Resolution, permitting the president to go to war against that country if he chose. But at no time before the Iraq vote did any administration official make the Korean declaration known, so Congress unwittingly authorized a war against Iraq, which allegedly possessed WMD *programs*, yet did nothing to deal with a country that perhaps possessed nuclear *weapons* and was known to be gearing up to produce more. On October 19, nine days after the congressional vote on Iraq and three days after the North Korea news leaked to the press, a Bush administration official commented to the *Washington Post*, "We do not need another crisis now."[3] North Korea thought otherwise. In December, it restarted its plutonium-producing reactor at Yongbyon and ejected International Atomic Energy Agency officials who were monitoring the site. Later that month, Secretary of State Colin Powell stated that the Korean developments were "not a crisis," leaving the world to wonder why, in that case, Iraq *was* a crisis.[4] In January, North Korea announced its withdrawal from the NPT.

In February 2003, the world got its first glimpse of the extent and progress of Iran's nuclear program. The International Atomic Energy Agency, after the disclosure months earlier by an Iraq opposition group of hitherto-unknown facilities in Iran for uranium processing, requested and was granted access to Iran's uranium-enrichment site at Natanz; IAEA confirmed the allegations. But this news, too, received only modest attention in the rush to war against Iraq.[5]

The administration's production of false evidence of WMD programs to justify the war in Iraq has been much discussed. The temporary concealment of evidence of North Korea's nuclear program at a critical moment in American decision making in October 2002 has received less attention. Both distortions were components of a policy that claimed to place the highest priority on the most advanced proliferators of WMD without actually doing so.

As a result, on the eve of the invasion of Iraq, the most dangerous proliferator was nuclear-armed Pakistan, already dispatching nuclear materials and plans to Iran, North Korea, and Libya; the second most dangerous was North Korea, busily making nuclear bombs; the third most dangerous was Iran, a country with a quarter-century-old nuclear power program and a likely interest in bomb making (despite its disavowals); the least dangerous was WMD-free Iraq. Yet the administration, forcing its counterproliferation policy into the framework of its war on terror, turned this list almost precisely upside down. Indeed, Pakistan was soon named "a major non-NATO ally" of the United States.

Nonproliferation and Regime Change

The absence of WMD weapons and programs in Iraq was a profound embarrassment to the Bush administration as well as a grievous injury to American political institutions, which propelled the nation into war in pursuit of a mirage. But it was not this mistake that delivered the fatal blow to the administration's broader nonproliferation strategy. On the contrary, if, as suggested by the *National Security Strategy of the United States of America*, the lesson of Iraq had really been that countries seeking weapons of mass destruction courted forcible regime change, then the broader policy might well have survived the unexpected absence of WMD in Iraq. Indeed, the spectacle of a United States so powerful and reckless that it was ready to go to war even in the absence of genuine proof of WMD might have terrified other target regimes even more effectively than a United States that had actually found such programs. But for this to happen, the administration would have had to succeed in setting up a stable, perhaps democratic, U.S.-friendly Iraqi government. America's intelligence services would still have been discredited, but its national will and the effectiveness of its military forces would have been vindicated. Bidding farewell to a grateful Iraqi people, the American military, mission at least half-accomplished, would have proved its competence at regime change and been ready and fit to overthrow more governments, such as those of Iran and North Korea—ones that actually did seek or possess nuclear weapons.

Of course, none of that happened. In a failure entirely distinct from the WMD error, the United States grossly miscalculated the feasibility of regime change in Iraq, mistaking regime *removal* for regime change. If I am to change the oil in my car, then after draining away the old oil, I must have new oil available to pour into the crankcase. If I am to change a regime, then after smashing the existing government, I must have another one available to set up in its place. In Iraq, regime smash was achieved; regime change was not.

If it was chiefly the WMD error that discredited the Iraq war, it was the regime-change error that knocked the legs out from under Bush's global imperial project. Not only did Iraq absorb all the troops that would have been needed for more proliferation-stopping invasions and occupations but the experience showed that even if troops had been available the overthrow of other regimes in other countries probably would have led only to new disasters. In this epic of self-defeat, the very first step may have proven to be the last.*

Some remarks made by Donald Rumsfeld in March 2005 show how tenaciously the administration held on to its idea that shocking and awing Iraq would also terrify other countries into submission, as required by the Bush doctrine. Two years into the occupation, he was still trying to squeeze some intimidating effect out of the spectacle. "The world has seen in the last three and a half years the capability of the United States of America to go into Afghanistan . . . and with 20,000, 15,000 troops working with the Afghans do what 200,000 Soviets couldn't do in a decade. They've seen the United States and the coalition forces go into Iraq. . . . That has to have a deterrent effect on people." And he added for good measure, "If you put yourself in the shoes of a country that might decide they'd like to make mischief, they have a very recent, vivid example of the fact that the United States has the ability to deal with this."[6] If such was his response to failure, we can only imagine what boastfully menacing language he would have used had the venture succeeded.

If regime change was impossible—owing to the recalcitrance of local peoples—then so were the disarmament wars whereby Bush hoped to save the world from nuclear, biological, and chemical terror. Both goals—forced democratization and forced nonproliferation— fell in a single heap. American military doctrine had called for the armed forces to be ready to fight and win two wars. There was no provision for sinking into two quagmires. The Iraq failure showed that

---

*We can reverse the hypothesis and wonder what might have ensued had the United States found WMD yet been unable to set up a successor government. In that case, it seems likely that U.S. public support for the war would have been more durable, leading to a longer war whose results would have been hard to foresee. If I am right that determining the political future of Iraq was beyond the power of the United States (or of any other country, for that matter), then the lack of WMD, by helping pull the rug out from under public support for the war, may have been a blessing in disguise, saving the United States from an even more protracted war.

regime change was untenable as a foundation for a global policy. Undoable in itself, it was no use for stopping proliferation, or for any other purpose, either.

National Defense or Global Empire?

The extent of these failures, many of them predicted by observers in advance, fuels a fundamental doubt: was the Bush counterproliferation doctrine advanced in good faith, or was it just one more mask put on to conceal other objectives? If the latter, then the failure to deal successfully with nuclear dangers would be unsurprising—they would never have been the point in the first place. This is not the place to analyze the many possible motives that underlay the administration's invasion of Iraq. A short list would include a grab for Iraq's oil reserves, perhaps as a beachhead for securing control of most or all of the Middle East's oil; defense of the United States' ally Israel; bringing democracy to the Middle East (indeed, the whole world); and demonstrating the omnipotence of American military power. If stopping proliferation was not at least very high on this agenda, our whole concentration on nuclear policy would be beside the point. There would be no reason to wonder about such questions as why the ranking of proliferators was turned upside down, or why the steps to dissuade nuclear competitors backfired, or why many other nuclear powers were refurbishing their arsenals and extending their targeting, or why policies supposedly aimed at strengthening the world's nonproliferation regime instead pushed it to the edge of breakdown.

There are substantial reasons for such suspicions. For one thing, two months after the invasion, Deputy Secretary of Defense Paul Wolfowitz commented to a journalist, "The truth is that for reasons that have a lot to do with the U.S. government bureaucracy we settled on the one issue [justifying the invasion] that everyone could agree on, which was weapons of mass destruction as the core reason. . . ." (On the other hand, he went on immediately to add that the "overriding" reason was "the connection" between terrorism and WMD, thus citing the "nexus" that the administration has consistently placed at the heart of its doctrine.)[7]

It is also suggestive that Donald Rumsfeld is reported to have proposed invading Iraq immediately after September 11, as if, instead of responding to the attack, he only wanted to exploit it to advance a preexisting agenda. And, as many opponents of the war have pointed out, such an agenda is easy to find. Fully four years before the attacks, the Project for a New American Century, a group including many future top officials of the administration, issued a public letter calling on President Clinton to remove Saddam Hussein from power. For several in the group, including Wolfowitz, overthrowing the Iraqi government had been a fixed purpose ever since the First Gulf War, when the administration of George H. W. Bush, after evicting Iraqi troops from Kuwait, declined to press on into Baghdad. At the center of these doubts, of course, is the mendacious presentation of the case for going to war, in which, as the famous British "Downing Street memo" describing high-level meetings in Washington put it, "the facts" were "being fixed around the policy." The suspicions prompt an obvious further question: if protecting the nation against WMD was not the aim of the policy, then what was?

There can be no doubt regarding the chief candidate for an answer. It is, in fact, liberally strewn as it is throughout every major document, classified or public, of the Bush administration: "full spectrum dominance," "unchallenged" global military might, backed by "Global Strike," with its capacity to attack "any target in any dark corner of the world"—in short, as some administration supporters have candidly avowed, global empire. In the words of the journalist Ron Suskind, in his book *The One Percent Doctrine,* "The primary impetus for invading Iraq, according to those attending NSC briefings on the Gulf in this period, was to make an example of Hussein, to create a demonstration model to guide the behavior of anyone with the temerity to acquire destructive weapons or, in any way, flout the authority of the United States."[8] This overarching goal is of course consistent with all the other possible motivations for empire, from securing oil to promoting democracy.

Two contrasting pictures can be drawn. In the first, put forward in vivid language by the administration as the decision for war in Iraq was made, we see a vulnerable, wounded nation, suffering from the worst single assault in its history, now bent on defending itself against further damage, especially from weapons of mass destruction. In the second, embodied in secret memos but also reflected in more general policy pronouncements, we see a global behemoth, throwing off its chains at last, striding out into a world it means to dominate. In the first picture, the attack is a tragedy that has befallen the United States, portending further harm if defensive steps are not taken; in the second picture, the attack is an opportunity to unleash the immense coiled power of the United States to remake the world in its own image. The question is whether the former picture was used to distract attention from the latter—whether an essentially aggressive strategy, aiming at planetary dominance, was falsely sold to the public as an essentially defensive one, aiming at keeping the American citizenry safe in their homes.

Dominance or Consent?

In order to address this question and its significance for nuclear policy, a few words are first necessary regarding the idea of dominance in the American context—dominance over the North American continent, over an empire, over the world. Historians inform us that this theme stretches in an unbroken thread from the founding of the Republic (or before) down to the present—that, in the recent words of the neoconservative historian Robert Kagan, "The United States has never been a status quo power; it has always been a revolutionary one, consistently expanding its participation and influence in the world in ever-widening arcs."[9]

On the advancing edge of those arcs are found, among many other events, the near-extermination of Native American tribes, the idea of manifest destiny and its fulfillment, including aggressive wars against Spain to acquire Florida and against Mexico to acquire Texas and then New Mexico and California; the long American hegemony over the Caribbean and Central America; the Spanish-American War of 1898 and the grab for imperial possessions in its wake; the immense extension of American power associated with the Cold War; and, now, the pursuit, in all but name, of global mastery. In short, episodes of preemptive attack, overthrow of regimes, and pursuit of dominance are common. On these points, many historians of both the right and the left are in surprising agreement—although the right has been applauding and the left deploring.

Yet historians also chronicle an equally long-lasting tradition of domination's opposite—the idea and reality of consent, leading to respect for law and the principled rejection of conquest and empire, whether by the United States or others. On this thread are strung the colonies' rebellion against the hated British empire; the Declaration of Independence's profession of a "decent respect for the opinion of mankind"; the constitution of the United States, which establishes consent as the foundation for domestic politics; George Washington's warning against "entangling alliances"; the foundation of the League of Nations and Wilsonian internationalism (regarded by Wilson as an application of American constitutional principles to the world); the foundation of the United Nations, based on Roosevelt's revived and revised Wilsonianism; the principles of international law established at the Nuremberg trials; American postwar antipathy to the surviving European empires, including the British empire; the array of economic and treaty arrangements with allies in the post–World War II years; the signing of the Geneva Conventions and their incorporation into domestic law; and the dense web of arms control treaties of the Cold War. Whether the tradition of dominance or the tradition of consent has been stronger in American history is a matter much debated. Possibly, the tradition of dominance has been stronger in reality and the tradition of consent stronger in myth—using that word to refer not merely to illusions but to the guiding ideals and self-understanding of the United States.

However that may be, for most of American history, the idea that the United States, sequestered behind its two oceans, might try to dominate the entire globe was as unthought of as it would have been unreal. Even Wilson's universal aspirations were (to the disappointment of many of his European supporters) based squarely on the tradition of consent, meaning extension of international law and other forms of cooperation, not the global deployment of America's already burgeoning economic and military power. In any case, Wilson's vision was opposed on the home front, where American membership in the league was rejected. It wasn't until the Second World War that inklings of global dominance acquired even the slightest color of reality.

During the Cold War, the idea of "world domination" was still regarded as an intrinsically evil goal, if not an absurd one, and, when mentioned at all, was identified as a Soviet idea and seen as heir to Hitler's similarly reprehensible ambitions. The United States still pictured itself as anti-imperial—opposed both to the old imperialism of the fading European powers and the new style, Soviet empire building, which it strove not to destroy ("roll back") but merely to "contain." Soon enough, of course, the phrase "American imperialism" became commonplace around the world, but in the United States it was rejected by mainstream and official opinion as a left-wing libel.

In any case, whatever elements of American empire in fact existed, at least three outsize obstacles stood in the way of realizing any such goal at the global level. The most conspicuous was the Soviet Union, flush with its victory in the world war and sitting secure in its eleven time zones. (Roosevelt had hoped to enlist it as one of his "four policemen" to manage the postwar world.) The second was the global movement of peoples all over the world to throw off imperial rule and achieve self-determination. By the end of the Second World War, this movement was well on its way to putting an end to all of the old European empires, including, eventually, the Soviet one, and it posed an impassable barrier to the erection of any new empire, American or other. In Vietnam, the United States had protracted, bitter, humiliating firsthand experience of the rise to power, universal and implacable, of local peoples in their own countries. This was the force that, in the utterly predictable and predicted form of resistance to American occupation in Iraq, would place regime change out of reach and, with it, implementation of the whole Bush doctrine, including its nuclear component.

A third obstacle was the advent of nuclear arms—our topic of concern. As the supreme embodiment of force, they naturally compelled reconsideration across the board of the balance between the tradition of domination and the tradition of consent. Whereas the Soviet Union was merely one superpower, and as such could (and did) disappear, nuclear arms, owing to their origin in imperishable laws of physics, could not, and, by revolutionizing warfare itself, lastingly wreaked havoc with the very composition of power, whether wielded by the United States or anyone else. Nuclear arsenals would stand athwart the ambitions not just of the American superpower but of any nation whatsoever, in the present or the future, that might dream of global dominance or even of lesser imperial conquest. Not just American dominance but dominance itself was the bomb's victim.

But that realization came slowly. In the first days of the bomb, its peculiarity was that it both fueled ambitions for dominance and thwarted them. On the one hand, it was an instrument of violence without limit, filling its possessors' minds with dreams of unlimited sway over other nations. On the other hand, also owing to that limitless violence, it sobered and terrified them, especially when other nations began to acquire it. Used against Japan, the bomb had seemed to be a war-winning weapon, yet Americans also immediately understood that it was a human-species-ending weapon. It was both the "master card" that Secretary of War Henry Stimson had said it was, and, as he also said, a thing that "went right down to the bottom facts of human nature, morals, and governments."[10] Stimson's contradictory reactions marked points of origin for two equally contradictory schools of thought. At the heart of the debate between them were questions that no weapon had ever posed before. Was the bomb usable or useless? Did it augment power or, surprisingly, reduce it?

To simplify greatly, whereas the nuclear-war-fighting school of strategic thought came to regard nuclear superiority as useful and nuclear arms as usable, another, the mutual assured destruction school, saw nuclear superiority as meaningless and nuclear arms as unusable. The war fighters wanted to prepare to win nuclear war—to "prevail" or "terminate the war on terms favorable to the United States" were more euphemistic phrases sometimes used—the other regarded victory as impossible in a war that would obliterate all participants. One of the greatest exponents of nuclear war fighting was General Curtis LeMay, the founder and commander of the Strategic Air Command, who once said, "I'll tell you what war is about. You've got to kill people, and when you've killed enough they stop fighting."[11] In 1956, he described "in cold terms what the United States [was] capable of doing to the Soviet Union today. . . . Between sunset tonight and sunrise tomorrow morning the Soviet Union would likely cease to be a major military power or even a major nation. . . . Dawn might break over a nation infinitely poorer than China—less populated than the United States and condemned to an agrarian existence perhaps for generations to come."[12] He once told an observer that if he believed a Soviet attack were imminent, he would not wait for a presidential order but order a preemptive attack on his own authority.

During the Cold War, no administration embraced either school unreservedly. All continued to rely on nuclear arms, even on the first use of nuclear arms, but all were deeply conscious that actual use spelled suicide. Yet over time the second school gradually predominated, and nuclear arms were confined more and more to the passive role of deterrence. A turning point was the education of

John F. Kennedy's secretary of defense, Robert McNamara. Kennedy's predecessor, Eisenhower, who believed (almost certainly wrongly) that he had ended the Korean War by indirectly threatening the use of nuclear arms, had sought to extract similar benefit from the immense American numerical nuclear superiority by extending the scope of those threats on a global basis in his policy of "massive retaliation." When McNamara got to the Pentagon, a briefing on the Single Integrated Operating Plan acquainted him with what SAC commander Curtis LeMay had wrought. He made the acquaintance of plan 1A, the annihilating, indiscriminate attack not only on the Soviet Union but on China and Soviet-occupied Eastern Europe, with its expected three hundred million deaths. Horrified, McNamara soon sought to restrict nuclear weapons to the more limited role mainly of deterring attack by other nuclear weapons. The policy of mutual assured destruction was born. As for far-flung Communist challenges, conventional arms would be used for those, as happened in Vietnam.

This long debate over the usefulness of nuclear arms seemed to reach a decisive moment when President Ronald Reagan, whose secretary of defense, Caspar Weinberger, had once declared that the United States must be able to "prevail" in a nuclear war, nevertheless declared jointly with Soviet general secretary Mikhail Gorbachev in 1985 that "nuclear war cannot be won and must never be fought." If Ronald Reagan did not believe in winning a nuclear war, then what president ever would again? The nuclear war fighting school appeared to have been dispatched to history's graveyard. Superior firepower was no longer the route to dominance. Certainly, global empire was out of the question.

Dominance Redux

With the end of the Cold War, one of the three major obstacles to global dominance, the Soviet Union, which most observers had thought would last indefinitely, collapsed in a cloud of dust. Suddenly, unexpectedly, global dominance became, for the first time, an alluring possibility and, for many in the administration of George Bush Sr., a conscious goal. The lesson drawn by Cold War hawks from the Soviet collapse was not that empire itself had become anachronistic but that one of the empires, the American, had proven itself superior to all others, thus fit for global supremacy. Instead of placing the Soviet disappearance in the centuries-long context of the decline of imperial rule, they placed it in the context of what they saw as the rise of irresistible American power. The United States' political and economic system had proved itself the best; its culture had swept the earth; and, most important, its military forces were, by every tally sheet of firepower and technical sophistication, superior to the rest of the world's combined. In this view, the twentieth century had been a kind of boxing contest among rival empires, leaving, at its end, one contestant standing—the United States, now seemingly the master of all it surveyed.

Somehow forgotten was the fact that Russia and six other countries still possessed nuclear arsenals and could, at some future moment, brandish them to check American ambitions. Also forgotten was the other main obstacle to global dominance. The lesson, taught above all by the Vietnam War, that the United States could not order the political affairs of even small countries by military force had not been a popular one. Strenuous, successful efforts were made to overcome it. Secretary of State James Baker said of the invasion of Panama in 1989, "In breaking the mindset of the American people about the use of force in the post-Vietnam era, Panama established an emotional predicate that permitted us to build the public support so essential for the success of Operation Desert Storm [the First Gulf War] some thirteen months later. Desert Storm, in turn, created the emotional predicate for President George Bush, Jr.'s Operation Iraqi Freedom."[13] After Desert Storm, President George H. W. Bush exclaimed, "By God, we've kicked the Vietnam syndrome."

The limits on global dominance imposed by nuclear arms also quietly slid out of view, while the nuclear-war-fighting school gained an unexpected new lease on life in Secretary of Defense Dick Cheney's discovery of new uses for nuclear weapons in the mission of global counterproliferation. The transition from the Soviet-aimed targeting of the SIOP to the planetary targeting of Global Strike had begun, all as part and parcel of the goal of global supremacy that had been made so tempting by the Soviet collapse.

This new ambition was crystallized in a document that won brief notoriety and then, when Bush Sr. lost his bid for a second term, was forgotten. Its importance for the present is that it outlined a scheme for global dominance a decade before September 11, 2001. Its sponsor was Cheney and its draftsman was Zalmay Khalilzad, who would become ambassador to Afghanistan in 2003 and of Iraq in 2005. The draft stated, "The number one objective of U.S.'s post–Cold War political and military strategy should be preventing the emergence of a rival superpower. Our first objective is to prevent the re-emergence of a new rival." Even strong regional powers should be suppressed, especially in areas "whose resources would, under consolidated control, be sufficient to generate global power. These regions include Western Europe, East Asia, the territory of the former Soviet Union, and Southwest Asia." The ambitions of others should, indeed, be nipped in the bud by "convincing potential competitors that they need not aspire to a greater role or pursue a more aggressive posture to protect their legitimate interest." Accordingly, the United States "must maintain the mechanisms for deterring potential competitors from even aspiring to a larger regional or global role.[14]

The draft also foreshadowed Bush Jr.'s policy of preemptive disarmament wars, stating that the United States "may be faced with the question of whether to take military steps to prevent the development or use of weapons of mass destruction." The draft was later released in revised form by Secretary of Defense Cheney under the title *Defense Strategy for the 90s.* In the words of James Mann, perhaps the most knowledgeable and careful chronicler of the careers of the Bush national security advisers, "What the Pentagon officials had succeeded in doing, within months of the Soviet collapse, was

to lay out the intellectual blueprint for a new world dominated—
then, now and in the future—by U.S. military power."[15] The *Defense
Strategy for the 90s* is important because, in combination with
Cheney's innovations in nuclear policies, it shows that the idea of
American global dominance, though never embraced by President
Bush Sr., was brewing in the minds of key officials who, a decade
later, would have a second chance and a preponderant influence
over the policies of his son.

A Defensive Empire

In light of this record, must we conclude that the justification for the
Iraq war in particular and of the campaign against proliferation in
general, namely defense of the nation from imminent danger, above
all from a mushroom cloud rising over one of its cities, was merely a
mask concealing a long-contemplated and tirelessly pursued agenda of
global empire? Careful analysis shows a more complex association of
sincerity and deception than either of these alternatives suggest. The
array of expectations that died in the Iraq war—including the belief
that there were weapons of mass destruction in Iraq, the belief that the
Iraqi population would welcome the arrival of American forces and
forthwith set about founding a liberal democracy under American
tutelage, and the belief that the resulting success would inspire the rest
of the Middle East to follow suit—have justly been criticized as delu-
sions. But our question is whether they were also deceptions.

Let us consider the debate regarding weapons of mass destruction in Iraq that took place before the war began. In September
2002, Vice President Cheney claimed that Saddam Hussein had "re-
constituted his nuclear program."[16] We know now that the evidence
for the claim was at least manipulated and possibly manufactured
outright. Findings contrary to the desired case were choked off as it
rose in the bureaucratic hierarchy, while disproven findings that
supported the case flew upward and were inserted in presidential
statements; high officials put lower ones under pressure to conform

to the White House line; critical footnotes expressing doubt in the classified versions of intelligence estimates never made it into the publicized versions of those estimates; and those who cast doubt on the case were sidelined or worse.

Yet the manufacture of evidence, though wrong in itself, does not prove absence of belief. A detective who is convinced of a suspect's guilt and plants a packet of heroin on him to "prove" it may perjure himself, but he is not without conviction. Indeed, he has too much conviction, and it often happens that the truest believers are the greatest liars. Not even facts can puncture their illusions. The most revealing case study is perhaps Secretary of State Colin Powell, who, although the closest thing to a war critic in the administration, wagered his reputation on the truth of evidence we now know to be false when he presented it to the world in his pre-invasion speech at the United Nations Security Council. It is difficult to imagine that as he did so he foresaw the day, which soon came, when indisputable facts would impeach his testimony and stain his reputation. It is far easier to imagine that he—and even more so true believers like Rumsfeld or Cheney or the president—was persuaded of the allegation even as he presented the false evidence for it to the American public. Indeed, the evening before his Security Council speech, Powell wondered aloud to an aide what they would all think if they combed Iraq from end to end and found no WMD.

Rumsfeld's insistence on going to war with an army much smaller than the one recommended by high military officers appears to tell the same story. Rumsfeld has been excoriated for his decision, and the judgment that the number of troops was too few has been borne out.*

---

*Let us be careful to note, however, that the obverse proposition—that a tactical decision to send in more troops would have brought success in Iraq—does not necessarily follow. It's often simply assumed that the war would have gone better with a larger force. My own opinion is that more troops would not have solved the problem, which was the inevitable resistance of a proud people to occupation by a foreign power plus the weak cohesion of the various ethnic and religious groups in the country. More troops would mainly have meant more targets and more casualties.

What is rarely asked is why Rumsfeld insisted on a small force. After all, we cannot suppose that he secretly wanted to fail in Iraq. One answer is that although the small force courted obvious risks, pointed out in advance by dissenting military officers, it was a requirement of the larger strategy of dominance, in which the Iraq war was to be but a first step. That invasion made global strategic sense *only if,* as a tactical move in the larger strategic effort, a small force could accomplish the mission, leaving other forces available for threatening or attacking the rest of the axis of evil as well as other targets around the world—the unnamed "regional adversaries" mentioned in the strategic documents.[17] Furthermore, the small force could win only if it turned out to be true that, as Rumsfeld's expatriate Iraqi advisers told him, an enthusiastic Iraqi population would indeed promptly set about remaking its nation along the lines of the "one model" set forth by the *National Security Strategy of the United States of America.* When the war began, its chief military planner, General Tommy Franks, announced to the American troops in Iraq that most of them should get ready to leave within four months, in the fall of 2003.[18]

Only under those circumstances was it possible to imagine the success of the administration's reverse version of the domino theory, in which one tyranny after another would fall to democracy. Rumsfeld's mistaken insistence on a small force is thus evidence of his real faith in swift and painless regime change. When the assumption proved false in Iraq, the Bush doctrine was dead; it could not even be tried out on its own terms, for the troops in Iraq, "few" as they were, astonishingly turned out to be all that the world's sole superpower had to spare (even with the National Guard and reserves included), leaving only air power available to deal with the rest of the "axis." But no air campaign in history had ever, by itself, brought about regime change even in a single country, much less sustained it. The double collapse of policy in Iraq—no WMD, no flourishing new regime—was thus part and parcel of the encompassing grand illusion that violent regime change could be the mainstay of a global strategy.

It is true that in most immediate decisions the administration chose empire over safety—war over diplomacy or police action; unilateral action over action in concert with allies; an attack on Iraq over a confrontation with Pakistan about its egregious proliferation policies, and so forth. It is also true that evidence was repeatedly manipulated, distorted, suppressed, or manufactured in the service of these decisions, giving the strong impression that the ship *World Empire* was sailing under a false flag emblazoned "National Defense." Surveying the ruins of the policy, it may seem that bad faith reigned supreme, that a gigantic con job was attempted and has now been unmasked.

However, such a conclusion cannot account for abundant evidence of the administration's sincere belief in its grand vision. And in that vision national defense and global dominance were not alternatives; they were bound together. In Bush's words, "We are led, by events and common sense, to one conclusion: The survival of liberty in our land increasingly depends on the success of liberty in other lands." Or, in what may have been his most utopian single sentence, "America's vital interests and our deepest beliefs are now one." In its identification of one nation with all that is positive and good anywhere, the statement transcends even imperial ambition and enters the zone of the eschatological. Doctrine (a guideline for policy) had clearly flowered into ideology (a comprehensive vision of History's progress and destination). Indeed, before long, Bush announced that he was engaged in an "ideological war." The men and women of his administration would not be the first to have sacrificed fact—both deliberately *and* unconsciously—to ideology. Like so many ideologues, they were too dazzled by their vision of the glorious future of their dreams to pay adequate attention to the sordid realities they were creating in the present.

In short, rolling defense and aggression into one ball, President Bush wished, without quite saying so, to establish a kind of defensive global empire. To be safe, the United States needed to dominate the world, and do so totally, without a single competitor on the farthest horizon. Nuclear danger, from rogues and terrorists, was by no means the sole reason for thus conjoining global offense with global defense, but it was the lynchpin of the scheme. Only the vision of the mushroom cloud over an American city, invoked repeatedly by administration officials as it took the country to war in Iraq, could justify such an ambitious enterprise.

If we picture the world Bush and his advisers foresaw after the invasion of Iraq, it becomes clear that in their view global dominance was the best and probably the sole path to safety for the United States in the new age. In this exercise, we must imagine that joyful Iraqis had indeed set up a flourishing democracy; that other countries in the Middle East and elsewhere, witnessing the uplifting spectacle, had followed suit; that a few holdouts, shocked and awed by the success of a nearly unbloodied American military, had been frightened into submission, or, failing that, subjected to prompt regime change; that democracy in the world had acquired a new lease on life; that the new democracies, now at peace with one another, were voluntarily turning away from weapons of mass destruction, and, of course, from support for terrorists, leading to the simultaneous reduction of both dangers; that an enlightened America, working mainly through example, yet holding its awesome, unchallenged, and forever unchallengeable military dominance, nuclear and conventional, at the ready, would be both the indisputable and the indispensable master of this new world order as well as its principal beneficiary. The path to safety, as Bush said so often, was action. The requirement of defense was preventive attack. The place to stop terrorists was abroad, "so we won't have to fight them at home." Even if the initial steps toward defense and toward dominance at first diverged sharply, they would gradually converge, and, fact lining up with faith, become, in the final stage, one and the same in Bush's grand conciliation of America's interests and its deepest beliefs.

None of that was remotely likely, but if it had been, then in *such* a world, regime change would indeed have been a feasible instrument for mastering nuclear danger. Even the choice of Iraq as the first disarmament war would have fallen into place. Attacking and defeating the axis's weakest adversary of evil would, by enhancing American prestige, increase its leverage in dealing with more difficult cases down the road.

Bush as a Model

The proportions of good and bad faith in the Bush doctrine are important to assess for reasons that go beyond fairness to those concerned. If, out of zeal to indict the administration's manifest failure, great as it is, we blind ourselves to the sincerity of their beliefs, we are at risk of missing the heart of the challenge that really does lie before the world. Comprehensive errors of policy of this kind are rarely, if ever, gratuitous. Almost always, they are at least in part misbegotten solutions to problems that are real.

Today, the central problem is what to do about the prospect of global nuclear anarchy. Let us give the Bush administration its due. It framed an audacious, comprehensive doctrine addressing this problem and acted resolutely on the basis of its beliefs. A plan for global dominance was a solution on the proper scale, for the problem was and is in its very nature global: the universal pretensions of global empire matched the universal availability of the bomb in the mind. A solution backed by a resolute will was essential, because the momentum of the bomb, which had defeated all comers, was obviously tremendous. A solution that required a virtual revolution in the way the world was run was a solution at the proper depth, for the problem cannot be addressed without deep, structural change in the international order. Moreover, the Bush doctrine was governed by a logic that was consistent, even necessary, if its key assumptions were accepted: first, that in a time when the worst weapon technologies are on the edge of falling into the hands of the worst people and regimes (and they are), an unmanaged world is no longer acceptable; second, that we still live in an era in which power in the last analysis is based on force; and, third, that the United States possessed greater force than all other countries combined. The conclusions followed. *If* force was the ultimate arbiter of proliferation as of other matters, *then* it was true that preemption would be necessary, since action after the fact would either be deterred by the proliferator's arsenal or lead to nuclear war. *If* preemption was necessary, *then* regime change had to follow, since a regime that had made nuclear weapons could build them again if it were left in power and waited out the storm. *If* preemption and regime change were necessary, *then* a global master capable of performing these tasks was required, not only for its own sake but for the sake of all peoples. *If* the need for a global master was accepted, *then* the United States, owing to its unmatched military might, was the only one in sight and, whether eagerly or reluctantly, must assume the burden. Finally, *if* the United States was to perform this service, *then* its hands should not be tied, in which case it made perfect sense to class "international fora," including the International Criminal Court, with "terrorism" as weapons deployed by "the weak" to oppose order and peace. And, as the Iraq war began, Richard Perle would have had good reason to celebrate the demise of the UN.

The magnitude of this administration's mistakes, you might say, gives us the measure of the problem the world faces. For notwithstanding the travesties of fact and judgment involved in the Iraq war and elsewhere, the idea of a global master, once duly recognized, is, at least theoretically, adequate to the administration's stated goals. As every political science major knows, dominance has been one of the very few remedies for anarchy. Since what threatens today is the worst of all imaginable sorts of anarchy, nuclear anarchy on a global scale (with the other weapons of mass destruction thrown in for good measure), this traditional solution at least recognizes the problem for what it is. The classic text on the subject is Thomas Hobbes's *Leviathan*, his name for a state that puts an end to the horrifying war of all against all by concentrating the means of violence in its own hands and bringing all rebels and rogues to heel. Before Hobbes, Jean Bodin, the French philosopher of absolutism, taught that power is a product of "the sword alone," which therefore must be wielded by a single authority, the sovereign. Peace in this scheme was not a casualty of dominance but the product of it. From early modern times down to the present, these tenets have been embodied in the concept of sovereignty, which rests on the idea that in every political system there must be a single, unified power whose decisions are final because it possesses a monopoly on the means of force. (The exponents of absolutism, then as now, have never lacked cogent defenders.)

With remarkable consistency, the Bush doctrine proposed this logic for our time. The idea of global dominance is to today's world what the idea of national sovereignty was to the time of the foundation of nation-states. It would constitute a system of something like Earth-rule by one nation.* In a very real sense, Bush was proposing the United States as a global Leviathan. (His unprecedented assertion of presidential powers at home, under the doctrine of the "unitary presidency," would, if accepted, have made the president a kind of sovereign over the United States at the same time.) In such a system, a double standard, in regard to nuclear weapons and much else, is not a flaw but a first principle and a necessity, as Bodin, Hobbes, and the other absolutists of their day well knew. Whether in the context of nation-state formation a half millennium ago or of international order today, as large a gap as possible in both rights and power between the lord and the vassals is essential, for it is precisely on this inequality that the system, promising law and order for all, relies. If there is no double standard, there will be no dominance, and if there is no dominance, there will be no peace, and if there is no peace there will be nuclear anarchy, and if there is nuclear anarchy there will be nuclear war. And is it wrong to suggest that today, in a widening sphere, the business of the world, going far beyond the management of nuclear danger, must be dealt with on a global basis or not at all? And if the dominance of a single power is to be rejected, has any serious alternative been recommended?

---

*We have to say "something like" because its exact workings, being prospective and also, in my opinion, phantasmal, have always been extremely blurry. That is why, in describing the scheme, it is difficult to choose among such words as "dominance," "hegemony," and "global empire."

In the early modern age, an alternative to dominance *was* proffered at the national level. It was the conception of the state based on law and the will of the people embodied in the tradition of consent. Articulated in the writings of John Locke and others, it took root in England, in the Glorious Revolution of 1688–89, and was developed further in the hands of the American revolutionaries of 1776 and the constitution builders of 1787. In responding to the universal danger posed by nuclear proliferation, the United States therefore had two suitably universalist traditions that it could draw on, one based on consent and law, the other based on force. Bush chose force. It was the wrong choice. It increased the nuclear danger it was meant to prevent. It engendered pointless—and unsuccessful—war and destruction. It set back democracy at home and abroad. It disgraced the United States in the eyes of world opinion. It launched the world into a vicious, escalating cycle of violence that could not attain its goal yet could not, as long as the doctrine was pursued, be abandoned. It collided head-on with the deep-seated conviction of peoples everywhere that, whatever else they may believe in, they are firmly resolved not to bend the knee to any imperial master.

Yet to invoke the tradition of consent is not to name a solution to the nuclear dilemma, for obviously none yet exists or has even been advanced. Bush has been taken to task for the stubborn willfulness of his leadership as well as the ambition and audacity of his doctrine, but those qualities are to his credit. They correspond to the immensity and urgency of the task at hand. In this respect, Bush is a model. It will be of no use to revive the tepid measures, vacillating and half-hearted, of the Clinton years, which created the vacuum that Bush so disastrously filled with his imperial doctrine. The deeper tragedy of our times is that no comparable ambition, no comparable audacity, no comparable will, has been mustered by the exponents of the tradition of consent and law. On the contrary, they fearfully offer only half a loaf of their prescription, or, worse, watered down Bushism. Their failing has been as great as his, and more contemptible, since they are the guardians of the path that in all likelihood alone offers hope for delivery from the multiplying nuclear dangers of our day.

PART III

A TREMENDOUS PARTY FOR THE WHOLE WORLD

CHAPTER 8

A REALM OF SHADOWS

The bold enterprise, founded on the principles of law and consent, that should take the place of the bold but misconceived enterprise of American global dominance, founded on the principle of force, can only be one thing: the elimination of nuclear weapons by global agreement. To paraphrase William James, nuclear abolition is the moral equivalent of empire. Like all equivalents, it has similarities with what it would replace. Like global empire, abolition is universal. Like empire, it decisively changes the structure of the international order. Like empire, it requires every nation on Earth to take its place in a "new nuclear world order" (to adapt Prime Minister Singh's phrase to a new purpose). Above all, like empire, it constitutes, if realized, a comprehensive solution to the problem it addresses, which is nuclear anarchy.

Of course, there are also the polar differences. Whereas empire requires a nuclear double standard, abolition requires—is—a single standard. Whereas empire is founded on the unremitting threat of force and use of force, abolition is founded on the principle of cooperation. Whereas empire is a structure based on domination, abolition can only be based in a structure of law. A final, perhaps obvious, difference is that abolition, though of course very ambitious, still is a much more modest goal than global empire. Whereas empire reaches into every sphere of life, from the military to the political to the economic to the cultural, abolition directly addresses only one sphere. However, because that one is located at the very heart of the global system, its reform would give decisive impetus to efforts to resolve a long agenda of other issues requiring cooperative global action. Not itself a full substitute for empire, it would nevertheless be the indispensable arch stone of that substitute. But before exploring the outlook for abolition in our day, let us examine the last historical moment it was seriously considered—the summit meeting between President Ronald Reagan and General Secretary Mikhail Gorbachev at Reykjavik, Iceland, in October 1986.

Abolition in the First Nuclear Era

Immediately after the event, an impression arose that the meeting between the leaders of the two superpowers had been a chaotic, dizzying bout of improvisation in which a clueless Reagan had somehow been lured into momentarily agreeing to nuclear abolition. In this telling, the whole negotiation, both embarrassing and futile, comes off as a freakish, almost whimsical episode in which the two leaders, departing from their briefing books, and perhaps their senses, somehow decided to give an airing to a proposal that all serious people knew to be quixotic.

It is true that the American delegation had not been prepared for negotiations as substantive as those that occurred. Yet both the Soviet and the American memoranda of conversation (memcon) of the event reveal a disciplined, searching, sincere exploration and negotiation of the possibility of abolishing nuclear weapons. Each leader knows exactly what he wants. Each is a master of his brief (though Reagan and his advisers are caught by surprise by the breadth of Gorbachev's initial proposals). Each listens carefully to the other.

When confusion arises, it is soon cleared up. Each is eloquent, even inspired, in his appeal to the other. Each is a rock-ribbed nuclear abolitionist. Each, indeed, has been an abolitionist for several years and has thought long and deeply about the subject. By the second day of the meeting, each is prepared to commit himself to surrendering his country's entire nuclear arsenal on the spot. Also—as we know from the memcons of their previous summit at Geneva in 1985 (which did not produce any agreement)—they have discussed the subject before, and at length: the Reykjavik conversation is the culmination of a longer conversation. Each strives to find common ground with the other. They extend their session in search of it. But their paths to the goal are different, and in the end—heartbreakingly—they cannot agree.

Just as important as this impressive performance, the negotiation, placed in a larger time frame, can be seen as the endpoint of a slow evolution of thinking as long as the Cold War. The problem presented by the advent of the bomb in 1945 was how to absorb such a disproportionate force as the energy released from mass into the fluctuating, frail, contingent realm of historical events. A protracted effort of translation was required—a slow sifting and weighing, in heart and mind, of each aspect of the nuclear dilemma. Or, to put the matter differently, the Cold War framework become a mirror in which the dread new object, though unused, was steadily held in view.

The Cold War thus was a pedagogical opportunity. For a modern historical era, it lasted a remarkably long time. Considered as a laboratory in which to examine the bomb, it provided ample leisure for investigation. You might say that it held the mysterious and elusive atomic fire steady in its tense grip long enough for people to discover some important things about it and to reflect on them quite deeply. (By helping to prevent the world war that might otherwise have ended the struggle, the bomb was itself a contributor to that longevity. It slowed history down—enough to permit processes other than war to work their way.) In the meantime, the bomb's nature was considerably clarified. Under the discipline of events, a slow evolution in policy and thought followed. It was in this period that the war-fighting school was gradually eclipsed by the mutual-assured-destruction school. Most important, the use-lessness of the bomb for war was impressed on its possessors. But it took four decades for the lesson finally to sink in—an event that was signaled when Reagan and Gorbachev made their famous joint statement at the Geneva summit: "A nuclear war cannot be won and should never be fought." The days of seeing nuclear arms as a source of military advantage had seemingly expired, and the days of seeing them as a common danger had arrived.

Observers might have thought that the mutual-assured-destruction school of deterrence had finally triumphed once and for all. For decades, right-wing politicians who rejected the doctrine had maintained that victory in a nuclear war was still possible. Now, their greatest champion, the ultraconservative Reagan, was standing beside the general secretary of the Communist Party of the Union of Soviet Socialist Republics declaring the opposite. The decades of danger had not passed in vain. The illusion that anyone could win a nuclear war or gain any advantage whatsoever from it was officially dead.

Yet Reagan had not, in fact, embraced this lesson's corollary in the conventional wisdom of the doctrine of deterrence. It so happened that he despised that doctrine, chiefly on moral grounds. He regarded nuclear weapons as "totally irrational, totally inhumane, good for nothing but killing, possibly destructive of life on earth and civilization."[1] Or, as he put it to Gorbachev a year later at Reykjavik, "Now . . . we have horrible missiles, whose principal victims are civilians. The only defense against them is the threat of slaughtering masses of other people. This is not civilized."[2] The long education in nuclear matters provided by the Cold War had indeed led him at last to assess the realities of nuclear war in the same way as his liberal opponents, most of whom were wedded to deterrence. His prescription for dealing with that situation, however, could not have been more different. Neither, of course, was he in agreement any longer with his own tribe of nuclear hawks. He was on his own. He was a fervent nuclear abolitionist.

It's not easy to trace the origins of Reagan's nuclear abolitionism. Historically, the first sign of it seems to have appeared in December 1945, when Reagan, then a movie actor, agreed to lead a rally for nuclear disarmament—only to bow to pressure from his studio, Warner Bros., to cancel the engagement. At the time, he was still a Rooseveltian Democrat and held many views he later discarded as he moved sharply rightward. As the Cold War got under way, he changed his mind about abolition, now judging that "we'll never obtain international control," and so "we must be strongest in atomic weapons." Yet the idea of abolition did not entirely disappear from his mind. In 1963, for example, he stated, "We can make those rockets into bridge lamps by being so strong that the enemy has no choice." (The idea of cultivating American strength as a path to abolition would never leave his thinking.)[3]

The abolition trail then goes cold until 1976, when President Gerald Ford, who had just won the Republican nomination, permitted a narrowly defeated Reagan to give a farewell speech to the convention. The theme of his peroration was what the world would be like in a hundred years—when people will "know all about us," though we "know nothing about them." He fretted about "the erosion of freedom that has taken place under Democratic rule" and "restrictions on the vitality of the great economy that we enjoy." All of this was familiar and expected. But Reagan had something else in mind. He went on:

And then again there is that challenge of which he [President Ford, who had addressed the convention earlier] spoke—that we live in a world in which the great powers have poised and aimed at each other horrible missiles of destruction, nuclear weapons that can in a matter of minutes arrive at each other's country and destroy, virtually, the civilized world we live in. And suddenly it dawned on me, those who would read this letter a hundred years from now will know whether those missiles were fired. They will know whether we met our challenge. Whether they have the freedoms that we have known up until now will depend on what we do here.

> Will they look back with appreciation and say, "Thank God for those people in 1976 who headed off that loss of freedom, who kept us now 100 years later free, who kept our world from nuclear destruction?"[4]

Reagan did not call for the elimination of nuclear arms, but the topic as well as the tone and sentiment of this abrupt intervention was so far outside the context of customary right-wing discourse that it was in effect inaudible to the world at large. How could a man of the right express, with considerable eloquence, antinuclear sentiments so often associated with the left? Later, Reagan's biographer Lou Cannon commented, "This clue did not lead us anywhere . . . because most of us in the journalistic community did not realize then that there was a mystery to solve."[5]

The theme went underground again until March 23, 1983, in the third year of Reagan's presidency, when, to the astonishment of most of his advisers, he made two radical proposals in yet another peroration to a speech—this time one devoted mainly to a defense of the arms buildup he had been engaged in since arriving in office. The first proposal, later named the Strategic Defense Initiative (SDI), and popularly known as "Star Wars," was a proposal to build a defensive system that would "intercept and destroy strategic ballistic missiles before they reached our own soil or that of our allies," thus rendering "these nuclear weapons impotent and obsolete." That accomplished, the world—and this was the second radical proposal crammed into Reagan's peroration—could proceed to "achieve our ultimate goal of eliminating the threat posed by strategic nuclear missiles," which in turn would "pave the way for arms control measures to eliminate the weapons themselves."

Reagan's double shock caught the top officials of his administration by surprise—and most were appalled. In the first place, they believed, quite correctly (as about a $100 billion in expenditures over the ensuing twenty-three years would show), that an impervious missile shield over the United States or any other country was a technological impossibility for the indefinite future. Reagan seemed to have escaped from one of the great illusions of the nuclear age—that a nuclear war could be won—into another: that a nuclear attack could be defended against. In the second place, support for abolition among the officials of his administration was close to the zero point. Seen from their perspective, Reagan had committed the United States to two impossibilities in the same speech.

The reaction of the Soviet leaders was even more unfavorable. SDI had several features that rendered it unacceptable to them. One of the often-avowed purposes of Reagan's arms buildup had been to spend the Soviet Union into bankruptcy. (Many believe to this day that he succeeded.) SDI appeared to the Soviets to accelerate this effort. They were not mistaken. In a press conference, Reagan explained that the Soviets "are no match for our industrial might—this is why they came to the table and are willing to negotiate with us."[6] After leaving office, he recalled, "The Soviets were spending such a large percentage of their national wealth on armaments that they were bankrupting their economy. We also knew that, if we showed the political resolve to develop SDI, the Soviets would have to face the awful truth: They did not have the resources to continue building a huge offensive arsenal and a defensive one simultaneously."[7]

The other feature of SDI that upset the Soviets was what they saw as the plan's strategic aim: gaining decisive American nuclear superiority after all. As they well knew, the Republican Party Platform of 1980, on which Reagan had run for president, had called for "overall military and technical superiority over the Soviet Union"—a right-wing tenet of long standing.[8] Yet just four days after his SDI speech, Reagan addressed at least the second issue, proposing a solution that, in the abstract at any rate, would have altered and radically expanded the scope of his proposal. He announced that if the United States developed effective SDI technology he would share it with the Soviet Union. Once the two countries were thus defended, he would declare, " 'I am willing to do away with all my missiles. You do away with yours.' "[9]

The proposal to share the United States' most advanced technology struck both his own administration and the Soviets as the most unreal element of the plan yet. Less noted at the time was that the sharing idea, however remote from realization (as was SDI itself), made conceptual sense. If enacted, it would have precluded any bid for superiority. This new twist on his proposal radically reduced the burden of proof on SDI. Even Reagan soon was required to recognize that a full, foolproof defense of the United States or any other country against a large arsenal of nuclear-armed missiles was chimerical. On the other hand, if offensive arsenals were eliminated, then defenses would face only the lesser and more feasible challenge of safeguarding against the tiny missile forces that a cheater on an abolition agreement might cobble together in secret.

Later, Reagan would repeatedly name exactly this objective as his principal rationale for his program. Even if nuclear weapons were abolished and the agreement were subjected to the most intrusive inspections, a "madman" might still build and launch a few nuclear weapons. SDI—now in the hands of any country that wanted it—would offer protection against just that. In refashioning his proposal in this way, Reagan was addressing the most frequently made and most potent objection to nuclear abolition: that if it were ever accomplished, the world might be held hostage by a cheater suddenly in possession of a nuclear monopoly and so capable of forcing the world to bow to its will. (Some might say, of course, that Reagan's amendment was a mere thought experiment. But then all nuclear strategy from 1945 on, including the most hallowed concepts of deterrence, have been nothing but one thought experiment after another.)

Reagan's proposal arose out of the confluence of several historical currents in the Cold War's last decade (although no one knew yet that it *was* the last decade). Perhaps most important was the greatly underestimated, active mind of Ronald Reagan. Rarely, if ever, has a major international initiative been more thoroughly the product of the solitary mind of a president, with almost no contribution being made by his top officials. In fact, throughout the period, his abolitionism had a certain furtive, freelance quality. The idea appeared mostly in the handwritten perorations to speeches, not the bureaucratically vetted main body, or in press conferences, or—most important—in the confidential precincts of summit meetings.

Another current was the broad nuclear freeze movement of the early 1980s, which demanded an end to the Cold War arms race through a bilateral agreement. Reagan had opposed the movement in harsh terms, calling it "a dangerous fraud" perpetrated by those "who want the weakening of America."[10] Yet as early as 1979, when Reagan was running for president, Martin Anderson, one of his campaign advisers, wrote in a memo that Reagan was politically vulnerable to charges that he was too prone to hawkish impulses, including "stockpiling nuclear weapons to blast the Soviet Union." (In the campaign, Reagan had charged that President Jimmy Carter had been "totally oblivious to the Soviet drive for world domination.") Anderson saw three possible remedies: "to rely on Soviet good intentions," to "match the Soviet buildup," or to "develop a Protective Missile System." He favored the latter, but the proposal was rejected at the time.[11]

Another current, closely related to the freeze, was the declining popularity of Reagan's nuclear buildup, approval of which had fallen in public opinion polls from 80 percent to 20 percent.[12] Administration officials hoped that the SDI/abolition package would steal the freeze movement's thunder—an aim in which it in fact appeared to succeed. Reagan's national security adviser, Bud McFarlane, wrote in a memo to Reagan in December 1984, two months after his reelection, "You have thrown the left into an absolute tizzy. They are left in the position of advocating the most bloodthirsty strategy—Mutual Assured Destruction—as a means to keep the peace." And although in May 1983, a freeze resolution passed in the House of Representatives, a year later the movement was well on its way to disappearing.[13] However, it is equally true that the freeze movement of that period created the political conditions that permitted Reagan's abolitionism, dormant until then, to revive. Unknowingly and unwillingly, the freeze movement and Ronald Reagan were partners in a power-ful, almost decade-long effort to lift nuclear danger.[14]

Then a new historical current, destined to absorb all the others, came into play. On March 11, 1985, Mikhail Gorbachev was elected general secretary of the Communist Party of the Soviet Union. The chain of events that would lead to the downfall of the Soviet Union had now been set in motion. Remarkably, Gorbachev was as fervent a nuclear abolitionist as Reagan. In January 1986, he proposed a three-stage plan to abolish nuclear weapons by the year 2000. His proposal was no less sincere for being much more conventional than Reagan's. The world would proceed to abolition in three five-year stages. In the first, the arsenals would be cut in half. In the second, the world's other nuclear powers would join the process. In the third, the world would proceed to abolition. The freshest element in the plan was Gorbachev's willingness to permit highly intrusive on-site in-spection on Soviet soil—Russian opposition to this had always been cited by U.S. officials as the chief reason for rejecting previous Soviet proposals for radical disarmament.

Gorbachev had arrived at abolition along a route of his own. He had already embarked on his program of liberalizing Soviet rule. His goal was a democratic Soviet Union at peace with the West, and, in pursuit of it, he sought, more insistently than Reagan, an end to the Cold War, including a reduction and even a liquidation of the super-powers' nuclear confrontation, which he desired for its own sake and also for the economic relief it would give his domestic reforms.

What his initiatives in fact turned out to bring was not just the end of the Cold War but an end to the Soviet Union. In 1985, how-ever, the Soviet Union was still intact, and the leaders of both super-powers were nuclear abolitionists. Thus it happened that in nuclear matters the Cold War, which began with the Baruch Plan, was book-ended by abolition proposals. But this second time around, the pro-posals were not the product of abstract thought and hope but of the long evolution of experience with the nuclear dilemma that the Cold War had provided.

Of course, abolition didn't happen in 1986 any more than it had in 1945. The climactic scene was the Reykjavik summit. At its opening session on the morning of October 11, both men agreed, in keeping with their public and private statements for some two years, that their objective was the elimination of all nuclear weapons. Gorbachev then startled Reagan with a handful of sweeping and highly detailed arms control proposals, one for a 50 percent reduction in strategic nuclear weapons, another for the elimination of intermediate range missiles. They were conditioned, however, on an agreement by the United States to confine the development of SDI to the laboratory and, for a period of ten years, not to withdraw from the Anti-Ballistic Missile Treaty, which would have prohibited the deployment of elements of SDI and, as currently written, could be annulled on six months' notice.

Gorbachev would not agree to the offensive cuts, he said, if defenses were permitted. He did not mention abolition in these proposals. Reagan, however, did in his response. Gorbachev was calling on him to restrict SDI for ten years, but SDI in his opinion was the very thing that "would make the elimination of nuclear weapons possible." His concrete proposal was an amendment to the ABM Treaty that would permit SDI's development—but not yet its deployment—in tandem with an agreement to "eliminate ballistic missiles." In response to the charge that SDI would give the United States a first-strike capacity, Reagan sensibly answered, "We are proposing a treaty which would require the elimination of ballistic missiles *before* SDI is deployed, therefore a first strike would not be possible."

Reagan then invoked what, by now, was his standard argument for SDI: after abolition, the world needed protection against "a madman like Hitler" who might "try to build nuclear weapons." And he promised to share any American SDI achievements with the Soviet Union. Gorbachev turned a deaf ear to this reasoning, expressing his hope that Reagan's comments were only "preliminary."

The fundamental terms of the negotiations were now set. In the course of the next few days, the two heads of state seemed to compete in bringing forward ever more radical proposals for offensive nuclear disarmament, only to see them dashed on the unbridgeable disagreement over SDI and the ABM Treaty. In the afternoon session, in response to Gorbachev's "concern," Reagan put forward a proposal to eliminate all ballistic missiles over a period of ten years. That way, Gorbachev could be certain that no first strike was intended. SDI, which would be permitted in the treaty, would serve only as a defense against possible cheating. Restrictions on SDI for a decade were unacceptable to Reagan because "with the progress we are making we do not need ten years. . . . We do not think it will take that long."

Of course, we now know that, even after twenty years of intensive R & D, the ability to reliably shoot down even one missile under battlefield conditions, not to speak of scores or hundreds of them, has not been achieved. But Reagan believed in quite a different future. Defenses, Reagan said, were like gas masks kept in reserve even after poison gas had been outlawed, for use in case someone cheated.

Gorbachev again brushed off Reagan's proposal, saying that he could not take the sharing proposal seriously. If the United States would not even share dairy and oil drilling equipment (as was the case at that moment), how would it share its most advanced technological secrets? What he left unsaid—and probably could not say— was that such an arrangement, in which one superpower turned to the other for the means of its defense, would also be humiliating in the extreme. Certainly, the United States would never have entertained such a proposal had it been made by the Soviet Union or anyone else.

The next day, it was Gorbachev's turn to raise the disarmament stakes. Each leader seemed to be trying to tempt the other to abandon his position on SDI by proposing ever-more-alluring accomplishments in disarmament. Now, Gorbachev proposed ridding the world of all strategic nuclear arms in two five-year periods. In response, Reagan tabled a proposal to get rid of half of strategic weapons in five years and all ballistic missiles in the next five years. Gorbachev's proposal was the more sweeping, as strategic arms include bombers and cruise missiles as well as ballistic missiles.

Reagan then returned to the central issue of SDI and the ABM Treaty, proposing the investigation of three issues whose resolution in detail might break the impasse: how could SDI be "synchronized with our shared goals of eliminating ballistic missiles"; "what should the conditions and timeframe be for increasing reliance on strategic defenses"; and "what common understanding" in the meantime "might be reached on activities under the ABM treaty on advanced strategic questions."

Had there been any interest on the Soviet side in arriving at a nuclear-weapon-free world safeguarded by defenses, these were indeed the questions to address, for their successful resolution could have guaranteed the Soviets that at no point in the process of disarmament would the United States gain defensive superiority. But again Gorbachev's interest remained nil.

Later in the conversation, however, when Secretary of State George Shultz asked whether withdrawal from the ABM Treaty would be permitted after strategic abolition, Gorbachev answered that it would. It was the only narrowing of the basic disagreement that occurred during the summit. Perhaps for this reason, the conversation on offensive arms galloped forward. When Shultz pointed out that if strategic weapons were to be scrapped, shorter-range missiles should also be dealt with, Gorbachev agreed, and these were thrown onto the great bonfire of nuclear weapons that now seemed to be in preparation.

Next, Gorbachev got around to noting that whereas he was proposing to get rid of all strategic delivery vehicles (and shorter-range missiles, too) in the second five-year period, the American proposal still targeted only ballistic missiles for abolition. Promptly, Reagan agreed to the comprehensive goal. This seemingly sudden and momentous shift revealed the depth of Reagan's abolitionism. The more limited proposal had been handed to him at the summit by antiabolitionist aides eager to preempt his abolitionism by providing him with a more limited but still dramatic alternative. Now, taking his cue from Gorbachev, he cast aside this plan and put forward his own goal. (Reagan gave Gorbachev an unconvincing explanation for his change of mind. He said he had named only ballistic missiles because he mistakenly had thought that the Soviet Union wanted them to have "special mention." The implication was that abolishing all strategic weapons had been his intention all along—true of him, but not of his aides.)

Still, he worried that not every last nuclear weapon would be eliminated. He asked whether Gorbachev was saying that "we would be reducing all nuclear weapons—cruise missiles, battlefield weapons, sub-launched and the like." For it would be "fine with [me] if we eliminated all nuclear weapons." Gorbachev responded, "We can do that. We can eliminate them." At this point, the memcon records that the normally sober, impassive Shultz burst out, "Let's do it!"

Of course it was not to be. SDI and the ABM Treaty reared their heads again. Gorbachev continued to insist that SDI research be confined to "the laboratory." Reagan continued to insist on the right to test the fruits of the research outside the laboratory. Was the abolition of nuclear weapons to founder on a single word—"laboratory?"—Reagan asked. It was, and it did.

Before that happened, though, Reagan articulated a vision of what might have been. It was then, as recorded in the memcon, that he made the comments cited in the epigraph of this book:

> Ten years from now, he would be a very old man. He and Gorbachev would come to Iceland and each of them would bring the last nuclear missile from each country with them. And they would give a tremendous party for the whole world. . . . He would be very old by then, and Gorbachev would not recognize him. The President would say, "Hello, Mikhail." And Gorbachev would say, "Ron, is it you?" And then they would destroy the last missiles.

As the summit meeting neared its tragic close, the Soviet foreign minister appealed to the parties. "Let me speak very emotionally," he said, "because we have come very close to accomplishing this historic task. And when future generations read the record of our talks, they will not forgive us if we let this opportunity slip by."[15]

With the passage of one generation, we can read that record, and it seems clear that the obstacles could have been overcome. Whether, had such an agreement been struck, it would have been implemented is a separate question, and an imponderable one. A strange "asymmetrical" struggle between the two superpower leaders on the one side and an almost unanimous phalanx of the nuclear establishment in the United States as well as a probably somewhat less united but still formidable phalanx on the Soviet side would have ensued. The outcome, whatever it might have been, would have been decided in a political struggle of the widest dimensions.

Perhaps the most distressing fact of all is that, as we know now (and almost all of the scientific community said at the time), SDI was a delusion for the foreseeable future. There was no need for Reagan to defend his right to deploy it as there would be no "it" to deploy. Especially mistaken was his judgment that anything would be ready to deploy in the real world within the ten-year time frame of non-withdrawal from the ABM Treaty that was the downfall of the summit. Had Reagan accepted the ten-year period (or even, as we also know now, a twenty- or thirty-year period), he would have been spared the embarrassment of creating a collapsing expectation for SDI. Gorbachev had stated in response to Shultz's question that the United States would be free to withdraw from the treaty after the ten-year period.

Equally, there was no need for Gorbachev to oppose Reagan's SDI dream. As early as February 1986, he had wondered aloud, "Maybe it's time to stop being afraid of SDI?"[16] By December 1987, he had decided it was, dropped his demand to stop SDI for ten years, and proceeded to negotiate the elimination of intermediate-range missiles and the deep reductions of ICBMs embodied in the START I agreement.

If further demonstration of the primarily psychological character of nuclear transactions were needed, SDI supplies it. For this technical fantasy stood at the center of the most important strategic decisions in the last years of the Cold War—and thereafter. Let us add, though, that SDI's influence was not entirely negative. It enabled Reagan to embrace abolition. And it led him to a vision of abolition safeguarded by defenses against cheaters that still has value for the world and, like certain aspects of the Baruch Plan, is almost certain to be resurrected if and when the idea of abolition is next seriously raised.

The deeper question brought up by the Reykjavik story concerns the relationship of the Cold War to abolition. Common sense would suggest that the end of the Cold War should have proved an ideally propitious atmosphere for nuclear disarmament. Isn't peace better for disarmament than war, however cold? But the record tells us that the opposite was true (once more showing what a poor guide to experience theory can be). It's a fact of history that the idea of abolition surfaced at one of the pinnacles of Cold War tension, the early 1980s. Reagan was in the midst of his military buildup. The Soviet Union had already conducted its own immense nuclear buildup in the wake of the Cuban missile crisis. In early 1983, its officials had walked out of nuclear arms reduction talks with the United States. Reagan officials were talking of "prevailing" in a nuclear war. Certainly, the collapse of the Soviet Union was not yet on anyone's map of the future.

It's also a fact that when the Cold War disappeared into history, the idea of abolition disappeared with it. We are forced to wonder, however counterintuitively, whether agreement on the elimination of nuclear weapons might have been achieved if the Cold War had continued or if, at the very least, the Soviet Union had survived in liberalized form, as Gorbachev wanted.

One reason for the surprising turn of events is that negotiations generally go best when the parties are in equilibrium; yet, as the 1980s proceeded, equality was eroding. The Soviet Union had never come close to the United States in overall economic performance, but by the early 1980s, it had—at punishing cost—achieved parity in the nuclear arena, seeming to remove once and for all any hope that the United States could win or "prevail" in a nuclear war. The new situation drove home the long-existing (but underappreciated) reality that the two nations, equally and redundantly menaced with prompt inexistence, were in the same boat, and it buried the idea that nuclear superiority was meaningful or could even be achieved.

Such was the backdrop to Reagan's and Gorbachev's historic joint statement that nuclear war can never be won and should never be fought. And it was this recognition that led both men to ask why, if that were so, it was necessary to have nuclear weapons at all. In Reagan's words in his 1984 State of the Union speech, "The only value in our two nations possessing nuclear weapons is to make sure they will never be used. But then would it not be better to do away with them entirely?"[17] It was one of the most fundamental, hardest-won lessons of the Cold War.

Nuclear war has often been likened to a chess game whose last few moves need not be played because everyone can see that the outcome is a foregone conclusion. The remarkable yet somehow fitting fact is that in the mid-1980s, this very conclusion was drawn by that game's two kings, who were now asking themselves why, if the known end of the game was destruction for all concerned, anyone should make even the intermediate moves. Why not supplement the tradition of nonuse—an invaluable but insufficient lesson to be drawn from almost four decades of nuclear danger—with a new tradition of nonpossession? Why play such a futile game at all? (The knights, bishops, and rooks—the members of the nuclear establishment—like good bureaucrats everywhere were apparently ready to play the game they were in forever. A shining exception on the American side was George Shultz, who quietly but consistently supported Reagan's abolitionist yearnings while defending him against his scheming subordinates. On the Russian side, Foreign Minister Eduard Shevardnadze, and Gorbachev's chief foreign policy advisers Anatoly Chernyaev and Alexandr Yakovlev were also exceptions to the rule.)

But the moment of equilibrium was perishable, and Gorbachev, in particular, knew it. At Reykjavik, he told Reagan, "A year ago it was not the case that the Soviet Union had advanced major compromise proposals. . . . I simply did not have that capability then. I am not certain that I will still have it in a year or 2–3 years."[18]

Above all, Gorbachev feared the weakness of his own side. It was in response to the "period of stagnation" under his geriatric predecessors that he had launched his project of reform. In a presentation to the Politburo in September 1985, he had said that if the Soviet Union did not head off a "new stage" of the arms race (meaning SDI), "the danger to us will increase. . . . We will be drawn into an arms race that we cannot manage. We will lose, because right now we are already at the end of our tether."[19]

Gorbachev was also aware that Reagan knew how weak the Soviet Union actually was and wanted to force it to accept his proposals from a position of superiority. Gorbachev insisted repeatedly that negotiations could proceed only on a basis of "equality" and he complained that Reagan seemed to entertain the "illusion" that the Soviet Union needed arms reductions more than the United States did. But the supposed illusion was, in fact, a kind of truth. The ground was shaking beneath Gorbachev's feet.

There was a larger dimension to the growing imbalance. Gorbachev's reforms were meant to cure ills afflicting the Soviet system, but the system was itself the illness, and instead of offering a cure for it, his genuinely salubrious measures put an end to it. The more he improved the Soviet Union, the closer to collapse it came. (What he deserves undying credit for is that he surrendered his goal of a reformed Soviet Union without unleashing the immense violence at his disposal.) This is the larger political context in which the Reykjavik summit took place. Gorbachev could not, in the end, accept SDI because he saw it as an *economic* assault upon a Soviet Union in jeopardy.

Seen from this angle, Reykjavik was a tragedy of timing. At exactly the moment when the harvest of a protracted nuclear education was being gathered, the Cold War laboratory in which it had been learned was on its way to being dismantled and its great lesson—that the only sensible thing to do with nuclear arsenals was get rid of them—shelved.

Instead, as one side sank on the scales of power—down, finally, to nothing—the other seemed to rise, to what looked to some like world dominance. The "sole superpower" was getting ready to proclaim itself. And soon enough the leaders of that power, feeling themselves triumphant, would lose any interest in surrendering what most of them had always considered to be a prime element of their power, their nuclear arsenal.

Nuclear Abolition in the Second Nuclear Era

With the end of the Cold War, the second nuclear era opened.* Once again, the tutorial began. Once again, a dialectic of pressures and counterpressures commenced. Once again, the bomb's eerie presence and compulsory logic needed translating into the more familiar language of policy. Once again, the nuclear dilemma, having further matured (some fifty nations were now capable of building the bomb if they so chose), was driven from hiding by political events. Once again, there were trials and errors. And once again, just as in the 1980s, an impasse appeared.

Of course, it was and remains of a different kind. The events of the new era have brought a new set of underlying contradictions to the fore—though without resolving the old ones. In the post–Cold War era, the main lesson so far seems to have been that the bomb

---

*Like others, I have previously used the phrase "the second nuclear age" to describe the post–Cold War period instead of, as here, the "second nuclear era." On reflection, it seemed to me that "nuclear age" should be reserved for the entire open-ended period following 1945. (Since, owing to the unrepealable nature of nuclear know-how, this period is likely to be without end, even "age" is not quite an adequate name for it.) Within such an age, there can be many nuclear eras, the second of which began with the end of the Cold War. If nuclear weapons were abolished, we would not have ended the nuclear age, since rebuilding nuclear arsenals would remain a possibility, but we would emphatically have entered a third nuclear era.

potentially is not only equally destructive to all but equally available to all competent producers, very likely including, one day not far off, terrorist groups. In the Cold War, the driving force was the bilateral arms race and the crises it generated; in the post–Cold war era, the driving force has been proliferation and *its* crises. The teaching aids for this new lesson have been, among other happenings, the nuclearization of South Asia, the attacks of September 11, 2001, the false claims regarding weapons of mass destruction in Iraq and the real war that followed, the discovery of the A. Q. Kahn network, the North Korean nuclear test, and the potential threat of the Iranian nuclear program.

Perhaps because this is the second time around, the lessons of the second nuclear era have been presented more quickly, for a critical moment of decision has already arrived. The Bush doctrine—this era's bible of the strategic school of nuclear war fighters—has failed, as all the world can see. Again, the search for advantage from nuclear arms has proven a worse than hopeless task. Again, the indivisibility of the nuclear dilemma has been demonstrated. Again, the central axiom of life in the nuclear age has been confirmed: nuclear weapons cannot be the source of advantage for any one nation or group of nations at the expense of the rest; they are inescapably a common danger that can only be faced by all together.

Momentum Redux

The prospects for nuclear abolition at this new turning point are in some respects more promising than they were in the Reagan years but in others less so. The arguments for maintaining large nuclear arsenals during the Cold War were clear and strong. One might disagree with them, and many did, but everyone knew what they were. Each superpower saw in the other an implacable ideological foe with global reach. Neither dared be without nuclear arms as long as the other possessed them. The path to mutual disarmament was strewn with enormous obstacles, not least the difficulties of inspecting each other's arsenals.

Today, the arguments for nuclear arsenals are far less clear. Consider the policies of the United States. If, reviewing the post–Cold War record, we ask why, in a Soviet Union–free world, the United States wants nuclear weapons, it's not easy to give an answer. Notwithstanding America's bid for global empire, there is no full-fledged global rivalry that can be cited to justify the risk of annihilation. Are the reasons, then, realist, romantic, or Wilsonian? Two realist reasons top the possible list. One is a lingering fear of the Soviet's successor, Russia. But why, almost two decades after the end of the Soviet Union, should the United States and Russia maintain more than twenty thousands nuclear warheads between them and nuclear materials for producing thousands more? Jack Matlock, Reagan's ambassador to the Soviet Union, has called this state of affairs "insane." Indeed, the Russian threat has been specifically disavowed by two administrations.

The second reason is the counterproliferation mission assigned to the arsenal in the *Nuclear Posture Review* and the Global Strike documents. Yet for all the talk about the need to smash underground bunkers, it is impossible to escape the suspicion that here, too, nuclear bombs have gone searching for missions rather than the other way around. It's difficult to suppose that the nation's leaders, unless they have truly taken leave of their senses, will attack "Nemazee" (North Korea) with nuclear weapons simply in order to dig a deeper hole in the earth in search of a fugitive mini-arsenal very likely hidden somewhere else. The alternative solutions are too many, the costs too unthinkably high. Even if, in a flight of irresponsible fantasy, one were to accept the proposition that nuclear weapons are needed to attack hidden bunkers, as the planning for Global Strike envisions, arsenals of thousands of weapons would scarcely be required.

The "romantic" yearning for greatness might conceivably inspire an administration aiming at the role of global master yet finding itself falling short; but the absence of any Indian-style boasting by the administration about the American nuclear arsenal argues against this interpretation. Likewise, while it is true that nuclear

Wilsonian arguments are detectable in the idea that the sole superpower will bring order to the world through the exercise of its military might, it is also true that the administration has turned more to
conventional forces (however vainly) than to nuclear forces as the
chief instruments of a *pax Americana.*

It would be a waste of time to rebut threadbare arguments that
are mere placeholders for some other, perhaps unacknowledged,
motive. But placeholders for what? A different sort of reason may
offer an explanation: perhaps those in charge of nuclear arsenals,
unlike Ronald Reagan, simply do not believe in and cannot conceive a world without nuclear weapons. In that case, the arsenals'
survival should be attributed not to any mission the weapons are
currently assigned but to the perceived difficulty of getting rid of
them—a perception that is not so much the fruit of argument but of
what is more powerful than any argument, an unexamined assumption. Nuclear arsenals may remain not so much because anyone
wants them as because a world without them is outside the imagination of the leadership class. They are kept for the same reason that
Truman dropped the bomb on Hiroshima: the tracks leading in this
direction are greased and heading downhill. In the other
direction—at that time toward the decision not to use the bombs
against Japan; today in the direction of nuclear abolition—the path
was uphill and strewn with boulders. Now (as then) the easier thing
is to submit to the momentum.

The vicious cycle thus continues in operation: possession of nuclear arms provokes proliferation, and both nourish the global nuclear infrastructure, which in turn enlarges the possibility of
acquisition by terrorist groups, which, in the United States, is rou-
tinely termed the greatest security threat to the country and the
world. All of which leads to a basic conclusion: with each year that
passes, nuclear weapons provide their possessors with less safety
while provoking more danger. The walls dividing the nations of the
two-tier world are crumbling. According to the *Wall Street Journal*
article, "A World Free of Nuclear Weapons," by former secretary of

state George P. Shultz, former secretary of defense William J. Perry, former secretary of state Henry A. Kissinger and former senator Sam Nunn, "Reliance on nuclear weapons for [deterrence] is becoming increasingly hazardous and decreasingly effective.... In today's war waged on world order by terrorists, nuclear weapons are the ultimate means of mass devastation. And non-state terrorist groups with nuclear weapons are conceptually outside the bounds of a deterrent strategy and present difficult new security challenges."

Yet if the reasons for keeping nuclear arsenals are weaker than in the Cold War, the reserves of political will to eliminate them also are weaker. Nothing like the nuclear freeze movement exists; and, so far, neither the president nor any major presidential candidate has adopted anything like Reagan's vision. On the other hand, a new policy vacuum has opened up, and politics, like nature, abhors a vacuum. Bush's nuclear policies and counterproliferation wars not only have been tried and failed; they were repudiated in the 2006 congressional midterm elections and may suffer deeper repudiation in 2008. The last abolitionist president was a Republican; the next could be a Democrat. As in earlier crises of the nuclear age, a new wave of public concern could arise. When people around the world are asked about abolition by pollsters, they favor it by wide margins. Surprisingly perhaps, considering the general climate of established opinion in the United States, the polls show that this is even true of the American public.

Of course, the significance of polls should not be overestimated. There is a world of difference between a favorable reaction to a poll taker's question and an active political will to make something happen. Still, the gulf between elite and mass opinion is striking, especially since the public almost never hears abolition advocated by an elected politician or by anyone in the news media. (The *Wall Street Journal* article is the exception to the rule, and could be a harbinger of things to come.) At the very least, if such a proposal were ever made, we know that it would not immediately meet with crippling public resistance.

Neither should we forget the 183 nations that have agreed under the terms of the NPT to do without nuclear weapons. For surrounding the nuclear archipelago there has always been the sea. Throughout the nuclear age, there have been broad and deep, if slow-moving, antinuclear currents. Beneath the surface, they continue to flow today. In view of the close call at Reykjavik, the new support for Reagan's vision in the *Wall Street Journal* article, the manifest weakness, if not downright absurdity, of the remaining arguments for nuclear arms, and the widespread global disgust with them, it even seems possible that, if a movement for abolition did arise, nuclear establishments around the world might yield to it much more quickly than anyone now imagines. The obvious precedent is the abrupt collapse of the Soviet Union, another structure of lavish violence that went to pieces with astonishing rapidity.

Yet trying to forecast public opinion on this or any issue is probably a vain exercise. Popular movements almost always arise unexpectedly. Who would have thought in 1979 that a nuclear freeze movement would shortly appear and win approval for its proposal in Congress, or that shortly thereafter the most right-wing president of the Cold War period would advocate the abolition of nuclear arms, or that in the Soviet Union a party chairman would come to power ready to champion abolition and democracy for the Soviet Union, which would then disappear? Where the will of either publics or their leaders is concerned, perhaps the best anyone can— or should—do is express one's own opinion in the matter at hand, hope for a cordial reception, and leave it at that.

However, a question that can be addressed and answered today is what broad shape a program for nuclear abolition should take in order to meet the specific conditions of the second nuclear era. If the will to act were to materialize, several broad principles could guide the effort.

At the outset, adopt the abolition of nuclear arms as the organizing principle and goal of all activity in the nuclear field.

It's a commonplace to say that reaching a goal depends on taking the steps that lead to it, starting with the first ones. That is as true for nuclear disarmament as anything else, yet the nuclear story has developed in such a way that the reverse has also now become true: success in taking the first steps depends on making a genuine, fully publicized commitment to the goal. The end must open the gate to the beginning.

At present, a host of modest, eminently sensible proposals to reduce nuclear dangers have been put forward by individuals, nongovernmental organizations, and governments, but the most important ones have not been enacted. The products of decades of study and experience, they fall into three familiar categories, which together comprise the whole of nuclear danger: proliferation, greatpower nuclear rivalry, and (the newcomer) nuclear-armed terrorism.*

I shall mention only the most venerable and significant of the proposals in each category. In the field of proliferation, perhaps the most important is placing all aspects of the nuclear fuel-cycle under some form of international control in order to preclude new sources of supply of nuclear-weapon-grade materials. Another is a ban on the further production of fissile materials, even by existing producers (a "fiss-ban" treaty). A third is a global inventory of nuclear materials and other nuclear assets, to be used as a baseline for measuring the progress of all nuclear disarmament measures. A fourth is internationally sponsored interception of any illicit transfer of nuclear materials on the high seas. (The Bush administration has already launched an effort called the Proliferation Security Initiative to do this, and more than seventy nations have joined it, but existing law bars seizures of cargo on the high seas.) Still other proposals call for strengthening the Nuclear Non-Proliferation Treaty with stricter protocols for inspections of nuclear power facilities by the International Atomic Energy Agency and amending the treaty to forbid withdrawal from it.

The main proposal for dealing with great-power arsenals, sometimes nicknamed "Deep Cuts," proposes that the current Strategic Offensive Reductions Talks, which will bring American

---

*I here mean nuclear *weapon* danger. There are in addition of course the very serious environmental damages and dangers caused by reactors and nuclear waste.

and Russian arsenals down to 1,700–2,200 warheads on each side, be followed by a new round of negotiations to draw the numbers down into the hundreds. Also in the traditional arms control field are proposals that would "de-emphasize" the role of nuclear weapons in the military policies of the nuclear powers. The hope is that proliferators, witnessing this "de-emphasis," will decide that nuclear weapons aren't invaluable after all. One such measure would be a commitment by the nuclear powers never to use nuclear weapons first. If no one uses them first, the reasoning goes, then no one will use them second, so they will be conceptually retired from active service and can be cut back more easily. Another measure of this kind would be to take all nuclear weapons off hair-trigger alert, in order to reduce the risks of an accidental launch.

Measures for keeping nuclear materials out of the hands of terrorists include an array of methods for tracking, securing, safeguarding, consolidating, and reducing fissile materials. One of these is the Nunn-Lugar Cooperative Threat Reduction Program, in which the United States funds efforts to safeguard Russia's nuclear weapons and fissile materials; the exposure and destruction (one hopes) of A. Q. Khan's international proliferation network; and the Global Threat Reduction Initiative, in which the United States seeks to recover nuclear materials from reactors around the world.

All of these steps would be assisted by broader measures applying to both proliferators and existing nuclear powers. Among them: a comprehensive test ban treaty, strengthened regimes of inspection by the International Atomic Energy Agency, and international sanctions in case of treaty violations. Some analysts also call for the nuclear powers to offer nuclear guarantees to nonnuclear allies, in order to discourage them from acquiring their own arsenals (though others observe that such proposals would actually increase the role of nuclear weapons in our world).

Sensible and obvious as these steps might seem, the most important of them are blocked at every turn. Many have awaited acceptance or implementation for decades. The Comprehensive Test

Ban Treaty has been on the international agenda for more than a half century, the fissile material production ban for almost as long. The internationalization of peaceful technology was first formally proposed in the Baruch Plan of 1946. The paired ideas of "deep cuts" and dealerting have moldered on the shelf at least since the end of the Cold War. The proposal that countries make a full declaration of nuclear assets has been consistently rejected by the nuclear powers. Progress on this agenda of modest, sensible measures is, in a word, stalled. Instead of a slow amelioration, we witness the nuclear renaissance, pushing the world away from nonproliferation and deemphasis, and toward the spread of nuclear technology, new great-power confrontations, new arsenals and new missions and new leases on life for old ones, and the use of nuclear arms.

What is it that prevents so many sensible, eminently sane steps from being taken? The answer cannot be in doubt. It is the imperturbable resolve of the world's nuclear powers to hold on to their nuclear arsenals indefinitely. Across the widening moat of the nuclear double standard, nations constantly point to the countries on the other side as a rationale for possessing or acquiring nuclear arms. Those who already have nuclear arms cite proliferation as their reason for keeping them, and those lacking nuclear arms seek them in large measure because they feel menaced by those with them—or because, like India and Britain, they seek an otherwise elusive greatness through possession of the bomb. Internationalization of the fuel cycle runs afoul of the same contradiction. As long as the nuclear powers will not surrender their right to this technology, other nations will not give up their right to acquire it. The fissile cut-off ban likewise fails because it would freeze inequality in place, permitting the great nuclear powers their large stockpiles while depriving the lesser powers of their right to even the score. The Comprehensive Test Ban Treaty goes unratified because lesser powers believe they might want to conduct tests, and the nuclear powers keep looking for the next "generation" of nuclear weapons, such as bunker busters, in order to stop proliferation by force.

In each of these confrontations, the desire to possess nuclear weapons eclipses the desire to reduce them and restrict their spread. All along the line of the nuclear divide there is suspicion, conflict, and the threat of war rather than the trust and cooperation that is needed for progress. Nor, as the great powers once again begin to rattle their sabers at one another, have they forgotten their old reasons for possessing nuclear arms. Again and again, they claim that the Cold War is over but they do not act that way. The great powers will not abandon first use, dealert their arsenals, or accept "deep cuts" because they still fear not only the proliferators but, in some vague sense, one another. The Nunn-Lugar Program succeeds up to a point—until it collides with Russia's fear that America will spy on its active nuclear weapons, which, after all, are aimed at the United States. In fact, by reviving and refurbishing their arsenals, the nuclear powers signal that they expect that great-power rivalries will return. When they do, everyone will be nuclear armed. At that point, nuclear arms races, now in abeyance among the greatest powers, are likely to revive—this time not only between Russia and the United States but between India, Pakistan, and China. To be sure, now and then there is a success: Libya denuclearizes; North Korea agrees to freeze a reactor; Russia and the United States reduce the numbers of deployed warheads; a few new countries accept stiffened IAEA inspections. But the overall drift in the new century has distinctly been in the opposite direction.

A double-standard regime is thus a study in futility—a divided house that cannot stand, a wheel without an axle, a journey without a destination, a car with no engine under the hood. Its advocates preach what they have no intention of practicing. It produces absurdity, and, with absurdity, frustration and contempt. Its moving parts clash: it perpetually defeats itself. It condemns the world to unending, unsuccessful wars, bringing all the consequences that perpetual war must have for human rights, democracy, and the global cooperation that is indispensable for the solution of other planet-spanning perils. "De-emphasizing" nuclear weapons will not be enough to repair these cracked foundations, nor will deep cuts.

The step that is needed can be as little doubted as the source of the problem. Oppenheimer, Bohr, Einstein, Truman, Reagan, and Gorbachev, to name just a few, would have known what it was. The double standard must be replaced by a single standard, which can only be the goal of a world free of all nuclear weapons. If the nuclear powers wish to be safe from nuclear weapons, they must surrender their own. They should collectively offer the world's nonnuclear powers a deal of stunning simplicity, inarguable fairness, and patent common sense: we will get out of the nuclear weapon business if you stay out of it. Then we will all work together to assure that everyone abides by the commitment. Sometimes it's said that the world could free itself from nuclear danger if only it developed the political will to do so, but the problem is misstated. That will is in fact overmatched by a counterwill among the most powerful nations to possess nuclear arsenals and, however vainly, to seek advantage from them. Not so much a lack of will as a collision of wills is at the root of the difficulty, leading to the fatal double standard. But the spread of nuclear technology, a mere potentiality in the late 1940s, has proceeded too far in the new century to be reversed by any league of powers who wish to keep it from others while holding on to it themselves. It was easier in the twentieth century to split the atom than it will be in the twenty-first to split the family of nations into two permanently unequal nuclear camps. What made the former accomplishment possible— availability of the scientific and technical know-how for accomplishing the task—makes the latter impossible.

Abolition thus must be imported from the future to rescue the chaotic present. The United States and the other nuclear powers, instead of merely championing limited measures to reduce nuclear danger in the vague hope that the destination will be reached in some distant and indistinct future, should at the outset make a firm, unmistakable commitment to abolition. That commitment should be so "credible" (to adapt a key strategic word to new circumstances) that proliferators, witnessing it, and realizing that the age of nuclear weapons is truly going to end, would be prepared to join in a rigorous, defined international process that requires them to freeze and roll back their actual or incipient nuclear programs. Only such a universal will, joining the resolve of the present nine nuclear-armed nations to the 183 nonnuclear nations, can check the universal danger born in 1945. The united will of the human species to save itself from destruction would be a force to be reckoned with. Sometimes, the best is the enemy of the good; in this case, the best is the good's only friend.

If a person gets lung cancer, a doctor may prescribe a harsh regimen of chemotherapy to prevent the disease's spread and save the patient's life. The patient may reject the recommendation, but then must expect metastasis and all its consequences. The diagnostician's advice regarding nuclear danger today must be of the same kind. Do you want to stop the spread of nuclear weapons? Then prepare yourself to get rid of your own. But perhaps you want to hold on to your bombs? All right, but then get ready for proliferation. Get ready for new cold wars—or hot ones. And get ready for nuclear explosions in your cities.

Join all negotiations on nuclear weapons—on nuclear disarmament, on nonproliferation, and on nuclear terrorism—in a single forum.

Today, nuclear disarmament talks and nuclear nonproliferation talks proceed on parallel tracks that never meet. They seem to occupy separate universes. The first go forward almost exclusively between Russia and the United States, if and when the two countries please. China, Britain, France, and Israel are engaged in no such deliberations. India and Pakistan have initiated only the rudiments of talks, aimed solely at improving the stability of their nuclear standoff. No ceilings on numbers are under consideration. Nonproliferation efforts, on the other hand, occur mostly within the framework of the NPT.

This bifurcation is a legacy of the Cold War and should be buried with that long-gone epoch. The two efforts should be conjoined, for the benefit of both. Proliferators will not take the possessors' commitment to a world without nuclear weapons on faith alone; nor are the possessors likely to commit themselves to such a world until they are persuaded that proliferation has truly been checked. On both sides of this divide, nations will require guarantees given by nations on the other side. The best way would be to create a grand forum linking nonproliferation and disarmament goals.

One means of effecting the consolidation would be to amend the Nuclear Non-Proliferation Treaty, which at present provides no venue in which the highly specific nonproliferation requirements of Articles II and III are linked to the nuclear power disarmament requirements of Article VI. (An attempt to create such linkage was made at a treaty review conference in 2000 by specifying thirteen steps that the nuclear powers must take toward disarmament, but these were later repudiated by the United States.) Another means would be to convene a Nuclear Weapons Convention, as proposed by the International Association of Lawyers Against Nuclear Arms in association with other anti-nuclear groups.[20] The existing conventions that outlaw biological and chemical weapons offer precedents. Amending the NPT has the advantage that the NPT already exists. Convening a Nuclear Weapons Convention has the advantage that its basic architecture would be designed with the fundamental goal of the enterprise, nuclear abolition, in mind from the beginning.

Either way, the impetus given nonproliferation would surely be decisive. The nuclear arsenals of the great powers would be the largest pile of bargaining chips ever brought to any negotiating table. More powerful as instruments of peace than they ever were or ever can be for war, they would likely be more than adequate for winning agreements that would choke off proliferation forever. The art of the negotiation would be to pay for strict, inspectable, enforceable nonproliferation and nuclear-materials-control agreements in the coin of existing nuclear bombs. What would be the price to the nuclear powers, for example, of a surrender by the nuclear-weapons-free-states of their rights to the troublesome nuclear fuel cycle? Perhaps reductions by Russia and the United States from two thousand to a few hundred weapons each plus ratification of the Comprehensive Test Ban Treaty? Further reductions, now involving the other nuclear powers, might pay for establishment and practice of inspections of ever greater severity, and still further reductions might buy agreements on enforcement of the final ban on nuclear arms. At zero, former nuclear weapon states and non-nuclear weapons states, abolitionists all, would exercise a unanimous will, overwhelming and unbrookable, to manage, control, roll back, and extirpate all nuclear weapon technology.

Other means of front-loading the endpoint of the process are possible. For example, if the effort were to originate in the United States, it could begin with an interagency review ordered by the president to confirm that the United States was truly ready to embrace this goal. In a matter of such importance, parallel Congressional hearings would of course be in order, as would events organized in civil society for the wider public. The pathway to a limit of two thousand weapons on both sides of the old Cold War divide has already been negotiated. The pathway from there to a few hundred weapons on each side has been largely traced out in studies. But the path from a few hundred weapons to zero has not been determined in any detail. No serious study of the question has ever been done, by the government or anyone else, of what might need to happen in each region of the world, what revisions would be necessary in the Nuclear Non-Proliferation Treaty, what safeguards would be required, and what political preconditions would have to be met.

A world from which nuclear weapons had been banned would, of course, not be without its dangers, including nuclear ones. But we must ask how they would compare with those now approaching. Today, waves of fear are transmitted in long chains of cause and effect from the great nuclear powers at the center of the atomic archipelago to lesser outliers, and thence to potential proliferators, not to speak of terrorists. The great powers then mount a rearguard action to stop proliferation at the tail end of the chains—thus waging misbegotten war on Iraq and threatening North Korea and Iran with sanctions and, perhaps, military attack. Or else they open negotiations in which the members of the nuclear club try to perform the difficult feat of pressuring Iran and others to stay out of that same club. Meanwhile, the next generation of proliferators—perhaps Japan, Syria, Egypt, even Brazil or Argentina—looms on the horizon.

Military force aimed at regime change has rightly been discredited as a way to respond to proliferation. But even when it comes to sanctions the great powers are disunited. The United States calls for strong measures; Europe is content with weaker ones; Russia and China are happy with even weaker ones or none at all. But let us suppose that the nuclear powers had agreed to move step by step toward eliminating their own arsenals. The iron chains of fear that link all the nuclear arsenals in the world would then be replaced by bonds of reassurance. Knowing that Russia and the United States were disarming, China could agree to disarm. Knowing that China was disarming, India could agree to disarm—on condition that Pakistan also did so. Knowing that India was ready to disarm, Pakistan could agree to disarm as well. (In this connection, it is noteworthy that throughout the nuclear age, both before and after acquiring their nuclear arsenals, India and Pakistan have taken the position that, in a world committed to nuclear abolition, they would surrender their arsenals. China has made the same commitment.)* Seeing that all the nuclear powers were disarming, proliferators could agree not to arm. They would no longer have cause to rebel against a double standard whose days were numbered. They would no longer have to bear the

---

*The case of Israel is singular. It is the sole country that possesses nuclear arms without being threatened by them. However, its commitment to a nuclear-weapon-free zone in the Middle East in the context of a full settlement of the Arab-Israeli conflict at least offers an approach to this admittedly thorny problem. No country in the world has a more powerful reason to favor abolition than Israel, a country so small that it could effectively be destroyed by one or two nuclear weapons in the wrong hands.

cost of building nuclear arsenals. Any who decided otherwise would find themselves up against the sort of united global will so conspicuous by its absence today. Certainly, the great powers, having staked their own security on a ban on nuclear weapons as firmly as they now stake their security on their nuclear arsenals, would be mightily motivated to preserve their unity in the face of proliferators. Which of them would permit an Iran or a North Korea to acquire or keep a nuclear arsenal while preparing to give up its own? At their backs would be the nonnuclear weapon states, as eager to stop the creation of new nuclear powers as to disarm the old ones.

Think of abolition less as the endpoint of a long and weary path of disarmament and more as the starting point for addressing a new agenda of global action.

When the bomb was born into the world, posing its threat to all life on Earth, it appeared in lonely isolation, like a single immense volcano that had unexpectedly thrust itself up in a flat plain. Since then, other peaks in the same range have broken the surface, and it has become clear that this first menace was part of a new family of threats that have been multiplying ever since. Their common origin is that they were born of a prodigious increase in human power relative to the ecological underpinnings that sustain the continuity of human and other life on the planet. Their common characteristic is their colossal scale, threatening not just huge numbers of people, creatures, and plants but also the ecological and genetic frameworks that make the continuation of these living things possible. At the moment, the most sweeping and dangerous peril apart from a full-scale nuclear holocaust is of course global warming. Like nuclear danger, it transcends the domain of traditional history, with its wars, famines, rising and falling empires, and other contingent events, which, however unfortunate, have never before threatened the foundations of life. The energy crisis caused by the progressive exhaustion of the same fossil fuels whose hydrocarbons are heating up the Earth is the other side of this coin. A wide variety of lesser yet still historically unprecedented ecological threats—to the oceanic environment, to avian, reptilian, and insect life—have also arisen. Rising alongside these is the new force of bioengineering, which could threaten the continuity of life forms in other, unexpected ways, though the shapes of potential danger from this quarter are still unclear. The common quandary the new dangers pose is that they must be addressed on a global basis—not because anyone has any special appetite for grandiose undertakings but because they can be dealt with only globally. These threats to the foundations of life are of course accompanied by an array of other dangers that almost must be addressed globally. The tasks that need addressing include, among a multitude of others, fortifying the conventions banning chemical and biological weapons, regulating an inequitable, precarious, accident-prone global market economy, and responding to pandemics, natural or engineered.

The abolition of nuclear arms should be seen as an indispensable foundation for dealing with this larger planetary crisis. The means as well as the ends of the project would set the stage appropriately for tackling the larger agenda. The procedures required—action in concert by all the nations on Earth—are exactly the ones needed. Attainment of the goal, by formalizing the end of war among the great powers, already claimed as an accomplishment of deterrence, would fortify this commitment to the peaceful means of solving international disputes. Most important, a decision to free the planet from nuclear danger would be the first and most important step along the path of securing the integrity of the ecosphere. It would signal, for the first time since 1945, that the human species finally understands the enormity of the danger we pose to ourselves and other forms of life. Eliminating nuclear weapons is not even the most difficult item on the broader agenda. That honor almost certainly belongs to global warming. Nuclear abolition is often described as utopian. It is anything but that. It would be no more than rolling up our sleeves in order to get down to the real work that lies before us.

Design a world free of nuclear weapons that is not just a destination to
reach but a place to remain.

Getting to zero nuclear weapons is one thing, staying there another. The first—a journey—is a finite task that, once accomplished,
sinks into the past. The second is a state of being, a way of life that,
like nuclear know-how itself, must go on indefinitely, maybe forever. Our basic language for nuclear remediation—"arms control,"
"nuclear disarmament," "nonproliferation," "abolition"—refers only
to the journey. There is scarcely a vocabulary ("nuclear abstinence,"
"nuclear prophylaxis"?) for life at the destination.

During the Cold War, the principal objection in the United
States to a nuclear-weapon-free world was that you could not get
there. That objection melted away with the Soviet Union, and today
the principal objection is that even if you *could* get there, you would
not want to *be* there. This critique grows out of deterrence theory,
which looks to nuclear arsenals as the source of safety from
themselves—and, in its nuclear Wilsonian version, even proposes
nuclear arms as a new foundation for world peace. Not surprisingly,
the theorists look askance at the idea of liquidating the basis of this
high hope. Their arguments usually begin with the observation that
nuclear weapons can never be disinvented. They proceed to assert
that a world free of nuclear weapons is therefore at worst a mirage,
at best a highly dangerous place to be. It is a mirage because, even
if the hardware is removed, the know-how remains, permitting the
reintroduction of nuclear arms at any time—a danger commonly
known as "breakout." It is highly dangerous because the miscreant
rearmer, now in possession of a nuclear monopoly, would be able to
dictate terms to a helpless, terrorized world or, alternately, precipitate a helter-skelter, many-sided nuclear arms race. At the same
time, large-scale, even global, conventional war, no longer suppressed by the balance of terror, might erupt again. In this portrait,
a supposedly nuclear-weapon-free world would soon prove no such
thing. It would be a kind of Baghdad street in which improvised

explosive devices (IED), including nuclear ones, might go off at any time.

Yet once again historical experience throws such theoretical conclusions into doubt. In the nightmarish depiction of a nuclear-weapon-free world, even small powers who suddenly acquire nuclear weapons are credited with an ability to have their way against great powers that lack them. In the kingdom of the blind, it's often said, the one-eyed man is king.

This conclusion seems reasonable until you notice that history has taught an opposite lesson. Nuclear monopolies have invariably proved useless. Repeatedly, even the greatest nuclear powers have actually lost wars against tiny, backward nonnuclear adversaries without being able to extract the slightest utility from their colossal arsenals. In fact, the use of nuclear weapons in these situations has rarely been given a moment's serious consideration at the highest levels. It was not that the superpower leaders weighed the pros and cons of nuclear attacks and decided against them; rather, they almost always simply considered the idea too outlandish or grotesque to be seriously entertained.

In 1954, for instance, military advisers to President Eisenhower recommended using nuclear weapons to help the French win the battle of Dien Bien Phu, but he summarily rejected the idea. In the Suez crisis of 1956, a nuclear-armed Britain found no use for its arsenal and was forced to abandon its objectives in Egypt. In 1968, General William Westmoreland ordered consideration of using nuclear weapons during the battle for the remote, besieged base of Khe Sanh, but Washington soon ordered him to disband the study. In 1969, newly elected President Nixon ordered planning for a massive air attack on Vietnam called Duck Hook, and a cover memorandum for an NSC study on the subject from Kissinger to Nixon raised the question, "Should we use nuclear weapons?"[21] However, in the face of mounting antiwar resistance that fall, the entire plan was dropped. In 1979, nuclear-armed China was soundly beaten by nuclear-weapon-free Vietnam in their border war. In the 1980s, the Soviet

Union was forced to abandon Afghanistan without finding the slightest advantage in its supposedly supreme military asset, nuclear weapons. Deterrence theory teaches that nations are stopped from using nuclear weapons because they fear nuclear retaliation. Surely, there is truth in this axiom, yet at the same time it may disguise another, far more pleasant possibility: that even when fear of retaliation is absent, the reluctance to launch nuclear strikes is very great. Leaders of states are human beings, too. They are not eager to kill countless millions of people at the first opportunity. Fear is a powerful force in human affairs. But there is more in the human soul, even in the politician's soul, than fear. The knowledge, for instance, that such use in any of the wars just mentioned would surely have occasioned worldwide disgust, horror, fury—that the world and posterity would have branded the user a pariah, an enemy of humanity, criminally insane—surely had its effect.

Let us recall, for instance, a passage in Eisenhower's Atoms for Peace speech. He said, "Surely no sane member of the human race could discover victory in such desolation. Could anyone wish his name to be coupled by history with such human degradation and destruction?" If this reluctance, having nothing to do with retaliation, is real—and why should we doubt it?—then the wide credence given deterrence theory masks another equally powerful force: the nuclear moral taboo. If, as this evidence suggests, a deep revulsion against nuclear destruction exists independently of deterrence, then it would certainly come into its own in a nuclear-weapon-free world and perhaps be its firmest foundation.

There is a second source of reassurance, which also lies deep in the nature of the nuclear dilemma. Theorists fear that the cheater will use nuclear know-how to breach an abolition agreement, but they seem to forget that the cheater's victims and the world at large will be in possession of the same know-how. If they should deem it necessary, they will be perfectly capable of rebuilding their nuclear arsenals, and so of restoring deterrence in short order. At best, the cheater would enjoy a monopoly for a brief period. Indeed, if one spins out these scenarios, it is difficult to imagine how a cheater could gain genuine advantage from its violation. There are only two ways of utilizing nuclear weapons—by threatening to use them or by actually using them. Threats can be met by defiance coupled with the threat of conventional or nuclear retaliation, though the latter would be somewhat delayed. Or they might be countered by defenses, as Ronald Reagan pointed out. Actual use would certainly lead to the prompt overthrow by an enraged world of the renegade state, now revealed as an enemy of humanity.

But the point is not that any of these dire scenarios would be likely to unfold or that a proper response to breakout would be nuclear rearmament but that the futility of breakout would be clear well in advance to those contemplating it and would prevent any such adventures in the first place. In short, even in a world without nuclear weapons, deterrence would, precisely because the bomb in the mind would still be present, remain in effect. In that respect, the persisting know-how would be as much a source of reassurance as it would be of danger in a world without nuclear weapons.

Perhaps that is what the Danish physicist Niels Bohr, a nuclear abolitionist, was hinting at when he told the scientist Victor Weisskopf, who worked on the Manhattan Project, that "every great and deep difficulty bears in itself its own solution." If, in the sixty years of the nuclear age, no great nuclear power has won a war by making nuclear threats against even tiny, weak adversaries, then how could a nuclear monopoly by a small country enable it to coerce and bully the whole world? The danger cannot be wholly discounted, but it is surely greatly exaggerated. A world at zero would not be a heaven on Earth, but neither would it be the one painted by today's terror-ridden nuclear strategic theory.

A Final Bomb in the Mind

However, it would be wrong to reduce the role of nuclear know-how in a zero world to a handful of new scenarios for deterring nuclear war. The deeper issue is how, in the long run, we can manage a world in which it is *possible* to build nuclear weapons without actually *doing* so. The question brings us full circle. How should we live with that inexpungible essence of the nuclear age that was born even before Hiroshima, the bomb in the mind? Acquiring that incorporeal entity was a misfortune. At the same time, it was a coming of age. A creature defining itself as *Homo sapiens* and living in a universe whose matter was stocked with energy was destined to discover the fact sooner or later. Now we have, and it is no more possible to return to innocence than it is for a grown person to return to childhood. Shall we, like a child, insist on multiplying the device merely because we can? Or is it possible, like an adult, to exercise a mature restraint? As I have sought to show in these pages, the bomb in the mind already has an extensive history. Even at Hiroshima and Nagasaki, at the very moments of the bomb's only use, the users were looking beyond physical damage to a wider "psychological impression," not only on Japan but on the Soviet Union and the whole world. At the same time, the Manhattan Project scientists who supported the Franck Report sought to render the bomb's impact entirely psychological by suggesting that the bomb should not be dropped on Japan but instead demonstrated in a barren place— hoping that a horrified world would thereby be frightened into a regime of international control. The high priests of deterrence in the Cold War sought a different sort of psychological impact: grasping that actual use meant suicide, they sought to prevent use with sheer threats, to deploy terror to stop war instead of waging a war they knew was unwinnable. This important recognition was the basis of McGeorge Bundy's concept of "existential deterrence," an idea that took one more step back from the brink by recommending reliance not on specific threats but on the generalized aura of terror that emanated from nuclear bombs. The "romantic" nuclearists retreated into psychology by another route. Downplaying specific threats, they sought an appearance of greatness in possession *per se.* Ronald Reagan and Mikhail Gorbachev wanted to rid the world of nuclear weapons altogether.

Is it too optimistic to see in this history a persistent, multiform effort to back away from our own creation, to detach it from actual events, to relegate it somehow to a realm of shadows? If so, might we not conceive the final destination of the nuclear age as the crystallization of one final bomb in the mind? In this insubstantial object, scruple would displace fear, terror would yield to horror, rejection would take the place of denial, and the tradition of nonuse would ripen into a tradition of nonpossession. The bomb was born in the mind. Let it return there. Such a destiny belongs to its nature. The bomb cannot be less than a thought in humanity's collective mind. But it doesn't have to be a thing.

Then hold a funeral for the device, mount a large tombstone over it (maybe at its birthplace in Alamogordo, New Mexico), and post a vigilant guard—the community of nations—over it to make sure it never rises from the dead. And then throw a tremendous party for the whole world.

NOTES

1: The Seventh Decade

1. A. V. Fursenko and Timothy J. Naftali, *One Hell of a Gamble: Khrushchev, Castro, and Kennedy, 1958–1964* (New York: W. W. Norton & Co., 1997), 236.
2. Richard Rhodes, *Dark Sun: The Making of the Hydrogen Bomb* (New York: Simon & Schuster, 1995), 401.
3. McGeorge Bundy, *Danger and Survival* (New York: Random House, 1988), 198.
4. George P. Shultz et al., "A World Free of Nuclear Weapons," *Wall Street Journal*, January 4, 2007.
5. AP/IPSOS poll, March 20, 2005.

2: A Power Out of Our Power

1. Richard Rhodes, *The Making of the Atomic Bomb* (New York: Simon & Schuster, 1986), 708.
2. Gerard J. DeGroot, *The Bomb: A Life* (Cambridge, Mass.: Harvard University Press, 2005), 172.
3. George F. Kennan, *The Cloud of Danger: Current Realities of American Foreign Policy* (Boston: Little Brown, 1977).
4. Rhodes, *Making of the Atomic Bomb*, 470.
5. Rhodes, *Dark Sun*, 476.
6. Ibid., 208.
7. Rhodes, *Making of the Atomic Bomb*, 13.
8. David Holloway, *Stalin and the Bomb: The Soviet Union and Atomic Energy, 1939–1956* (New Haven: Yale University Press, 1994), 82.
9. Ibid., 204.
10. Bundy, *Danger and Survival*, 177.
11. Avery Goldstein, *Deterrence and Security in the 21st Century : China, Britain, France, and the Enduring Legacy of the Nuclear Revolution* (Palo Alto, Calif.: Stanford University Press, 2000).

12. James Carroll, *House of War: The Pentagon and the Disastrous Rise of American Power* (Boston: Houghton Mifflin Co., 2006), 67.

13. "Thos. T. Handy to General Carl Spaatz, July 25, 1945," U.S. National Archives, Record Group 77, Records of the Office of the Chief of Engineers, Manhattan Engineer District, TS Manhattan Project File '42 to '46, Folder 5B (Directives, Memos, Etc. to and from C/S, S/W, etc.).

14. Ibid.

15. Martin J. Sherwin, *A World Destroyed: The Atomic Bomb and the Grand Alliance* (New York: Knopf, distributed by Random House, 1975), 5.

16. Carroll, *House of War*, 65.

17. Margaret Gowing and United Kingdom Atomic Energy Authority, *Britain and Atomic Energy, 1939–1945* ([New York]: St Martin's Press, 1964).

18. Carroll, *House of War*, 65.

19. Ibid., 67.

20. Barton Bernstein, "The Atomic Bombings Reconsidered: The Questions America Should Ask," *Foreign Affairs* (January/February 1995).

21. Bundy, *Danger and Survival*, 78.

22. Lawrence Freedman, *The Evolution of Nuclear Strategy*, Studies in International Security 20 (London: Macmillan, 1981), 19.

23. Bundy, *Danger and Survival*, 70.

24. Gar Alperovitz, *Atomic Diplomacy: Hiroshima and Potsdam*, 2nd expanded ed. (London: Pluto Press, 1994), 524.

25. Fletcher Knebel and Charles W. Bailey, "The Fight over the Atom Bomb," *Look* 27 (August 13, 1963), 20.

26. Glenn Theodore Seaborg and Benjamin S. Loeb, *Stemming the Tide: Arms Control in the Johnson Years* (Lexington, Mass.: Lexington Books, 1987), 67.

27. Robert S. Norris and Hans M. Kristensen, "Global Nuclear Stockpiles, 1945–2006," *Bulletin of the Atomic Scientists* 62, no. 4 (2006).

28. Ira Chernus, *Eisenhower's Atoms for Peace*, Library of Presidential Rhetoric (College Station: Texas A&M University Press, 2002), 38.

29. Ibid., 55.

30. Ibid., 112.

31. Dwight D. Eisenhower, "'Atoms for Peace': Speech Delivered before the United Nations General Assembly," 1953.

3: Nuclear Realists, Nuclear Romantics

1. George Perkovich, *India's Nuclear Bomb* (Berkeley: University of California Press, 1999), 273.

2. Ibid., 250.

3. Gordon Corera, *Shopping for Bombs* (New York: Oxford University Press, 2006), p. 51.

4. Ibid., 122.

5. Ibid., 18.

6. Ibid., 93.

7. Ibid., 25.

8. Ibid., 45.

9. Issue Brief, Carnegie Endowment 8, no. 8 (September 7, 2005), 7.

10. Corera, *Shopping for Bombs*, 119.

11. Issue Brief, Carnegie Endowment, 6.

12. Corera, *Shopping for Bombs*, xiv.

13. Perkovich, *India's Nuclear Bomb*, 229.

14. Strobe Talbott, *Engaging India* (Washington, D.C.: Brookings Institution Press, 2004), 55.

15. Praful Bidwai and Achin Vanaik, *New Nukes* (New York: Olive Branch Press, 2000), 57.

16. Perkovich, *India's Nuclear Bomb*, 13.

17. Ibid., 29.

18. Ibid., 179.

19. Ibid.

20. Ibid.

21. Ibid., 2.

22. Bidwai and Vanaik, *New Nukes*, 63.

23. M. V. Ramana and Rammanohar C. Reddy, eds., *Prisoners of the Nuclear Dream* (Hyderabad, A.P.: Orient Longman, 2003), 325.

24. Kenneth J. Cooper, "Premier Says India Capable of 'Big Bomb,'" *Washington Post*, Saturday, May 16, 1998, A01.

25. Bidwai and Vanaik, *New Nukes*, xxiv.

26. Ibid., 52.

27. Ibid., xxiv.

28. Ibid., 54.

29. See Michael A. Levi and Michael E. O'Hanlon, *The Future of Arms Control* (Washington, D.C.: Brookings, 2005), 20. They write, "The ability of the nuclear superpowers to promote restraint among other countries through force of example alone will be limited. Second, and even more important, most states make their decisions about acquiring nuclear weapons primarily on the basis of their immediate security environment, together with calculations of the diplomatic and economic costs of doing so."

30. DeGroot, *Bomb*, 222.

31. Ibid.

32. Ibid., 217.

33. Andre Bendjebbar, *Histoire secrète de la bombe atomique française* (Paris: Le Cherche Midi Editeur, 2000), 160.

34. Ibid., 182.

35. Ibid., 324.

36. Bundy, *Danger and Survival*, 499.

37. Bendjebbar, *Histoire secrète*, 113.

38. Quoted in Julian Barnes, "The Odd Couple," *New York Review of Books* 54, 5 (March 29, 2007), 6.

39. DeGroot, *Bomb*, 233.

40. Margaret Gowing, assisted by Lorna Arnold, *Independence and Deterrence: Britain and Atomic Energy, 1945–1952* (London: Macmillan, 1974), 407.

41. Robert Jervis, *The Meaning of the Nuclear Revolution* (Ithaca: Cornell University Press, 1989), 174.

42. Ernest R. May and Philip D. Zelikow, *The Kennedy Tapes* (Cambridge: Harvard University Press, 1997), 133.

43. Ibid., 91.

44. Federation of American Scientists, "Nuclear Weapons," http://www.fas.org/main/home.jsp.

45. Kurt M. Campbell, Robert J. Einhorn, and Mitchell B. Reiss, *Why States Reconsider Their Nuclear Choices* (Washington, D.C.: Brookings Institution Press, 2004), 60.

46. Ibid.

4: Nuclear Wilsonians

1. McGeorge Bundy, "To Cap the Volcano," *Foreign Affairs* (October 1969), 10.

2. Richard Rhodes, "'A Great and Deep Difficulty': Niels Bohr and the Atomic Bomb," in *Symposium on "The Copenhagen Interpretation: Science and History on Stage"* (Washington, D.C.: National Museum of Natural History of the Smithsonian Institution, 2002).

3. Bohr's idea of "complementarity" forms a leitmotif in Richard Rhodes's *Making of the Atomic Bomb*.

4. All quotes from James Franck, "Report of the Committee on Political and Social Problems, Manhattan Project," June 11, 1945.

5. Kai Bird and Martin J. Sherwin, *American Prometheus: The Triumph and Tragedy of J. Robert Oppenheimer* (New York: A. A. Knopf, 2005), 299.

6. James Hershberg, *James B. Conant: Harvard to Hiroshima and the Making of the Nuclear Age* (New York: Knopf, 1993), 293.

7. Ibid., 280.

8. Rhodes, *Making of the Atomic Bomb*, 532.

9. Jonathan Schell, "The Folly of Arms Control," *Foreign Affairs* (September/October 2000), 38.

10. Scott Sagan and Kenneth Waltz, *The Spread of Nuclear Weapons* (New York: Norton, 1997), 44.

11. Jacques Chirac, "Speech during His Visit to the Strategic Air and Maritime Forces at Landivisiau/L'Ile Longue," January 19, 2006.

12. Ibid.

13. Jim VandeHei and Dafna Linzer, "U.S., India Reach Deal on Nuclear Cooperation," *Washington Post*, March 2, 2006.

14. William C. Potter, "India and the New Look of U.S. Nonproliferation Policy," *Nonproliferation Review*, Summer 2005.

15. Jo Johnson, "U.S.-India near End of Nuclear Freeze," *Financial Times*, December 8, 2006.

16. "Agni-III Tested," *Financial Times Information*, April 13, 2007.

17. Talbott, *Engaging India*, 82.

18. Ibid., 81.

19. Ibid., 58.

20. David Stringer, "Blair Unveils Plan for Nuclear Missiles," *Washington Post*, December 4, 2006.

21. "Parliamentary Statement on Trident by Tony Blair, December 4, 2006," *Guardian*, http://politics.guardian.co.uk/homeaffairs/story/0,,1963820,00.html.

5: Rise of the Imperial Idea

1. Janne E. Nolan, *An Elusive Consensus : Nuclear Weapons and American Security after the Cold War* (Washington D.C.: Brookings Institution Press, 1999), 51.

2. Ibid., 40.

3. Ibid., 38.

4. These arrangements are described in Bruce G. Blair, *The Logic of Accidental Nuclear War* (Washington, D.C.: Brookings Institution Press, 1993), 187–91.

5. Bruce G. Blair, "The Logic of Intelligence Failure," *Forum on Physics and Society*, April 2004, 2.

6. Hans M. Kristensen, "Global Strike: A Chronology of the Pentagon's New Offensive Strike Plan" (Washington, D.C.: Federation of American Scientists, 2006), 158.

7. Hans Kristensen, "Targets of Opportunity: How Nuclear Planners Found New Targets for Old Weapons," *Bulletin of the Atomic Scientists* 53 (September/October 1997), 23.

8. David Armstrong, "Dick Cheney's Song of America: Drafting a Plan for Global Dominance," *Harper's Magazine*, October 2002.

9. Richard P. Feynman and Jeffrey Robbins, *The Pleasure of Finding Things Out: The Best Short Works of Richard P. Feynman* (Cambridge, Mass.: Perseus Books, 1999), 91.

10. Kristensen, "Targets of Opportunity," 23.

11. Nolan, *Elusive Consensus*, 50.

12. Ibid., 50.

13. Kristensen, "Targets of Opportunity," 23.

14. Ibid., 24.

15. Ibid.

16. Ibid.

17. William A. Arkin, "Agnosticism When Real Values Are Needed: Nuclear Policy

in the Clinton Administration," *Journal of the Federation of American Scientists* 47, no. 5 (September/October 1994).

18. Joel S. Wit, Daniel Poneman, and Robert L. Gallucci, *Going Critical: The First North Korean Crisis* (Washington: D.C.: Brookings Institution Press, 2004), 210.

19. Kristensen, "Targets of Opportunity," 25.

20. Christopher Paine, "The Bush Administration's Misguided Quest for Low-Yield Nuclear Bunker Busters" (New York: Natural Resources Defense Council), May 2003.

21. Nolan, *Elusive Consensus,* 77–83.

22. Seaborg and Loeb, *Stemming the Tide,* 368.

23. John Wilson Lewis and Litai Xue, *China Builds the Bomb,* Isis Studies in International Policy (Palo Alto, Calif.: Stanford University Press, 1988), 36.

24. U.S. National Security Council, *The National Security Strategy of the United States of America,* September 2002.

25. Amy F. Woolf, "U.S. Nuclear Weapons: Changes in Policy and Force Structure," in *Congressional Research Service, CRS Report for Congress,* August 10, 2006, 13.

26. Nina Byers, "Physicists and the 1945 Decision to Drop the Bomb," *Cern Courier,* November 2002, http://arxiv.org/html/physics/0210058.

27. Francis J. Gavin, "Blasts from the Past: Proliferation Lessons from the 1960s," *International Security,* Winter 2004/05.

28. John Lewis Gaddis, *We Now Know: Rethinking Cold War History* (New York: Clarendon Press, 1997), 249.

29. "U.S. Will Unilaterally Withdraw from A.B.M. Treaty," *CNN Live Event,* December 13, 2001.

30. U.S. Mission to the United Nations, press release no. 63, April 27, 2004, www.usunnewyork.usmission.gov/04_063.htm.

31. Hans M. Kristensen, Robert S. Norris, and Christopher E. Paine, "National Insecurity: A Critique of the Bush Administration's Nuclear Weapons Policies," (New York: National Resources Defense Council, 2004), 32.

32. Senate Committee on Foreign Relations, *Testimony of Secretary of State Colin S. Powell before the Committee on Foreign Relations,* 107th Congress, 2nd session, July 9, 2002.

33. Noah S. Leavitt, "Can Conservatives Take a Page from Liberals' Playbook and Use International and Foreign Law in U.S. Courts? John Bolton, Condoleezza Rice, and the Schism among Conservatives," *FindLaw,* April 21, 2005.

34. U.S. Department of Defense, *The National Defense Strategy of the United States of America,* March 2005.

35. Richard Perle, "Thank God for the Death of the U.N.," *Guardian,* March 21, 2003.

36. Woolf, "U.S. Nuclear Weapons," 1.

37. Kristensen, "Global Strike," 103.

38. Senate Committee on Foreign Relations, *Testimony of Carnegie Non-Proliferation Project Director Joseph Cirincione before the Committee on Foreign Relations*, May 16, 2002, 107th Congress, 2nd session.

39. Keir A. Lieber and Daryl G. Press, "The Rise of U.S. Nuclear Primacy," *Foreign Affairs* (March/April 2006).

40. Senate Committee on Armed Services, *Statement of the Honorable Douglas J. Feith, Undersecretary of Defense for Policy: Hearing on the Nuclear Posture Review*, February 14, 2002, 107th Congress, 2nd session.

41. C. Paul Robinson, "A White Paper: Pursuing a New Nuclear Weapons Policy for the 21st Century," March 22, 2001, http://www.sandia.gov/media/whitepaper/2001-04-Robinson.htm.

42. Kristensen, "Global Strike," 125.

43. U.S. Department of Defense, *Nuclear Posture Review Report* [excerpts], hereafter referred to as USDD, *NPR*, http://www.globalsecurity.org/wmd/library/policy/dod/npr.htm.

44. USDD, *NPR*.

45. Kristensen, "Global Strike," 114.

46. USDD, *NPR*.

47. Global Security has published excerpts from the classified version, at http://www.globalsecurity.org/wmd/library/policy/dod/npr.htm.

48. Senate Committee on Armed Services, *Feith Statement*.

49. USDD, *NPR*.

50. Kristensen, "Global Strike," 3.

51. Ibid., 143.

52. Ibid., 97.

53. Ibid., 115.

54. Ibid., 101.

55. Ibid., 93.

56. Ibid., 90.

57. Ibid., 88.

58. Ibid., 53.

59. Ibid., 5.

60. Ibid., 109.

61. Ibid., 70.

62. Ibid., 84.

63. Ibid., 95.

64. Peter Grier, "U.S. Weighs Its Role in Weapons Development," *Christian Science Monitor*, April 20, 2005.

65. Kristensen, "Global Strike," 138.

66. Chairman of the Joint Chiefs of Staff, "Doctrine for Joint Nuclear Operations," 2005, 41.

67. Tim Weiner, "Air Force Seeks Bush's Approval for Space Arms," *New York Times*, May 18, 2005.

68. Kristensen, "Global Strike," 96.

69. Hans Kristensen, "Global Strike Command Becomes Operational," August 8, 2006, The Nuclear Information Project, www.nukestrat.com/us/stratcom/globalstrike.htm.

70. North American Aerospace Defense Command and United States Northern Command, "Vigilant Shield/Global Strike 06," November 2005, http://www.nukestrat.com/us/stratcom/GlobalLightning-05.pdf.

71. William M. Arkin, "Russia Nukes the United States," *Washingtonpost.com*, Early Warning, http://blog.washingtonpost.com/earlywarning/2005/10/russia_nukes_the_united_states.html.

72. George Perkovich et al., "Universal Compliance: A Strategy for Nuclear Security" (Washington, D.C.: Carnegie Endowment for International Peace, March 2005), 137–38.

6: A Nuclear Renaissance

1. William J. Broad and Daniel E. Sanger, "Eyes on Iran, Rivals Pursuing Nuclear Power," *New York Times*, April 15, 2007.

2. Joseph Cirincione, "Controlling Iran's Nuclear Program," *Issues in Science and Technology*, Spring 2006.

3. Ibid.

4. Selig S. Harrison, "Why the India Deal Is Good," *Washington Post*, August 15, 2005.

5. Don Oberdorfer, PBS, *The NewsHour with Jim Lehrer*, October 9, 2006.

6. Warren Hoge and Sheryl Gay Stolberg, "Bush Rebukes North Korea; U.S. Seeks New U.N. Sanctions," *New York Times*, October 10, 2006.

7. Edward Cody, "Tentative Nuclear Deal Struck with North Korea," *Washington Post*, February 13, 2007.

8. Thom Shanker and Norimitsu Onishi, "Japan Assures Rice That It Has No Nuclear Intentions," *New York Times*, October 19, 2006.

9. Graham Alison, "Flight of Fancy," *The Annals of the American Academy of Political and Social Science* (September 2006).

10. Kurt M. Campbell, Robert J. Einhorn, and Mitchell B. Reiss, *Tipping Point: Why States Reconsider Their Nuclear Choices* (Washington, D.C.: Brookings Institution Press, 2004), 277.

11. Ibid.

12. Ibid., 229.

13. Shanker and Onishi, "Japan Assures Rice."

14. Charles Krauthammer, "World War II Is Over," *Washington Post*, October 20, 2006.

15. David Frum, "Mutually Assured Disruption," *New York Times*, October 10, 2006.

16. Lally Weymouth, "A Conversation with Shinzo Abe," *Washington Post*, April 23, 2007, B03.

17. Corera, *Shopping for Bombs*, 168.

18. Drake Bennett, "Critical Mess: How the Neocons Are Promoting Nuclear Pro-liferation," *The American Prospect*, July 2003.

19. Liz Palmer and Gary Milhollin, "Brazil's Nuclear Puzzle," *Science*, October 22, 2004.

20. William J. Broad and David E. Sanger, "Fraying of Old Restraints Risks a Sec-ond Nuclear Age," *New York Times*, October 15, 2006.

21. Dr. Thomas Cochran and Christopher Paine, "Peddling Plutonium: Nuclear Energy Plan Would Make the World More Dangerous" (New York: National Resources Defense Council, March 2006), 4.

22. Office of Defense Programs, National Nuclear Security Administration, U.S. Department of Energy, "Complex 2030: An Infrastructure Planning Scenario for a Nuclear Weapons Complex Able to Meet the Threats of the 21st Cen-tury," DOE/NA-0013, October 23, 2006, 5.

23. Frida Berrigan and William D. Hartung, "Complex 2030: The Costs and Con-sequences of the Plan to Build a New Generation of Nuclear Weapons" (New York: World Policy Institute, April 2007).

24. Robert S. Norris and Hans M. Kristensen, "Russian Nuclear Forces, 2004," *Bulletin of the Atomic Scientists* 60, no. 03 (May/June 2004).

25. Robert S. Norris and Hans M. Kristensen, "Russian Nuclear Forces, 2005," *Bulletin of the Atomic Scientists* 61, no. 02 (March/April 2005).

26. Ibid.

27. Robert S. Norris and Hans M. Kristensen, "Russian Nuclear Forces, 2006," *Bulletin of the Atomic Scientists* 62, no. 02 (March/April 2006).

7: The Fall and Its Uses

1. Robert Jay Lifton, *Superpower Syndrome: America's Apocalyptic Confrontation with the World* (New York: Thunder's Mouth Press/Nation Books, 2003).

2. Corera, *Shopping for Bombs*, 152.

3. Doug Struck and Glen Kessler, "Hints on N. Korea Surfaced in 2000; U.S. Informed East Asia Nations of Nuclear Effort," *Washington Post*, June 22, 2005.

4. John Roberts, CBS News, *Face the Nation*, Interview with Colin Powell, De-cember 29, 2002.

5. Corera, *Shopping for Bombs*, 166.

6. Ann Scott Tyson, "U.S. Gaining World's Respect from Wars, Rumsfeld As-serts," *Washington Post*, March 11, 2005.

7. U.S. Department of Defense news transcript, "Deputy Secretary [Paul] Wolf-owitz Interview with Sam Tannenhaus, Vanity Fair," May 9, 2003, http://www.defenselink.mil/transcripts/transcript.aspx?transcriptid=2594.

8. Mark Danner, "Iraq: The War of the Imagination," *New York Review of Books* 53, no. 20 (December 21, 2006).

9. Robert Kagan, "Cowboy Nation: Against the Myth of American Innocence," *New Republic*, October 23, 2006.

10. Lieberman, *Scorpion and the Tarantula*, 58.

11. Rhodes, *Dark Sun*, 586.

12. Ibid., 566. However, this supreme hawk of the nuclear era was also devoted to deterrence. Of his goal in building SAC, he later said, "My goal was to build a force so professional, so strong, so powerful that we would not have to fight. In other words, we had to build a deterrent force."

13. Jim Mann, *Rise of the Vulcans: The History of Bush's War Cabinet* (New York: Viking, 2004), 180.

14. Michael Lind, *The American Way of Strategy* (Oxford and New York: Oxford University Press, 2006), 128.

15. James Mann, "The True Rationale? It's a Decade Old," *Washington Post*, March 7, 2004.

16. David Barstow, William J. Broad, and Jeff Garth, "How White House Embraced Suspect Iraq Arms Intelligence," *New York Times*, October 3, 2004.

17. Lawrence S. Wittner, *Resisting the Bomb* (Palo Alto, Calif.: Stanford University Press, 1997), 433.

18. Michael Kirk, *Frontline*, "The Lost Year in Iraq," 2006.

8: A Realm of Shadows

1. Shultz et al., "A World Free of Nuclear Weapons."

2. Memorandum of conversation between Reagan and Gorbachev, October 11, 1986, Reykjavik, Second Meeting, U.S. memcon, 13. All quotations from the Reykjavik summit are taken from Russian and American Memoranda of Conversation which can be found in the National Security Archives' Reykjavik File at www.gwu.edu/~nsarchiv/NSAEBB/NSAEBB203.

3. Paul Vorbeck Lettow, *Ronald Reagan and His Quest to Abolish Nuclear Weapons* (New York: Random House, 2005), 16.

4. Ronald Reagan, "Remarks at the 1976 Republican Convention," August 19, 1976.

5. Lettow, *Ronald Reagan*, 31.

6. Ibid.

7. Ibid.

8. Frances FitzGerald, *Way Out There in the Blue: Reagan, Star Wars, and the End of the Cold War* (New York: Simon & Schuster, 2000), 118.

9. Lettow, *Ronald Reagan*, 118.

10. DeGroot, *Bomb*, 307.

11. FitzGerald, *Way Out There*, 101.

12. Ibid., 256.

13. Ibid., 251.

14. A personal note may be in order. In the early 1980s, I wrote two books on the nuclear question, *The Fate of the Earth* and *The Abolition*, both of which called for elimination of all nuclear weapons. Noticing in the mid-1980s that Reagan had embraced this same goal, and agreeing that antinuclear defenses were

a logical measure to safeguard it, I went to Washington to explore the subject for the *New Yorker*, for which I then worked. I got as far as one very interesting and friendly encounter with Reagan's special adviser on arms control, Paul Nitze, who at the time was seeking to frame Reagan's abolitionist ideas in concrete terms that would be more acceptable to the national security bureaucracy. Regrettably, I parted ways with the *New Yorker* shortly thereafter, and the project died. In 1999, Nitze, known for most of his life as a hawk's hawk in nuclear as well as other matters, wrote a *New York Times* op-ed called "A Threat Mostly to Ourselves," in which he called not just for nuclear abolition but for unilateral nuclear disarmament by the United States.

15. Memorandum of conversation between Reagan and Gorbachev, October 12, 1986, Reykjavik, Fourth Meeting, Soviet memcon, 7.

16. FitzGerald, *Way Out There*, 408.

17. Lettow, *Ronald Reagan*, 138.

18. Memorandum of conversation between Reagan and Gorbachev, October 12, 1986, Reykjavik, Third Meeting, Soviet memcon, 3.

19. Anatoly Chernayev, *My Six Years with Gorbachev* (University Park: Penn State University Press, 2000), 81.

20. See the International Association of Lawyers Against Nuclear Arms' Model Nuclear Weapons Convention at www.ialana.net.

21. "Nixon White House Considered Nuclear Options against North Vietnam, Declassified Documents Reveal: Nuclear Weapons, the Vietnam War, and the 'Nuclear Taboo,'" *National Security Archive Electronic Briefing Book*, No. 195, ed. William Burr and Jeffrey Kimball, http://www.gwu.edu/~nsarchiv/NSAEBB/NSAEBB195/index.htm.

ACKNOWLEDGMENTS

For almost ten years, the Nation Institute has been the bedrock of my working existence. I wish to thank its president, my friend Hamilton Fish, for that.

I want to thank Beccah Golubock Watson and Molly Bennet for their research assistance.

And—once again—I want to express unreserved gratitude to my editor, Tom Engelhardt, whose dedication to getting things right goes so far beyond what any writer should reasonably expect.

INDEX

ABOUT THE AUTHOR

JONATHAN SCHELL is the author of *The Unconquerable World* and *The Fate of the Earth*, among many other titles. He is the Harold Willens Peace Fellow at the Nation Institute, the Peace and Disarmament Correspondent for *The Nation*, and also writes for *Harper's Magazine, The Atlantic, Foreign Affairs,* and Tomdispatch.com. He is also a Senior Visiting Lecturer in International Studies at Yale University, where he teaches a course on the nuclear dilemma.

THE AMERICAN EMPIRE PROJECT

In an era of unprecedented military strength, leaders of the United States, the global hyperpower, have increasingly embraced imperial ambitions. How did this significant shift in purpose and policy come about? And what lies down the road?

The American Empire Project is a response to the changes that have occurred in American's strategic thinking as well as in its military and economic posture. Empire, long considered an offense against America's democratic heritage, now threatens to define the relationship between our country and the rest of the world. The American Empire Project publishes books that question this development, examine the origins of U.S. imperial aspirations, analyze their ramifications at home and abroad, and discuss alternatives to this dangerous trend.

The project was conceived by Tom Engelhardt and Steve Fraser, editors who are themselves historians and writers. Published by Metropolitan Books, an imprint of Henry Holt and Company, its titles include *Hegemony or Survival* by Noam Chomsky, *The Sorrows of Empire* by Chalmers Johnson, *Crusade* by James Carroll, *How to Succeed at Globalization* by El Fisgón, *Blood and Oil* by Michael Klare, *Dilemmas of Domination* by Walden Bello, *War Powers* by Peter Irons, *Devil's Game* by Robert Dreyfuss, *In the Name of Democracy* edited by Jeremy Brecher, Jill Cutler, and Brendan Smith,

Imperial Ambitions by Noam Chomsky, *A Question of Torture* by Alfred McCoy, *Failed States* by Noam Chomsky, and *Empire's Workshop* by Greg Grandin.

For more information about the American Empire Project and for a list of forthcoming titles, please visit *www.americanempireproject.com*.